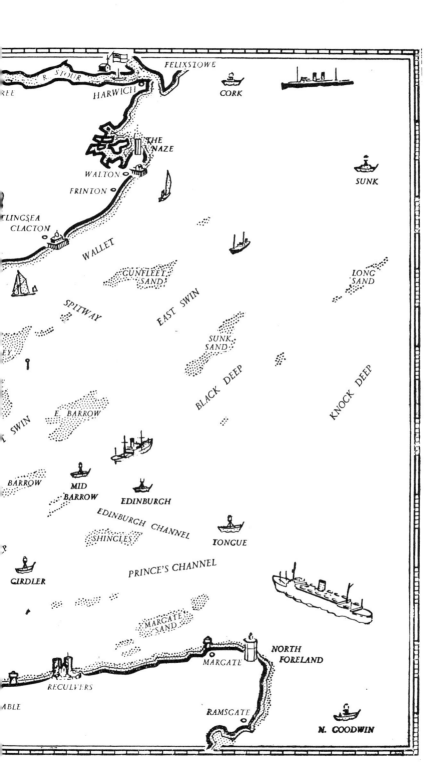

# LAST STRONGHOLD OF SAIL
*The Story of the Essex Sailing-Smacks,
Coasters, and Barges*

Hervey Benham brilliantly evokes the old days of
sailing-barges and smacks, of cutters and ketches, and of all
the craft which have sailed on the rivers of Essex and along the
East Coast. 'It is the end of an age, a tradition, a way of life,'
declares the author, and that tradition he has described with all
the understanding and affection of the real enthusiast, and
preserved for posterity in the lively, humorous and salty style
that is peculiarly his own.

Hervey Benham, author of many other well-known East
Coast books, including *Down Tops'l* and *Once Upon a Tide*,
has sailed on the East Coast for over fifty years in all types of
craft. He worked on local papers in Essex for over forty years,
and was the Editor–in–Chief of Essex County Newspapers Ltd
for many years until his retirement.

## OTHER BOOKS BY HERVEY BENHAM

*Last Stronghold of Sail* (Harrap)
Stories of the Colne and Blackwater

*Down Tops'l* (Harrap)
The story of the East Coast sailing-barges

*Once Upon a Tide* (Harrap)
East Coast shipping in the 18th and 19th centuries

*The Big Barges* (with Roger Finch; Harrap)
The story of the 'boomies', schooners, ketches and square-rigged barges

*Two Cheers for the Town Hall* (Hutchinson)
A study of the structure of local public affairs before reorganization, based on Colchester

*Some Essex Water Mills* (Essex County Newspapers; 2nd ed. Mersea Bookshop)
The mills of the Colne, Chelmer and Blackwater, and the coastal tide mills

*The Stowboaters* (Essex County Newspapers)
The story of the Thames Estuary sprat and whitebait fishermen

*The Codbangers* (Essex County Newspapers)
The story of the Icelandic and North Sea cod fishermen in the days of sail

*The Salvagers* (Essex County Newspapers)
The story of wreck and rescue on the Essex coast

*The Smugglers' Century* (Essex Record Office)
The story of smuggling on the Essex coast, 1730–1830

(Essex County Newspapers titles are now distributed by Boydell Press Ltd, P.O. Box 9, Woodbridge, Suffolk)

High Water : a fleet of loaded sailing-barges gets under way in Colne

# Last Stronghold of Sail

## Sail

The Story of the Essex Sailing-smacks
Coasters and Barges

*by*

HERVEY BENHAM

*with a chapter on Wildfowling by*

J. WENTWORTH DAY

*With thirty-one plates in half-tone*

**HARRAP**
LONDON

First published in Great Britain 1948
by HARRAP Ltd
19-23 Ludgate Hill, London EC4M 7PD

This edition first published 1986

ISBN 0 245-54486-0

Printed and bound in Great Britain
by R.J. Acford, Chichester

# PREFACE

EVER since he had a rag to his back and an idea in his head, man must have been sailing about the Essex rivers for one purpose or another. Now, in our time, he is ceasing to do so, except to amuse himself. This seems to me important. It is the end of an age, a tradition, a way of life. So I have tried to consider what is passing away on two such estuaries, Colne and Blackwater.

With all the Essex coast crying out to have its story told, it has sometimes been difficult to limit myself to such narrow confines, yet I have done so (with a few exceptions) because only so could a scale large enough to show up detail be employed, and because I wanted to demonstrate, by taking just one tiny fragment of the English coastline, what an inexhaustible treasury of local record and reminiscence is even now disappearing as the old heads in which these memories are stored are laid one by one beneath the earth. I hope others may make similar records in their own favourite watery realms; I know of no counties, with the exception of Suffolk (to which Major E. R. Cooper, writing as "Suffolk Coast," has done full justice), where such literary neglect is not regrettably complete.

This is neither a guide-book nor a yachting book. Look elsewhere for the dates of the parish church or an account of how the jam and the paraffin oil got mixed up in a highly localized yachtsman's cyclone-cum-tornado. It is a story of smacks and barges that still survive; of old sailing coasters and yachts that are dead.

I have connected 'salvaging' and wrecking chiefly with Brightlingsea and Rowhedge; old-style yachting with Wivenhoe, and its later phases with Tollesbury; oysters with Mersea; colliers and the coasters with Maldon; barges with Colchester, smuggling with Bradwell, and so on. This is partly for convenience, for in varying degrees all the little ports, of course, shared in almost all these activities; but I have found it better to think generally in terms of places than of subjects, though a few matters are so general as to have demanded chapters to themselves. One of these, wildfowling, I have left in the capable hands of Mr James Wentworth Day, for I should have gone very hungry had I had to rely on my own prowess with the gun.

To me the sailing-ship has always stood pre-eminent in beauty among man's achievements, and here I include the humble little craft just as much as the deep-sea windjammers, whose memory is queasily enshrined in a thousand calendars and Christmas-cards. Down the centuries men have marvelled at " The way of an eagle in the air ; the way of a serpent upon a rock ; the way of a ship in the midst of the sea ; and the way of a man with a maid."

Only the ship among man-made things enters the company of nature's mysteries, and among ships those evolved for the elements they live in must rank to me before mere toys designed for casual pleasure. Once there were many ; all round the coast sailed ketches and schooners, brigs and barques, cutters and luggers. Now the ketches of Brixham and Lowestoft and Grimsby have gone, the pilot cutters of the Bristol Channel and the Solent, the coasters and the river barges of the West Country, the scaffies and zulus of Scotland, the yawls of Suffolk and Kent, the Whitstable traders, the Sussex hog-boats, and the Cornish drifters—all have disappeared. It is a startling, saddening, and solemn reflection that of them all the Colchester cutter and the Thames Estuary sailing-barge are practically the last survivors. It is for this reason that these yarns have been claimed to describe the " Last Stronghold of Sail."

Well, if it had to happen, two lovelier survivors could hardly have been chosen. In her class the Colchester cutter, it seems to me, need fear no rival for elegance and ' breeding' ; the spritsail barge is unique in the whole wide world. For those who would know more of these matters a list of books is appended. But for the only real learning and understanding of ships I commend Belloc's pregnant injunction : " Read less ; sail more."

H.B.

*Thornfleet*
*Fingringhoe*
1947

# ACKNOWLEDGMENTS

MUCH of this book was first published in the *Essex County Standard*, and the old files of that paper have provided a great proportion of the material.

I have found particularly useful the following publications, which I recommend to those interested : the *Essex Review* ; *Maldon and the River Blackwater*, by E. A. Fitch (1894, etc.) ; *A History of the Town of Brightlingsea*, by E. P. Dickin (Barnes, 1913) ; *Vanishing Craft* (Country Life, 1934) and *Sailing Barges* (Hodder and Stoughton, 1931), by Frank Carr ; *Sailorman*, by E. G. Martin (Oxford University Press, 1933) ; *History of the Thames Estuary*, by Muir Evans ; *The River, the Sea, and the Creek*, by F. A. Smythies (Sampson Low, 1884) ; the Badminton *Yachting* ; *Coastwise Cruising from Erith to Lowestoft*, by F. B. Cooke (E. Arnold, 1929) ; *The Colchester Oyster Fishery*, by H. Laver (1916) ; *Shoalwater and Fairway*, by Sir H. Alker Tripp (John Lane, 1924) ; *The Magic of the Swatchways*, by Maurice Griffiths (E. Arnold, 1932) ; *The Modern Fowler* (Longmans, 1934) and *Farming Adventure* (Harrap, 1943), by J. Wentworth Day ; *Oyster Biology and Oyster Culture*, by J. H. Orton (E. Arnold, 1937) ; publications of the Kent and Essex Sea Fisheries Committee ; and the *Victoria County History of Essex* (vol. ii).

The individuals who have contributed speak for themselves throughout these pages, but I should especially like to acknowledge the help of Mr Joshua Francis, Managing Director of Messrs Francis and Gilders, Ltd, of Colchester, and Mr R. C. Jarvis, Librarian of the Custom House, London.

The majority of the photographs are by Douglas Went, of Brightlingsea. Those of the *Jullanar* are reproduced by courtesy of Mrs E. E. Bentall, of Maldon ; old prints are included by courtesy of the Colchester and Essex Museum ; the reproduction of the revenue cutter *Badger* is from a hand-coloured copper engraving in the possession of the Honourable the Commissioners of Customs and Excise. The end-papers are by F. B. Harnack, of West Mersea.

# CONTENTS

*Chapter* I. A Nick on the Map                               *page* 15

II. The Last of the Sailing-ships                            24

III. Brightlingsea Smacks and Wrecks                         31

IV. Quee: Harvests of the Sea                                44

V. Work and Play                                             47

VI. Wivenhoe's Century of Splendour                          51

VII. Alresford and the Flounder Fishers                      61

VIII. Rough Days at Rowhedge                                 66

IX. Mersea and the Dredgermen                                73

X. Farms under the Water                                     83

XI. Out with the Oyster Dredgermen                           90

XII. Where Plough meets Sail                                 96

XIII. Tollesbury—where the Yachtsmen
come from                                                    102

XIV. The Salty Town of Maldon                                106

XV. All Quiet at Heybridge Basin                             120

XVI. Some Notable Fliers                                     123

XVII. The Free Traders and the Oyster Pirates                130

XVIII. Wind and Tide                                         143

XIX. The Wildfowlers                                         154

XX. The Man who saw a Sea-monster                            170

XXI. The Last Fleet                                          175

XXII. Passages Good and Bad                                  180

XXIII. The Future—if Any                                     188

Index                                                        196

# ILLUSTRATIONS

Barges getting under Way       *frontispiece*

Evolution of the Sailing-barge : Nineteenth-century
  Types at Colchester      *page* 24

Colchester Hythe in the Eighteenth and Twentieth
  Centuries          25

Barges in a Breeze     *following page* 62

Fitting-out for the Sprat Season at Brightlingsea

Spratters and Scollopers preparing

' Stow-boating '

The Sprat Harvest at Brightlingsea

Sky, Land, and Water : a Blackwater Study

Full Moon and Low Water in Brightlingsea Creek

At Wivenhoe

Work and Play in Colne : Yachts, Barges, and Ferry

Oyster-dredging in Colne

The Saltings : a Mersea Idyll

Oyster Smacks of Mersea and Brightlingsea

Mersea Smacks sailing    *following page* 126

Sailing Work-boats at Brightlingsea and Mersea

Maldon Yesterday and To-day

Timber Barges at Heybridge

The Schooners *Essex Lass* and *Wave*

The Brigantine *Jessie Annandale* and the Yacht *Firecrest*

The Yacht *Jullanar*

The ' Boomie ' *Record Reign*

Wintry Weather in Brightlingsea Creek

' Calm as a Clock ' at Brightlingsea Creek

Colne Police Boats and the Revenue Cutter *Badger*

13

Barge Cargoes : Timber at Heybridge and ' Stackie '
at Mersea Strood
Wildfowling : the Opening Day at Mersea
Wildfowlers : Linnett, of Bradwell, and Cook, of
Mersea
Shipbuilders and Sail-makers of Wivenhoe and Bright-
lingsea
Days in a Bargeman's Life : the *Audrey* in Trouble and
Modern ' Stackies '

IN TEXT

The *Gem*, Last of the Passage-boats            30
Early Nineteenth-century Sailing-barge          30
The *Pearl*                                     60

# I

## A NICK ON THE MAP

*A Sail down Blackwater and Colne—Fifteen Little Havens, and a Score of Islands—The Ancient Church on the Saxon Shore—Where Henry VIII was contented—The Magic of the Waterside*

THE map of the east coast of England shows quite an appreciable nick between Harwich and the Thames.

It represents an area of water bounded to the south by Bradwell Point and to the north by Colne Point, and comprising the estuaries of two rivers, the Blackwater and the Colne. Rather curiously, in an area where almost every point, bank, and creek is amply and picturesquely named, this indentation has no title or description to distinguish it. But to console it for its anonymity it includes in its two rivers the three inhabited islands of Mersea, Osea, and Northey, as well as perhaps a score of uninhabited ones ; fifteen distinct minor ports (for Colchester, Rowhedge, Wivenhoe, Fingringhoe, Alresford, Brightlingsea, St Osyth, Maldon, Heybridge, Bradwell, Lawling, Goldhanger, Tollesbury, Salcot, and West Mersea each entertains its own maritime traffic) ; two of the finest oyster fisheries in the world ; a leading interest in the Thames Estuary sprat fishery ; the best wildfowling grounds south of Norfolk ; some of the saltest water in the country ; a wonderful breeding-ground for all the finny tribes in 'Pont' ; the most attractive little fishing-boat class left around these coasts ; one of the best fleets of sailing-barges ; and enough history and local lore to fill volumes.

It is enchanting and enchanted country. On a brisk June morning the great heaped white clouds go sweeping across the wide skies, and the peewits wheel below them ; a summer afternoon finds the floodtide rippling and searching among marshes shimmering with that most exquisite of carpets, the mauve-tinted sea-lavender ; at evening the descending sun casts a spell over the

15

moisture-laden waters and sends land merging into sea and bathes it all with rose, pearl, and gold ; on a bitter winter's night the wild swans strain low over the creaking ice-floes, lit in weird, ghostly spasms as the ragged clouds race across the moon.

And through all its creeks and inlets the tides ebb and flow as they have since time began—through all the " bays, channels, roads, bars, strands, harbours, havens, rivers, streams, creeks, and places within the said limits contained," as the old Customs records put it.   They are the very pulse-beat of eternity, the tides, and to dwell awhile in a realm ruled by their unchanging, unhasting tempo guides the mind, uneasily attuned to the fevered rhythm of a modern world, into a contemplation of things wide and infinite, a sympathy with natural forces which is an experience as profound, stimulating, and satisfying as a man can know.

Let us take a look at this watery realm which we propose to explore more fully in these chapters.   The Blackwater is the finer of the two rivers, so we shall start away from Maldon in a trim little smack on the top of the flood, with a nice westerly wind (since in print we can allow ourselves luxuries).   As we go aboard we note with what grace and dignity Maldon on its hill looks down on the river.   It is a lovely picture from the water, a tumble of old houses up the steep streets, and dominating it all St Mary's massively buttressed brick tower with a jaunty little spire on top.   It was a Roman colony ; the Vikings twice fought the Saxons here, and in Norman times it became the chief seaport of Essex, with a ship to its credit in *Domesday Book*.   It reminds one of old Rye in the way it now slumbers and dreams of past glories.

But our mainsail is set, and Maldon is already dropping astern. The river is narrow here, and the smacks lie at low water listing against a sandy beach.   Above them are several yards, where history has been made and they now build little yachts, and against the quays lie a few sailing-barges.

As we clear the first reach Heybridge opens out on the port bow.   Here is the lock giving entry on the Chelmsford canal, now used as a laying-up station for yachts and a haven for timber-barges and Dutch eel-boats, which often spread their eel-boxes over a wide area of the canal.   There they stay till the eels are all sold.

Opposite Heybridge lies Northey Island, whither came the Danes to attack the Saxons in the famous battle of Maldon in 991. They landed on Northey Island and found the Saxons drawn up on the mainland. For a time the tide confined the encounter to an exchange of arrows and insults, but presently, when the ebb permitted them to wade over, the Saxons retreated far enough to allow the Danes to obtain sufficient foothold for both sides to start level. 'Playing the game' with the aggressor has had the same results for a thousand years, and the Saxons were handsomely defeated. The great Anglo-Saxon poem which commemorated the battle (called by some the greatest war-poem in our language) contains the lines that were to ring so true in Anglo-Saxon ears all but a thousand years later:

> The will shall be harder, the courage shall be keener,
> Spirit shall grow as our strength falls away.[1]

Osea Island, a little lower down, had a pair of ravens living in an elm-tree which was known as "Raven Tree" as late as 1889, and more lately had the comical distinction of being turned into a home for inebriates by a brewer. This island is full of the charm that only islands boast, and in the midst of its diminutive village is a letter-box whose "Time of Next Collection" is indicated as "According to Tide." A pleasant way to regulate the life of a community.

Over across the narrows, where such a lop of sea arises when an easterly gale meets a spring ebb, lies Stansgate Point, where there existed a Cluniac priory, Stansgate Abbey, from 1176 till Wolsey's day, and where there was, till it was reclaimed in the latter half of the nineteenth century, a creek which nearly enclosed meadows still known as Ramsey Island.

Lawling and Mayland creeks still remain, opposite Osea Pier, and many small craft are kept in them and a few built by their side. The story of the building of the sea-walls is a fascinating one, of which little is known. It is safe to assume, however, that when the Romans sailed into these estuaries they must have been huge sheets of water, for few of the present defences can have existed in those days, though Roman remains have been found within their bounds, which suggests that there were at least some.

[1] *The Battle of Maldon*, edited by W. J. Sedgefield (Harrap, 1904).

Marshes were being reclaimed up to fifty years ago ; only in the past thirty years has the reverse process set in and breaches in many carefully preserved defences been allowed to spread and send acres of grazing back to coarse, brown-tufted scrub. A whole book might be written on the story of the walling and the mystery of the red hills, those strange, low mounds of red earth found all about the saltings. Many theories have been advanced as to their origin, the likeliest being that they were ancient salt-pans. Hard by the main Colchester-Mersea Road, just after Pete Tye Common is passed, is a place where disused walls ridge the pasture, evidence of the gradual course of reclamation, and here may be seen a red hill. Though the hill is now much flattened by the excavations of rabbits, the strange colour of the soil is still clearly to be seen.

The most famous tidal inundation occurred in 1707, when Northey Island was ' sunk,' and the Dagenham Breach caused a sea-wall gap which through neglect became a four-hundred-foot breach costing over forty thousand pounds to repair. On November 28, 1898, a bore on the ebb breached many of the Essex walls, and other great tides are recorded as occurring in 1324, 1376, 1448, 1527, 1690, 1874, and 1881.

In days gone by the flooding of hundreds of acres since re-claimed probably robbed the big tides of some of their menace ; otherwise it is difficult to see why some old houses were built in places so liable to turn the parlour into a paddling pool. Indeed, there is evidence that this was so from the way certain recent breaches in the Colne to-day ' take the top off ' danger tides and save places which would previously have suffered.

To get back on our course again, however : behind Osea lies Goldhanger Creek, little used now that the barges no longer come that way after a stack, and just below is Thurslet Creek, where an oyster-watch-boat lies, indicating that we are now entering the preserves of the Blackwater and Tollesbury Oyster Fishery Company.

Tollesbury Pier—now derelict, and, I believe, never used since an optimistic railway company was persuaded to build it back in 1907—lies on our port bow, and to starboard is Bradwell Creek, delightful little inlet leading to a barge quay and the hamlet of Bradwell.

The river here is used for the laying up of ships in times of depression. In the thirties no fewer than forty-three great steamers swung to their anchors, making a strange picture in so rural a scene. During the Second World War a single Finnish barque, *Alastor*, lay forlorn off Tollesbury Pier ; now the gaunt, rusty collection of war cripples and superfluous shipping again accumulates.

On Sales Point, the lowest extremity of the river's south shore, stands what at first appears to be a barn—and was, indeed, used as such for centuries—but what is in fact the Saxon chapel built by St Cedd when he was planting missionary centres in this part of the country. It is thus one of the most ancient churches in the British Isles. But St Peter's-on-the-Wall, as it is called, stands on history going back further still, for around it are the remains of one of the Roman forts of the Saxon Shore, prob-ably the Castellum of Othona,[1] which in Cedd's time became Ythancestir. The seaward side of the fort is gone, but a portion of the walls may still be seen on the southern side. A force of five hundred to a thousand Roman braves here made a last stand, fighting off the invasion of the English in the last days of the Roman occupation (about A.D. 410).

Across on the north shore the Nass Beacon (a good old Danish word, that!) marks the entrance to an inland archipelago, through which creeks run up to West Mersea, Salcot and Virley, and Tollesbury. This array of creeks, running far inland, is a wonder-ful paradise for small craft, and to-day as many small yachts as can find room are stationed where the Romans gathered oysters, and Vikings wintered their longships when they held the island in the tenth century. Cobmarsh and Packing Marsh Islands are formed by Thornfleet, Mersea Fleet, and Besom Creeks, while above the Hard the waters divide again to enclose Ray Island, immortalized in that colourful melodramatic novel *Mehalah*, by S. Baring-Gould.

Salcot Creek, winding away to where the unspoiled twin ham-lets of Salcot and Virley are linked across it by a little bridge, is a perfect example of the charm of the Essex marshlands, and Tollesbury Creek weaves tortuously inland to provide an

---

[1] Another theory holds that old Walton, to the north, was the site of Roman Othona.

unexpected arrival at a thriving little yachting centre, with twelve-metres and big schooners and power yachts hauled up in winter on the slipways of its yards. At low water the creek dwindles to a trickle, and one wonders how ever they got there.

Such is the Blackwater, treasury of beauty and of history of every kind.

Colne may seem by comparison featureless, but has much to interest. We shall miss not one tide but many if we linger to explore Colchester, oldest recorded town in the British Isles, with its unequalled Roman wall, its huge castle keep, and history clinging to every stone of it, where King Coel reigned and revelled in legend and Boadicea in bitter fact rebelled against the Roman invaders. So we will let these wait till another time, and be away while there is still water from its Hythe quays, less picturesque than those of Maldon, unfrequented by smacks or yachts, save the flotilla of local motor-boats, known variously as the " Royal Hythe Y.C." or (to the bargemen) more tersely as the " little bloody hundred," yet full of picturesque life at tide-time, when the barges are swinging and dropping away down river as the incoming deep-laden craft slide into the berths they vacate.

The first few tortuous reaches are dully dominated by gas-works, petrol-yard, and sewage-farm, and it is not till we have passed the quays of Rowhedge on our starboard hand (now deserted by shipping, though the riveting hammers ring out busily from the ironworks yard, and the adze still chunks into timber lower down where Peter Harris built the *Firecrest*) that there is much to stimulate the eye. Then to starboard breaks off Fingringhoe Creek, swinging in wide sweeps up to the mill, and to port lies historic Wivenhoe, showing a mellow old face which is somehow reminiscent of the sleepy dignity of a little Dutch waterside town, where we pass the yards which built wooden walls and famous yachts and the brick-and-plaster houses of the men who owned and sailed them.

Now we are under the lee of Alresford's wooded shore, and all of a sudden the river broadens into an estuary of real dignity and splendour. The ballast quays of Fingringhoe are to starboard, and to port below the buoys where once the grand steam yachts were moored and where the globe-trotting *Cap Pilar* now passes her last years of retirement in solitary inactivity is Alresford Creek, approached through a railway swing-bridge.

Already that fine landmark and sea-mark Brightlingsea church tower shows away inland to port, and in a moment we are running through the anchored barges at the mouth of the estuary, catching a glimpse of the shipping and yards up Brightlingsea Creek, which we may follow inland on the tide right up to St Osyth Mill and Priory. There to starboard lie the entrances to the attractively deserted maze of the Geeting Creeks, and there, where the oyster smacks are working, with the packing-house on Peewit Island beyond, is Pyefleet Creek, the home of the most famous oysters in the world, the Colchester Natives.

So, between Colne Point and East Mersea, with its wonderful fishing and dredging ground, 'Pont,' the Colne sweeps boldly into the sea—a stretch of water preferred to Harwich by no less an authority than Henry VIII; for, in the words of Katherine Parr's brother, "His Highness has perused and seen two notable havens, and specially the water which is called Colne water contenteth his Highness best." (Perhaps it is a good thing he did not look at the Blackwater as well, for in 1565 Maldon Channel was described as "delvern up and divided with sand, sea ooze, and shingle.") Under King Henry Colne water became a naval station, whence sailed his fleet against Scotland. It may have been one before, for in 1344 the *Elayne* was sent to the port of Colchester for the King's use, but in 1544 there were many royal ships lying in the haven, and in the same year the *Pauncey* (400 tons) took in provisions for 140 men before leaving Colne for the narrow seas. Among his new navy was the *Barbara* of Brightlingsea (140 tons). Brightlingsea shipwrights and caulkers were also impressed for the building of the famous *Henry Grâce-à-dieu* at Woolwich. There was a good deal of timber from the Colneside in this famous ship, including two great trees, weighing fourteen tons, from the Abbot of St Osyth for her mainmast.

These, then, are the waters we propose to explore. They represent one of the last strongholds of sail around these coasts, for among them all there is no steam- or motor-coaster owned, and the few Scandinavian steamers which visit the Blackwater with timber, and the British and Dutch motor-vessels that come with coal and clay to Colchester, the latter carrying on the price-cutting tradition of the bilanders which came from Holland two hundred years before, are far outnumbered by the local spritsail barges. Most of the larger smacks are now mainly motor-driven, but the smaller craft of Mersea and Maldon remain faithful to sail even when purely auxiliary engines are installed, and a fisherman still sets up a lugsail in his boat as a matter of course to take him about his business.

It is, as I shall hope to show, a poor shadow of the lively scenes of half a century ago, but it remains a survival of a past age only paralleled about our English coast to my knowledge at Whit-stable, where also the sailing-barges running into the East Swale pass the smacks dredging under their cutter rig. But both are in smaller numbers and less variety than in Essex.

The people of Colchester and Maldon are not interested in all this. They glance over their bridges, and perhaps they wonder why so few industries have ever been attracted to their towns' water-sides. They notice at Colchester a trim motor-coaster unloading gas-works coal, at Maldon in summer a few pleasure-skiffs disporting themselves on the tide—otherwise there is nothing to see but a few old barges.

On Sunday mornings, however, young Tommy may be ob-served dragging his parents along the quay. Mother watches anxiously lest her precious should trip on the big bowlines which lift and heave in their ring-bolts as the barges sheer and surge uneasily at their moorings. Father, bored in his bowler hat, would like to get back to his armchair and his favourite astrologer. "Why must the boy insist on coming down here for his Sunday walk?" he asks for the hundredth time.

But Tommy is adamant. He will not budge. Wide-eyed, open-mouthed, he watches the big ships. He says nothing. The barges tell him nothing. Skippers and crews are ashore; every sail is neatly stowed and stopped up. Every rope is neatly coiled away. Smoke wisps up from the stove-pipes of the few which are away from their home ports—from the fo'c'sle stove, where the traditional Sunday duff is bubbling in the pot; from the cabin aft, where the men make ready to eat.

High over the huddle of insignificant buildings lining the quays float the house-flags on their topmast heads, gay splashes of coloured bunting crowning the forward-straining spars, which, scraped and oiled, gleam bright as butter. They lift and fall languorously, as if disdainful of their surroundings. Thus the barges lie resting, asleep.

Young Tommy feels something he cannot express. Creaking springs and mooring-lines whisper of days in summer creeping along the Maplin sands; of nights in winter running in an easterly gale for the shelter of Colne or Harwich, topsail down, mainsail brailed to the sprit, sandbanks ready on either hand to bring the ruin of shipwreck; of men who do not measure their toil by the tyranny of the clock or the factory whistle, but by the still more imperious but so much nobler time-table of the tides; whose concern is not with ledgers and typewriters, but with wind and weather; of quiet men with the dark-blue jerseys and bright-blue eyes of the sailor, ignorant men in the eyes of the world, but wise and strong in the sight of nature.

"Come along, Tommy. Your father wants his dinner." Dragging unwillingly behind his parents, Tommy disappears up the hill, but he carries a picture with him.

I shall try to fill in some details of that picture for you, Tommy, and for those other Tommies, who run out along the promenade at Brightlingsea to Bateman's Tower to see the vessels at anchor in the estuary; who linger on the sea-walls at Tollesbury or the quays at Wivenhoe and Rowhedge long after Mother has begun preparing trouble for those not home by bed-time, or who sit wide-eyed in Dad's oyster-skiff at Mersea as he dredges.

For I, like you, believe there is something irresistibly fascinating about these places. What it is neither I nor you will ever be wise enough to put into words, but I shall try to show a little of what lies behind it all; to spin a few of the yarns which, trivial in themselves, go to make up the magic and the romance of the water-side.

# II

# THE LAST OF THE SAILING-SHIPS

*Colchester Coasters before the Barges—The 'Swim-headers'—Old-time Cargoes—The Barge that just fitted—'Boomies' and Passage Boats—A Hundred Sail a Tide—Before the Tow-boats*

It is just over a century since Colchester began to know the 'sprittie,' for it was not until 1830 that barges began to develop in length and set tops'ls and mizzens, and some ten years later when the round bow began to supersede the swim-head, such as is still usual in London river lighters. The older bargemen can still remember swim-head sailing-barges, which are said to have blundered along surprisingly well, though they pounded so much that one is said to have "busted in her swim," punching into a head sea, but this type can hardly have been in general use for trading as far afield as Colchester, even though in those days the Havengore route had much more water and was far more commonly used, and the first barge to reach Marriage's Mills in 1865 was of this type.

Whether any small lee-boarded, flat-bottomed vessels beside the Dutch bilanders were in fact in use before the nineteenth century for carrying the grain from the farms to the local mills it would be interesting to know. So far I have been unable to find reference or picture suggesting that this was the case, and accordingly we must suppose the trade of the Colne to have been in the hands of little, round, tubby sloops and cutters of the hoy type, averaging perhaps fifty tons, mostly working from London, with a motley fleet of brigs and brigantines, schooners and ketches, and now and again a barquentine, engaged in the coal trade and in general coasting, as well as venturing farther afield on deep-sea work.

The hoys in turn were descended from the little square-rigged, one-masted crayers, thirteenth-century coasters which

...lution of the Sailing-barge. (*Above*) A cutter-rigged craft, with square-sail yard ...-billed, at old Hythe bridge, Colchester, in 1820, showing also two small lighters, in ...h, presumably, grain was then taken on to East Mills. (*Below*) The *William and Mary*, the first sailing-barge to reach East Mills in 1850. She was a swim-header.

24

Colchester Hythe Yesterday and the Day Before. (*Above*) Craft by the quay, from an eighteenth-century 'prospect' of the town. (*Below*) A big fleet in the heyday, just before the First World War. The big vessel in the centre, with a vane at her mizzen masthead, is a 'boomie.'

25

were perhaps the first to use the present Hythe, first mentioned in that century. The Roman corn-ships, the Saxons' double-ended clinker-built rowing-boats, and the town's balingers, barges kept in the time of Richard II for trading in time of peace and sending to the wars at the King's command, would have unloaded lower down the river, at the old Hythe, a name now corrupted from the Saxon 'Hythe' (Harbour) to Old Heath, by which name a district of Colchester is to-day known. In 1623, though dredging had been in progress thirty-one years before, ships could not get above Rowhedge, and dues were levied for clearance.

In the fifteenth century Colchester, and to a less extent Bright-lingsea and Bradwell, were great wool-exporting centres. By the sixteenth century cargoes were interesting and various. In addition to the staple imports of Newcastle 'sea-cole,' foods, fish, salt, and wines were coming in, and exports included corn, bacon, butter, and cheese (chiefly sent to London). Holland was sending pots, brown and white paper, mill-stones, and dyes for the local wool-trade, including copperas, which suggests that the Essex industry referred to in Chapter IV had then hardly started. Prunes, figs, raisins, currants, and oranges are also mentioned. Cargoes named in a scale of port dues of 1698 include " Bay, Say, or Perpetuane," timber, chalk, lime, paving-stone, tobacco-pipe clay, ashes, and " pan-tyles," Fuller's earth, "oyle," wines, and brandy.

During the hard times of the following century exports of corn from Colchester caused such feeling among the hungry population that an escort of Dragoons had to protect the carts carrying the cargo to the Hythe.

A hint of some of the old-time riverside activities is given by the Customs' records, which in 1681 describe the common quay on the west side as extending from the " Lime Kilns on the south end to the old Salt House at the end of the Middle Row on the north end," while in 1823 a " Grocers' Quay " is mentioned as bounded on the south side by a shipyard. Shipbuilding at Colchester came to an end about the middle of the nine-teenth century.

To return to more recent times, however : while there was a Francis among the Colchester shipowners in 1846, it is the name of Beckwith that is perhaps most closely associated with the early days of Colchester sailing-barges. Sixty years ago Mills and Beckwith owned a fleet of vessels of all rigs, including one barquentine and seven or eight small barges, among them the *Jessie*, *Exact*, *Arnold Hirst*, *Empress*, *Spy*, and *Pride of the Colne*. A schooner owned in the port at this time, the *Margaret*, is remembered as a prize from the Crimea.

*Exact* was the only barge ever built at Colchester. She was built on beer-barrels in the field that is now part of Francis and Gilders' yard, and after her launch she would not go under Hythe Bridge. So they cut an inch and a half off her stemhead, shoved her under, and with that unerring deftness of humour which is an Essex characteristic named her *Exact*.

These craft were engaged in bringing grain to the mills, timber and oil cake, and in stack-work, and they also ran a regular carrier service weekly to London in competition with the railway. In the days when the modern sea-side resorts were building, thousands of tons of building material were unloaded by the barges on the open beaches of Clacton, Frinton and Walton. A condition of the work was that unloading must be completed in one tide, but even so it must have been worrying work in unsettled weather. The Kent barge *Favorite*, built in 1803 and the oldest barge afloat, did a lot of this work, and though sometimes blown up on to the beach always got away unscathed.

The gas-works coal-trade was mostly in the hands of the Harwich boomie-barges, which had developed out of the old cutter-rigged barges. One of these, the *Jabez* (with the *Faith* and *Rebecca* the only boomies actually owned in the port), was lost in the great gale of 1881. Other booms'l barges working to Colchester were the *Alice Watts*, *Startled Fawn*, *Hesper*, and *Gloriana*, trading up and down the East Coast from the Tyne with ancient dry compasses from which the card would be removed when out of use, a cork being placed on the head of the battered pin to protect what was left of its point. Their galleys were no more than primitive stoves lashed to the rigging on deck, and they had tiller steering—even the *Alice Watts*, the largest, which carried a fore-topmast square-sail. Old Ralph Hatcher, the *Hesper's* skipper, was totally deaf, and all remarks made to him had to be in writing. They carried a slate on deck for the job.

Yet the ketch barge skipper had no doubt of his superior status as compared with the sprittie sailorman. Old Captain Dove, of Brightlingsea, told me, with a zest that belied his ninety-three years, of experiences with the boomies *Masonic* and *Matilda Upton*, which he commanded, and both of which were sunk under him, though not before he had voyaged in them to nearly every port between Hull and Dublin, and across " the other side " to " Amsterdam, Rotterdam, and various other cuss-words." He admitted that in their own weather the spritties were faster, but said that when without a ship he always turned to the smacks, not (with withering scorn) to " those sprits'l barges." " Why ? I'll tell you why," he added. " Those things aren't fit to go to sea. They haven't a reef point about them. I know they do go to sea," he admitted, " but what can they do if they get caught in a breeze ? Why, only act like a blessed woman—lift up their skirts and run ! "

In the days just beyond memory's span the port of Colchester must have looked very different from what it does now, for there was a lock-gate by the present maltings, and from about 1719 to soon after 1800 this enabled vessels at the quays to lie afloat at low water. There was also a timber dock on the site of the present Corporation yard.

The craft of the middle of the nineteenth century would mostly seem poor things to modern eyes both in size and quality. The *Arnold Hirst*, for instance, was only of sixty-five tons, and she was an exception if she was not leaky, while to illustrate the beggarly living conditions of the times, a tale is told of the Colchester shipowner who was so notoriously mean that when he ordered his hundredweight of ' hard bread ' (ship's biscuits) from Last, the Hythe baker, he stipulated " flat both sides and no holes in them " in order to save the barrel of treacle which (when it was not forgotten) went aboard with them.

Throughout the latter half of this century as the hoys and schooners disappeared the sailing-barges were increasing in size, quality, and number, and the modern fleet of Francis and Gilders, combining practically all the small Colne and Blackwater barge fleets into one numbering over thirty vessels, is the biggest single fleet these rivers have known.

About 1902 Beckwith's had introduced the steamboats *Gem* and *Eager* for their London carrier service.  Of these the *Gem* is specially well remembered, and I am indebted to her former skipper, Mr David Francis, for much of this information.  The last of the Colchester passage-boats, she was a rare little old-timer, this 100-ton ketch-rigged steamer, and even thirty years ago, in her coasting days, she would recall the era of " down funnel and up screw " by setting her sail and turning away down Channel in the bargeman's time-honoured fashion—two hours standing offshore, one hour on.  The town's groceries, its beer, and its paraffin oil were among the goods regularly carried by the *Gem* and her sister-craft, which made two trips one week and one the next, this one being via Mistley.  Three calls were made in the London docks, so it was a busy life, and as any delay meant missing a week-end at home, it had to be a bad gale to interfere with the time-table ; indeed, it was rarely that anything but fog caused these little craft to upset their schedule.  It seems surprising that so economical a way of carrying heavy goods ever ceased, for, according to her old skipper, her deck cargo paid the *Gem's* expenses and everything below hatches was profit, but this last of the passage-boats turned over to ordinary coasting work in 1912, and was running everywhere between Plymouth and Hull and over to Holland up to 1914, when she was taken over for Admiralty service.  She was the last in a long tradition, for four passage-boats are mentioned in 1619, and a weekly service is referred to in 1714 as exempt from payment of dues towards the repair of the famous Dagenham sea-wall breach, save on four entries a year, when they were to pay three shillings.  Since the *Gem* no power coaster has belonged to Colchester.

It was about this time, just before the First World War, that the little harbour of Colchester was at its busiest.  The *James Renford* and *Essex*, both steamboats, were competing with the *Gem* and *Eager*, while in addition to Beckwith's, Francis's, and Marriage's barges, there were many craft belonging to Owen Parry's oil mills, the closing of which after the First World War was a sad day for the Hythe.  Owen Parry's fleet included that well-known racer the *Queen* and her sister-ship, *King*, but they also kept many other craft busy bringing in linseed in big, cylindrical drums, some of which were carried on deck.  One of the liveliest memories of his own sailing days recalled by Mr Joshua Francis, Managing Director of Francis and Gilders, Ltd, is of a deck cargo of these drums which broke loose one wild night down Swin and careered back and forth up and down the deck chasing himself and his mate in all directions till finally, having broken nearly every spoke off the wheel, they carried away the bulwarks and restored peace and quiet on deck by plunging overboard.

Jarvis and Gibbs also owned barges on Colne at this time, and Mr Thomas Ward had one bearing his own name. Shead's had the *Prosperous* and *Faith*, two of the oldest Colchester barges, and a local farmer, Mr Littlebury, two or three craft working with the produce of his fields, so that with the Maldon, Ipswich, London, and Kent craft there were often thirty barges loaded in London at one time for Colchester. And after a spell of southerly winds a hundred barges would muster from Colne and Blackwater to be joined at the Spitway by as many more streaming out of Harwich. Then began something like a barge race up Swin.

Since 1919 there have been motor tow-boats on the Colne, which have robbed the river of much of its laboriousness to the bargemen—indeed, it is already difficult to realize just how craft were got up the narrow reaches before their introduction. It is impressive enough to see the barges sail up to the quay to-day, and check alongside without sinking the vessel ahead or going stem first into the bridge in strong fair winds—but when the wind was foul how was it done ? It must be remembered that the average size of the barges even thirty years ago, before the millers with their modern siloes demanded 500-quarter lots, was much smaller than to-day, and these little craft would keep turning or, when that was impossible, sailing and luffing with a " Gravesend nip " and with the aid of booms to shove their heads round in extraordinarily narrow waters. Then, when at last there was no room at all, it was " down gear and out booms," and with mast and sails on deck the dead weight had to be shoved along. There were 'hufflers' in plenty in those days to come aboard and lend a hand, but even so there was a cruel amount of hard shoving. Tortuous, twisting Fingringhoe Creek, now negotiated effortlessly in a half-hour's towing, often took three tides of heartbreaking effort in those days.

Beckwith's passage barges before the introduction of the *Gem* and *Eager* used to employ trace-horses on the sea-wall. One walked each bank, but of course only the ' windward horse' could pull. The ' lee horse ' took his ease till a bend in the river gave him his turn. The horses would take the barges as far as Wivenhoe or Rowhedge. Manpower hauling on lines was used in similar fashion for the other barges.

The colliers and timber-ships would bring up in the estuary and await a slant, but as they could make Colchester only on spring tides it often became necessary to tackle a foul wind if one was not to wait another fortnight or unload at the buoys at Wivenhoe. Then the boat would be manned and sent ahead to tow, and the schooners and brigantines would, if there was not too much wind, fill away on the better tack and get some way on while the oarsmen did their best and let go a kedge to wind-ward. The ship would haul over to this, and then, breaking it out on the old tack again, would make another board. The brigs would box about, fore-yards back, mainmast sails drawing, filling and jilling almost without way, but just able to make over the ground and keep off the mud.

No wonder that the old-timers tell their younger brethren, " Work ! There is no work on the water nowadays ! " Especi-ally as they, unlike the bargeman to-day, had to turn out and help to work the cargo out when they finally got alongside.

THE " GEM," LAST OF THE       EARLY NINETEENTH-CENTURY
PASSAGE-BOATS               SAILING-BARGE

*From contemporary engravings*

# III

# BRIGHTLINGSEA SMACKS AND WRECKS

*The Boat that struck the Mast-head—A Queer Piano-stool—" You Brightlingsea Sharks "—A Tale that made an Audience weep*

BRIGHTLINGSEA men have never been afraid of going to sea. Their smacks earned a wonderful reputation for daring (and sometimes for piratical practices) in the last century.

Originally all these Brightlingsea smacks were cutters. Most of them were built by Aldous, most famous and productive of all the builders of Colchester fishing-boats. Every one, when built, was provided with a Bible and had a box to hold it built in the cabin. They ranged from eight to forty tons, and many of the smaller ones for oyster-dredging were built not to order but on speculation, and handed over for quite a small deposit. As conditions were, they were soon paid for, for ten-tonners which are still in service after seventy years were turned out for a hundred pounds, hull and spars.

But as the Brightlingsea seamen ventured farther afield, down Channel, up to Scotland, or to dredge the deep-sea oysters that lay off Terschelling, on the Dutch coast, involving a winter voyage of a month's duration, it came to be found that these cutters were not man enough for the job, even with Brightlingsea toughs aboard, and many were lengthened and re-rigged as ketches.

The nineteenth century saw the great days of the Brightlingsea fishing-fleet. As early as 1377 a commission on Essex fishing found fault with the " wunderthons," eight- to ten-feet beam trawls, which were taking so many fish that they were being sold to the swine, and in 1488 stow-boating was condemned by Parliament enacting that " stall-boats fastened by anchors having with them such manner of unreasonable nets and engines " be not allowed. Despite this, however, ' stall-boats ' were in use in 1547, and in 1662 sprats were being caught and brought to Colchester

" in incredible abundance." Fishing-boats and coasters were not distinct types up to the end of the eighteenth century, for throughout the French wars the Admiralty protection certificates against impressment refer constantly to vessels " fishing and coasting." Most smacks then were about twenty tons ; the biggest coaster was the *Nottingham* (1776) of 110 tons.

The Brightlingsea ships' names of this period are as lovely as a poem to read. There were the *Mary Fortune* and the *Anne Gallant* and—a lovely touch of quaint humour among so much serene dignity—the *Green Lettuce*.

By this time the day of the deep-sea voyage from such little havens as the Colne was done ; no longer did barques of Brightlingsea set out to Bordeaux with Essex fleeces or the Colchester weavers' cloth. The age of the specialized coaster and the specialized fishing-smack had come. In 1811 only three smacks were protected, but in 1848 there were 160 of fifteen to forty tons, and in 1861 the peak of 200 was touched. By 1929 that total had dropped to fifty-six, and it is to be feared it will have been halved again by the time the present post-war fit-out is completed to tell its tale.

A century ago they ranged far afield. In the eighteen-forties about sixty went in February or March to Falmouth and the Channel Islands for two or three months, dredging deep-sea oysters. The *Hebe* was taken by French cruisers, working in the three-mile limit, and the crew turned adrift ; an account of a Scottish adventure will be found in Chapter X.

Another favourite fishing-ground lay off the Terschelling Light, on the Dutch coast some 180 miles east-north-east of Orfordness, where in over twenty fathoms of water lay the deep-sea oysters which up to the time of the First World War were fished from Brightlingsea.

Originally this fishing was carried on with quite small cutters, but as these proved unequal to the work much larger, ketch-rigged smacks came to be employed. Some of these were specially built, about sixty feet long by seventeen feet beam ; some were old cod-smacks from Grimsby, similar in form to the Humber sailing-trawlers, which were the largest of their class in the British Isles, as much as eighty-five feet long. Some of the ketches were made by sawing the old cutters in two and lengthening them.

These vessels were known as ' skillingers '—a corruption of Terschelling—and went to sea and stayed at sea in any weather. Large dredges were handled by three men and towed on a sixty-five-fathom, three-inch warp.   A winch was used to haul, but it must have been cruel work.   Dredging continued without ceasing day and night while the weather was fine ; when there was too much sea to work the smack would be hove to.   These ketches went to sea for as much as three to four months at a stretch, never for less than three to four weeks.   All had wells in which the oysters were stored in string bags ; the *Austria* in one trip brought home thirty-two thousand.

Mr Frank Carr, in his *Vanishing Craft* (which also contains a fine picture of both inshore and deep-sea oyster-smacks in Brightlingsea Creek), gives an account by Captain Walter Pittick of the dismasting of one of these skillingers, the *Hawthorne*, one February night when hove to in a North Sea gale.   The smack was stated to be riding well when a tremendous squall caught her and broke off both mainmast and mizzen-mast short above the deck.   A steam trawler found her next day and towed her after an anxious trip into Cuxhaven.

Deep-sea oystering came to an end some years before the First World War.   So hard a game was not found worth the candle, and it is said that a poisoning scare killed the demand.   The skillingers then became scollopers, working out of the French Channel ports, principally Boulogne, and going to sea only by day.   The daily haul was sent to London on the night steamer. It seems, however, that a few Brightlingsea boats were engaged in this trade as early as 1887.   The Government inspector's report of 1899 credits Brightlingsea with ten first-class smacks scolloping from January to March inclusive.   The dredges used were the same as for the deep-sea oysters, though after a while the Brightlingsea men took a leaf out of the Frenchmen's book and equipped them with spikes as well as a hoeing edge—somewhat against their better judgment, as the destruction caused by these spikes was appalling and had much to do with the ultimate extinction of the fishery.

By this time, however, the old sailing-ketches had had their day.   Their place was taken by veteran Yarmouth steam drifters, with which several scolloping voyages were undertaken from

Brightlingsea. Remains of the old ketches can be seen in various stages of decay in Pyefleet and other creeks, and also at Emsworth, in Hampshire, a considerable home of the scolloping industry. The fleet included the *Excellent*, the biggest of them all, which was at work scolloping less than thirty years ago, *Vestal*, *Christabel*, *Test*, and *Fiona*, which, originally a Jersey coaster, is to end her days as a Sea Scout guardship in Colne. That there were clippers among them is proved by the fact that the cutters *Norman*, *Recruit*, *Welfare*, *Wave*, and others were employed as fish-carriers for the North Sea fleet at a weekly wage of twelve pounds.

The terrible losses in the great gales of 1883 and 1884 had as much as anything to do with the end of the ' skilling.' Five smacks, *Mascotte*, *Conquest*, *Recruit*, *Pride*, and *William and Henry*, and twenty-seven men from Brightlingsea were lost in two gales in those years, days of disaster which the tablets round the church walls recall.

From Charlie Death, a grand old veteran of the place, I heard how the cutter *Express* came as near being lost as was possible in the 1884 gale. At about seven in the morning they were in a gale of wind with a seven-cloth jib set abaft the mast, when a sea broke aboard and took everything out of her except the mast and bow-sprit. One hand, Walter Crampton, was washed overboard and lost. Sails, boat, spars, and bulwarks were gone, and, believe it or not, even the cross-trees from the mast. The ballast, dredges, and eight thousand oysters in her hold had shifted so that she lay with her upper dead-eyes in the water.

They let go a couple of dredges over her bow to try to bring her up to the sea, but it was to no avail, and as fast as they tried to get the ballast back it shot up into her side again. At two o'clock in the afternoon another sea swept them, taking the hatches and ripping up the decks. Now they were a floating wreck, and the men felt inclined to give up, but Death got them to set a five-cloth jib abaft the mast, and, having done this, they left him with some rum at four o'clock in the afternoon lashed to the tiller. Once he was swept away by a sea, but at dawn the battered *Express* crept into Yarmouth Roads and anchored. Next day they sailed her home—and drew four shillings a head !

Death and two of his cronies, Harry Bragg and Shedric Spar-ling, told me one day, sitting round the stove in the Water

Bailiff's office, tales of the 'salvaging' (pronounced for some reason with the accent on the second syllable) which was such a staple of the Essex coast in the youth of many an old salt still living. What tales they were ! Of how the *Excellent* was once in a sea which washed a short iron ladder out of her cabin and overboard, and, incredible as it sounds, carried her boat up and damaged it on the mizzen mast-head ! Of how the *Vestal* was driving out of control on to Haisborough Sand and had got into the shallow water when a breaker broached her to and brought her head to wind, hove-to, whereupon she shook herself, and, seeming to take a fresh resolve to fight it out, sailed herself clear of the sand.

This salvaging was a piratical business, but often a heroic one, for the looting of wrecks was inextricably connected with the rescue of crews of ships stranded on the Thames Estuary sandbanks till less than a century ago ; indeed, in 1866 Captain John Salmon, of the *Emily*, was presented with a telescope by the Board of Trade for the rescue from a wreck, at great risk to himself and his crew, of five men who had given up all hope after sixteen hours' exposure.

Though the N.E. Gunfleet was buoyed in 1628 (the first buoy on the Essex coast), and the Swin Spitway a few years later, many other channels and sands remained unmarked for many years after this, while not till 1845 was a lifeboat placed at Harwich, the first on this perilous stretch of coast, and even then it saved no lives for six years and was withdrawn. No doubt the interest of the salvagers, who regarded a wreck as something altogether too precious to be wasted on a lifeboat, had something to do with that. In any case it was not till the terrible wreck of the emigrant ship *Deutschland* on the Kentish Knock in 1875, with the loss of sixty-four lives, that the resulting outcry brought about the final provision of a lifeboat.

Four years later, when the Norwegian barque *Nef* was wrecked on the Long Sand and abandoned (September 24, 1879), Lloyd's agent found two days later that her fore- and main-mast had been cut away, and all her gear, rigging, and provisions even to the brass locks and hinges of the doors had been taken. You may be sure the Colne men had had their share, for the Colchester Receiver of Wrecks subsequently reported on their methods. These smacks worked in company, he said. One or two went to the wreck and another went fishing or stayed in harbour. Then these made a rendezvous at sea, and most of the stuff was transferred to the smack which had not been to the wreck, the others running in with some trifles or with something too large to be concealed, and reporting to the Receiver. Meantime perhaps the goods would be transferred to a smack from some smaller port, or if not the smack would return and say they had never been near the wreck, but had been in quite another direction. The Harwich Receiver said that this practice had been going on for years, and it was most difficult to deal with it.

In December 1738 the Maldon Customs Collector was contesting a claim that " wrecked coals pay but half duty. . . . The coals were in good condition when brought on shore and sold cheap to the detriment of the merchants ; therefore we think that they ought to pay the whole duty."

" I don't suppose anyone can go back to the Knock John[1] ship ? " I asked those ancient mariners, mentioning perhaps the richest of all the windfalls that an ill-wind ever blew ashore for the good of Brightlingsea and Rowhedge. That was in 1856, yet I was among men with long memories, and longer family traditions. " Well, seeing that I took my drop of medicine out of a Knock John glass just before I came here," said Bragg, " I dare say I ought to know something about it." And he told me how his family had secured these glasses, one of which had been given as a wedding present at the time of every marriage in the family since, and how there were men in the town who secured the rich cloth aboard " and never did a stroke of work again as long as they lived," and how a woman who informed on the plunderers was burned in effigy.

Well remembered too is the wreck of the full-rigged ship *Indian Chief*, which went ashore on the Long Sand head in the fearful gale of January 1881, when the Harwich lifeboat was capsized in the harbour, and Walton pier was washed away. The smackmen saw the crew of that ship, frozen and exhausted, fall from her yards into the sea, and when later they got near her they found

[1] The name is taken from the Thames Estuary sandbank on which the wreck occurred.

rats crushed between the swollen balls of jute which she was carrying. Death was there in *Ripple*, and recalled a noted Brightlingsea sailor named Pallett, who came from the Channel Islands, and, being of French stock, " could speak no English till he learned to say dammit," getting down her royal yard though the lifts had parted.

Bragg, who was in *Tartar*, told me that one of the salvagers looked aloft as they stripped her gear, and commenting, " What a fine piano-stool that topmast truck would make ! " went aloft and secured it. What a strange fancy in all that wild waste of sand, water, death, and destruction ! I should like to know what happened to that piano-stool, though.

Those three have promised to show me some of the linen and engraved silver that came off the *Ingerid*, a Rotterdam steamship bound from Norway to Naples, which finished her days on the Sunk in that same gale. She struck the sand on a Monday, and after a boat's crew had been lost trying to leave her the following day, and other men been lost overboard trying to get a second boat out, the captain and six men sought refuge on the foremast. Here they lashed themselves on the Tuesday, and remained till Friday morning, when they were got into Harwich by the lifeboat. According to the contemporary report in the *Essex Standard* :

> The faces of the four shipwrecked sailors were so blackened with frost that they looked as if they had all been in a horrible fighting affray, whilst their limbs were stiff and useless. The legs and feet of all seven men were severely frost-bitten, being black and red from the exposure to the cold, whilst the flesh under the nails of their hands and part of their fingers were also blackened.

Yet my old smackmen introduced a note of comedy even into such a tale as this, for they recalled that the *Ingerid* was loaded with herrings in barrels, and that they made special screws on boat-hooks to get them out. After she had lain on the sand a month a smack bound down Channel took a cargo of them aboard. A man named Joe Tillett gave them " a drop more smoke to freshen them up a bit " and sold them to the navvies in the streets of Newhaven. " They could allus put a bit of beer away, them Newhaven navvies—but, my word, we give 'em a thirst that night." Shead's crew smuggled her linen wrapped in their mainsail and drew £4 a head on it, while Bragg had, till recent years, one of those herrings nailed up over his door for a souvenir !

In those days a marine-store dealer's stood next to the Custom House. Oh, tempting conjunction ! A lovely hawser was coming up the road on a barrow. The Custom House doors stood open. So did the marine-store dealer's. "Keep her going, boys. Keep her full," the word went round the crew of barrow-shovers. " Altogether, now—run her in ! " In she went, and the doors shut to behind—but not the doors of the Custom House.

In the spratting season the smacks organized themselves into 'companies,' or groups of six or seven smacks which worked together and pooled their catches. The sprats were transferred by towing one or more of the detached sleeves of the stow-boat net beneath the rowing-boat. A pull with, say, four sleeves, each nine yards long and chock-full of fish, was indeed a long pull and a strong pull if the carrier-smack was up-tide.

These companies were known by such picturesque names as the Short Blue Company, the Cob Company, and the Peg Leg Company. One day the last-named company, including *Eileen*, *Recruit*, *Express*, and *Dauntless*, spotted a brig go ashore on the ' Burrows,' as the Barrow Sand is always called. Argument ensued as to whether she was on the Swin side or the Black Deep. They decided she was in the Swin—but they were wrong, and as, with the tide on the ebb and the wind sou'west, they could not now get back, they brought up, rowed ashore on the Barrow, and set out to carry the boat across the sand. But on completing that exhausting journey they found they had for once met their match. The Scottish skipper sat on the quarter and roared with laughter at their efforts. He refused to be scared by their gloomy comments on his dangerous position, and when they hopefully asked his cargo he replied with a guffaw, " Chalk ! Worth about five bob a hundred tons ! " He added, " She'll come off the same way as she went on," and sure enough as the tide made he got his headsails set, and her head canted off, and away he went. So did the Peg Legs, but not in such good humour, for his parting words in rolling Scots were, " That's one for you Br-r-ightling-sea shar-r-ks ! "

The smack *Honour* put Bob Tillet aboard a wrecked Dutch schooner and sailed into Harwich for a tug. In her absence the schooner capsized. Bob drove up by the Mouse on the wreckage and was picked up by a P. and O. liner. He got back to Brightlingsea to find the *Honour* with a flag in her rigging for him.

A similar incident occurred when a smack put one John Sharpe aboard a water-logged ship on the Gunfleet, and, a gale springing up, had to leave him there four days. He survived the ordeal, but showed the effect of the shock all his life.

One of the strangest ' wrecks ' remembered was seen sixty-eight years ago by Bragg when he was stow-boating as a boy in the *Greyhound* in the Rays'n. He saw a full-rigged ship come right up the Wallet, through the Knoll Channel, and go ashore on the ' Main.' She had no idea where she was and did not know she was aground till they looked overboard and saw she had stopped. She only stayed there till the next spring tide, but the disgraced captain jumped overboard and drowned himself.

Another skipper who was lost (but knew it !) brought up near a Brightlingsea smack in the Black Deep and asked his position. The " shark " offered to tell him for ten pounds and was refused. In the end, however, the skipper compromised and gave him ten pounds to pilot him clear—a job worth something in those days of inadequate buoyage.

A vivid account of a salvage carried out as long ago as 1834 is recorded in a now forgotten little book called *The River, the Sea, and the Creek: Sketches of the East Coast*, by " Garboard Streyke " (Mr F. Smythies), published in 1884. This recounts how on November 10 of that year the Colne smack *Eagle*, with William Easter master, was hove to on the look-out in the Swin off the Crouch. It was about eleven in the morning, blowing a hard gale from the E.N.E., and thick with rain, when they saw a vessel go ashore on the Middle Sand. Letting draw, they found her to be the 600-ton barque *Marquis of Huntly* sailing from Leith to London with Government stores. She had a pilot on board, but had no idea of her position. Other smacks were already on the scene, including the *Batchelor*.

It was a terrible business getting aboard, and in doing so the *Batchelor's* boat was swamped, the master, Lawrence, being washed out of her and rescued with great difficulty. However,

they got under her lee and aboard in the end, and Easter was put
in charge.  He had the main try-sail and spanker set and got her
head to wind ; then the jib and fore-topmast-staysail were set to
drive her off, but when the fore-tops'l filled the yard carried away.
The salvagers then turned attention to lightening the ship and
managed to get six heavy cannon and some chests of ammunition
overboard, a Herculean task as they had to dump them to windward to save her smashing in her lee bilge on them.  All this time
the barque was pounding violently, decks awash.  Now they let
go the starboard bower anchor and awaited the next tide.

The captain wanted to send to Sheerness for a steamer.  Easter
disagreed, saying they would be afloat or broken up before she
could arrive.  Two brothers named Cook and a man called
Samuel Wisbey manned their boat, however, and attempted to
get back to the smack for the purpose.  The boat capsized, and
the three were drowned under the eyes of their mates.

When the tide came the anchor-chain crushed the iron fairlead
and nearly took the stem out, but they got a spring on it.  When
this parted she bore off the wrong way, and they lost three more
boats alongside, and nearly a lad with them, for he was in the
water for twenty minutes.  Eventually they wore her round, and
at half-past six that evening she was afloat in Swin without her
false keel.  They pumped all night, and next day Easter took her
to Gravesend.

The most dramatic story of all, however, is the salvage by John
Dowman, of Brightlingsea, dredging the Channel oysters out of
Fécamp in the 42-ton *Wave*, when the 180-ton billy-boy schooner
*Wesleyan* was wrecked on Beachy Head.  The weather was such
that the Dieppe steamer service was suspended, and the lifeboat
could not go out.  As the *Wesleyan* was wallowing and crashing
on the sand, loaded with Portland stone, some lumps of which
weighed five tons, there was no hope of getting her off, and Dowman and his mate, Causton, told the skipper to come aboard the
*Wave* with them.  He, however, said he had " something else "
below, and when they went down into the cabin they found there
his wife with five children round her and a three-months-old baby
in her arms, naked as he was born.  The cabin was knee-deep in
water, and they had been in that state all night and the day before.
Now they were half dead with cold and shock, and the men had

to drag out the children one by one and throw them in the wildly pitching boat. Then the half-crazed skipper refused to leave, saying the schooner was all he had, and he would not go home to an empty house—for even his bedding was aboard—but would stop and go down with her. There being no time to argue, they flung him in the boat too. The schooner settled by the stern and sank so rapidly they had to cut the boat adrift.

So they set out for Newhaven, doing their best for the children and the mother, who kept crying out she knew this ship would go down like the other. It was a dead beat to Newhaven, but they got there about nine in the evening and were given a great reception. A collection was made and five pounds raised, which Dowman gave to the schooner skipper.

News of the deed had preceded them to Colne, and on their return Sir Claude de Crespigny, of Wivenhoe, raised another fund of thirteen pounds. Dowman also received a gold medal, and there was a civic reception in Colchester Town Hall at which some of the audience are reported to have wept as the smackmen described what they saw when they went below in the *Wesleyan's* cabin.

Now lifeboats and better buoyage and pilotage have made an end of salvages. The deep-sea oysters, " as big as a straw hat," like that one which at a Peldon wedding is recorded as having been divided into eight good morsels, are forgotten. The timbers of the deep-sea ketches lie mouldering in the mud, and Brightlingsea devotes itself to the quieter delights of yachting.

Yachts have been stationed in the creek for more than a century and built there nearly as long. Lord Wharncliffe's *Romulus* was the first yacht to belong to the place, and in 1849 she had been joined by the famous *Pearl* (of which more will be said when Wivenhoe is described), and *Darling, Dove, Christobel, Fleur-de-Lys*, and *Satanella* were other early yachts. The first to be built in a local yard was the ten-tonner *Fawn*, which was built by Aldous in 1846, though in 1839 eight yachts had competed in the first recorded race for a " handsome silver cup."

While yacht-building never attained the same importance as it did higher up the Colne, the chronicle of the vessels belonging to Brightlingsea in the last century would fill a book longer than this, for by 1882 there were more than seventy, and in the nineties about a hundred and seventy vessels, and all through the years since the creek has been packed each summer with small yachts and the river with big ones, while in the winter the long beaks of the racers and the clipper stems of the steamers hang over the road by the slipway in a long panorama of curves.

The schooners *Tamesis* and *Heartsease* are among the last to maintain the old tradition, while the fine eighteen-foot one-design class, well suited to the boisterous conditions of the estuary, worthily represents the new.

Though in 1946, just a century after the building of the *Fawn*, Aldous' Successors, Ltd, announced the end of the firm's interest in boat-building, the Brightlingsea yachting tradition will be kept alive by James and Co., incorporating the yard where Stone built so many a staunch boat.

I have tried to suggest what has gone into the making of that tradition, but I believe that the most vivid impression of all will be gained by sitting a while in the quiet of Brightlingsea church, still a splendid building, even though less glorious than before that night in 1814 when the clerestory crashed through the roof without warning.    For around the walls are tablets commemorating the Brightlingsea men whom the sea has claimed since 1872, when the Rev. (later Canon) Arthur Pertwee started these memorials.    There are nearly two hundred of them in all, and that number will be exceeded when the men of the Second World War are commemorated.    Each tells in simple language of some humble tragedy ; some in the far-away waters of the great oceans, some in the rivers and creeks of the Essex coast. There were Brightlingsea men in such disasters as the loss of the *Titanic* and of H.M.S. *Vanguard*, but most recall more intimate affairs—of the *Greyhound*, lost in collision in the Swin in 1884, taking Charles Barber and his two sons aged sixteen and fourteen with her, or of " John Goddard, Lost with his Barge *Frances*, Flushing to London, December 4, 1896," and " Maurice Goddard, 16, Perished with his Father " ; or, perhaps more pitiful still, the time when the father survived to break the news of a tragedy— " Leonard Wellum, 17, Drowned from his Father's Barge *James Garfield*, off Ramsgate, 1891."

Ships of every kind are named : the ketch *John and Charles*, 1891 ; the cod smack *British Workman*, 1889 ; the emigrant ship

*Kapunda*, 1887 ; the sloop *Friends*, of Goole, 1880 ; the brig *Edward*, 1881 ; the brigantine *Daniel* ; the schooner *William* ; the lugger *Mascotte*, barges, yachts, smacks, all contributed their toll of Brightlingsea lives to that hard master the sea.

No fewer than forty lives were lost in the dreadful years 1883–84, which had much to do with the final abandonment of the Terschelling deep-sea oyster fishery. The *Recruit* sailed then with a skipper of thirty-five and a crew aged thirty-three, twenty-eight, twenty-three, twenty-two, and eighteen. None of that brave young company returned ; all are commemorated here.

Days when dredging off the French coast was a commonplace are recalled by the loss of the smack *Norman* in Caen Bay in 1894, but most of the smacks—including, in addition to those mentioned, *Oyster Girl*, 1895, *Neddy Campbell* and *Gipsy Queen*, 1894 —were recorded simply as " claimed by the North Sea." Sometimes, as in the case of the smack *Perseverance*, 1889, the terse obituary " Particulars Unknown " hints at some last fight alone, unwitnessed and unrecorded.

The whole way round the walls of the church the tablets go, a frieze most moving in its undramatic simplicity ; and above the tablets march the words " In the midst of life we are in death. Out of the deep have I called unto Thee, O Lord. Thou art the hope of all the ends of the earth and of them that remain in the broad sea. He shall send down from on high to fetch me, and shall take me out of many waters. The sea shall give up her dead."

So be it. Yet I believe, for all the cruelty that the sea has shown to Brightlingsea men, none would be more sad at heart should they come to " a new heaven and a new earth, and there was no more sea."

# IV

## QUEER HARVESTS OF THE SEA

*Cement-stone and Copperas Dredging—The Romans' Building Material
—How not to clean a Knife—Literally Vitriolic*

ALL that was dredged from the sea by Colne fishermen in the nine-teenth century was not fish by any means. Brightlingsea smacks in particular were also occupied in the curious pursuits of cement-stone and copperas dredging.

Ever since Cardinal Wolsey was granted permission to take stone from Harwich cliffs for his college at Ipswich, building-stone has been gathered from the Essex shores, but in 1796 James Parker, of Northfleet, Kent, took out a patent for Roman, Parker's, or Aquatic cement, the making of which from the cement-stone, or *septaria*, to be found off Harwich and Walton became a very considerable industry. At first the stone was mostly taken from the foot of the cliffs, and so much was carried away that coast erosion was seriously aggravated. Then when these deposits were worked out it became the practice to dredge from smacks on the so-called " West Rocks," which were in fact an accumulation of cement-stone deposited off Walton Naze by the tide. (So much for the oft-repeated tale that the smacks were dredging stone from the ruins of ancient Walton buildings now beneath the sea.)

These *septaria* were broken into small pieces which were burned in a kiln with breeze, just as chalk is burned for lime. The pro-duct was ground very fine, sifted, and barrelled. When used it was mixed with the correct proportion of sand and water, and though it deteriorated quickly, and so had to be used fresh, it was extremely valuable in that it quickly set hard even under water, and so was widely used for stopping broken water-pipes or as damp-proof stucco for facing buildings. It was, in fact, the fore-runner of the modern Portland cement, which ultimately replaced it. Incidentally, in Roman days these *septaria* formed the only local building material.

The real home of the industry was Harwich, whence cement-stone was exported all over the country and to all Northern Europe, and where in 1845 between four and five hundred men were employed in the trade at five factories. There were, how-ever, factories at Colchester and Brightlingsea as well as in other parts of Essex and Kent ; indeed, in 1859 Cobb and Taylor, of the Hythe, Colchester, were one of the only two Essex firms remaining.

In 1851 it was estimated that three to four hundred cutter-rigged smacks were at work on the West Rocks, racing each other on and off its grounds morning and evening. Most of these boats were from Kentish ports, but some were from Harwich and Brightlingsea. The dredgermen received about five shillings a ton for this stone, which was described as providing a " very pro-fitable day's work " under favourable conditions. It must also have been an uncommonly hard one. In the seventies the fleet was also a familiar sight to holiday-makers on the Walton beaches, but though at the turn of the century Roman cement was still being made at Faversham, it was by then almost entirely super-seded by Portland cement. The older generation on the Colne, however, can still remember the barges *Fortitude* and *Gratitude* trading in this cargo, and it is recorded that in 1848 some stone was dredged off Brightlingsea.

The story of the copperas industry is rather similar. This con-sisted of the gathering, or dredging, of nodules of copperas (bisulphide of iron) and the manufacturing of them into green copperas, or green vitriol, which is used for dyeing cloth and leather black and for making black ink.

Like cement-stone, copperas is a product of the London clay. It occurs all round the Essex coast (and occasionally inland) in the form of small cylindrical blocks varying in size from that of a small twig to the size of a man's thumb, so closely resembling pieces of wood (even the bark being distinguishable in some cases) as to suggest that wood formed the nucleus on which the copperas was deposited. It was worth in raw form from fourteen to eighteen shillings a ton. Copperas is mentioned among the sixteenth-century imports, but by 1770 the Brightlingsea factory, which was busy throughout the seventeenth and eighteenth centuries, employed a great number of smacks and vessels to dredge the stones along this coast.

It was a stock joke in olden days to advise boys to dig their knives into the "copperas grounds" and leave them over night to clean them of rust. When the knives were removed in the morning the blades had disappeared, converted into green copperas—for this action was precisely the secret of the manufacture. The copperas was gathered into heaps and packed with alternate layers of scrap-iron. It was then wetted, and in a few hours the copperas was oxidized into green vitriol and sulphuric acid, which acted on the scrap-iron to produce more copperas. The liquid drained into pits, into which more scrap-iron was thrown till all the free acid was exhausted, and the liquid was then boiled in lead pans with still more iron to evaporate the water, the copperas crystallizing in cooling-tanks. So literally vitriolic was the process that fifty years ago the old site of the industry in Walton High Street was described as still an open space, bare of vegetation, and it was said that the floors of the near-by houses quickly became corroded.

Though it is over a century since the manufacture was practised in Essex—it is surmised that its extinction coincided with the decline of the local wool trade and tanneries—the gathering of raw copperas from the beaches at low water continued an occupation for women and children all the year round, and for the men in winter as late as the seventies, when the crowds of copperas-gatherers at Walton were still to be seen. One of its last uses was in sulphuric acid making at Ipswich.

It remains perpetuated to-day in many names, including Copperas Grounds, in the Wallet, Copperas Bay, on the south bank of the Stour, and a Copperas House Field marking the site of the works at Brightlingsea.

# V

## WORK AND PLAY

*A Smuggler and a Magistrate—Latch-keys but No Admittance—Kippered
Herrings with Marmalade—" Whose Turn to get drunk ? "—How Many
Kidneys has a Pig ?*

SUCH, then, were some of the things that went on out of Brightlingsea in the boyhood days of the veteran mariners who now sit
out on sunny mornings in the shelter by the Hard. They can
picture that same Hard cluttered up with wreckage—anchors and
chains, tobacco, ships' boats brought in by the salvagers, stacks of
timber lost from the deck cargoes of the water-logged Norwegians
—and with tons of cement-stone newly dredged off Walton.

The only causeway then was an old ship's keel let in the mud
(which was knee-deep where now there is firm ground), and close
by where the present causeway is was the Coast Guard hulk. Over
across the river on the Mersea shore lay the Hospital Ship and,
stranded on the mud, the Bakers' old barge, *Pandora*.

Schooners, ketches, and brigs lay on the Hard, their crews
working out their cargoes of coal, and crammed in the narrow St
Osyth channel lay the great fleet of smacks—a hundred and
twenty in all, moored two or three or four together, with a few
lower down the creek—the big ketches, the long-boomed stow-
boating and salvaging cutters, and the half-hundred little oyster-
smacks.

Monday morning would see forty or fifty smacks' boats on the
Hard for water, which the men had to fetch all the way from a
spring in Coke's Lane, at the east end of the town, till a tap was
provided on the Hard.

Many of the men who moored against that picturesque background were in one way or another of a type we shall not see
again. Daredevil sailing was a commonplace. Walter Welham used to sail his father's ketch *Antelope*, though his father had

47

to come along as often as possible to draw the freight money, or
there was small chance of his seeing any.  He came away from an
Irish port with a load of mackerel and carried away his jib in the
Irish Sea.  Heave to and get it in ?  Not he !  There was a fair
wind, so he just kept coming and towed it under the lee bow all
the way up Channel !  The tatters when he got home were " as
white as a hound's tooth."  His way of coasting was to be in port
till he was spent out ; then put to sea in any weather and crack on.
His luck was as steady as his nerve.

Less lucky was another daredevil skipper, William Fance, son
of Captain Fance, of the boomie-barge *Masonic*.  He coasted
about in a barge of his own without even a compass.  He was
skipper of the smack *Express* when she was lost, and his body was
found ashore at Haisborough, naked.  It is thought that he had
tried to swim ashore.

One of the most stirring tales of old-time Brightlingsea seamanship concerns Charles Barnes, who as a seventeen-year-old apprentice was the only survivor left aboard a smack in the Channel
when his five mates were washed overboard and she lost her gear
and hatches.  The boy got up sails, which he nailed over the
hatches, and sailed single-handed to Shoreham, being rewarded
with an inscribed silver watch by the Brightlingsea Smack Club.
(These clubs were, of course, not social institutions, but co-operative insurance societies.)

On the lighter side the renowned George Orman (" Dawley ")
deserves a mention.  He could not read or write, but was a rare
barterer and recorded his deals in a system of characters of his own
made with chalk on his door.  He was a brave and energetic man
and did a lot of work in his smack *Emblem* in the Downs, grappling
for ships' anchors and gear.  One great anchor he brought in to
Brightlingsea, with a wooden stock and a huge ring for bending
on a rope cable, is now in the Colchester Museum.  He had a
dump of contraband in the sand on Brightlingsea Stone and
generally dodged the Revenue men, but on one occasion he found
himself in Colchester police court and was cautioned by the
magistrates' clerk, who told him he must answer questions.
" Naow, naow, booy," he answered, " my owd tongue own't
on'y wag when I tell it, and when thet do thet on'y saie what
I want it to."

When these smacks went to sea they put the tea in the kettle and the kettle on the stove. The stove was kept in and the kettle on, more tea being added till there was no room for water, and then they started again. My old friend Sparling was used to this style of living, yet he told me he was surprised when he went to sea with Johnny Underwood in the *Lady of the Isles* and Johnny proceeded to smother two kippered herrings with marmalade ! But then it was this same Johnny who left his smack trawling in the Rays'n and rowed into Brightlingsea for water in a punt caulked with seaweed !

The Davies brothers were the complete twins. They converted an old ship's boat, called her *Odd Times*, and in her went winkling. They got drunk on alternate Friday nights, and the sober one assisted the other off in the punt. This turn-and-turn-about routine was most carefully maintained, and as the pair came ashore with their winkles the boys on the Hard called out, " That's the one whose turn it is this week." They were parted once only, when one was sent to prison.

I want, however, to avoid giving the impression that these men who saw the last days of a real long-shore community by the Colne were merely quaint, obsolete eccentrics. An adventurous, lively turn of mind has always made these men ready to try anything once. Fred Salmon, of the *Emily*, tried putting an electric light in the mouth of his stow-boat net. He got plenty of whiting, but no sprats, perhaps because sprats lie head to tide and thus enter the net stern first, so that those in a position to do so could not see the light. Tom Poole, the Water Bailiff, tried the same scheme on a trawl-beam when Colchester first had electric light, but could not find it made any difference either in attracting or repelling the fish.

Spring Wyncoll, a retired Mersea shipwright, had a fancy when he was landlord of the Fingringhoe Whalebone to cycle on the water, and mounted the cranks of a ' penny-farthing ' in a punt, in which he voyaged to Colchester.

A few tales of the smackmen ashore will illustrate the gaiety and zest of life in those days of hard toil and uncertain livelihood. They centre largely round the pubs, and certainly too much time and money were spent in these places. Yet I do not know that it was so much worse to drink, jest, and yarn than it is now to come into Colchester on the bus and gape a couple of hours away hanging dumbly on the mouthings of Hollywood's latest crooner.

Every smackman had to go through the ordeal of ' shoeing ' in these pubs when he came of age, and I am told (and can well believe) it was a painful business having your foot lifted and every husky smackman present ' drive a nail ' in the sole of your boot.

" What game shall we play to-night ? " they used to ask on those winter Saturday nights when the yachts were laid up and the men had to make their own fun.   Some outlandish tricks were tried.   One party went to a butcher who had just killed six pigs and got him to cut one kidney out of each.   Then they started an argument as to how many kidneys a pig had and took on a five-shilling bet with every man who said two.   To settle it they repaired to the slaughter-house, proved their point to the fuddled gamblers, and got paid for their trouble.

Another night the party was going well, and a man went round the houses of all present to collect the latch-keys and tell the women to go to bed.   Being a bit far gone himself, he distributed the keys indiscriminately, and not one man could get in !   They were dodging about all night swapping keys, and still at it when their wives opened up next morning !

Rough days, uneducated days.   But virile days.   These men, who worked hard, lived dangerously, and played like boys, were simple by Ministry of Education standards.   They were not sophisticated—but they were not spoon-fed.

# VI

## WIVENHOE'S CENTURY OF SPLENDOUR

*The Marquis and the Smugglers—Yacht that made a Town's Fortune—*
*The Cutter with Two Masts—A Surprise for an Owner—Lightship that*
*went voyaging—A Millionaire's Queer Ways—Miraculous Draughts of*
*Fishes*

IN the year 1820 the Marquis of Anglesey, fresh home from the
French wars after losing a leg at Waterloo, wanted a yacht.
What made him turn to a tough little village on the river Colne
for it we are never likely to know, but perhaps he himself had a
taste for toughness, since the yacht he wanted was to be a 130-ton
cutter.

Anyway, he sought out Philip Sainty, the chief Wivenhoe
boat-builder, a man whose hobbies Wivenhoe tradition still
declares to have been smuggling and polygamy. As to the latter
there is no evidence, but it is true enough that Sainty was unfortunately detained in Springfield Gaol just then, and when the
Marquis secured for him a full pardon he declined to come out till
his brother and his brother-in-law (a man bearing the good Essex
name of Pullen) were also released from Maidstone Gaol, where
they were lodged for similar offences.

By releasing that trio of gaol-birds the Marquis not only
secured for himself the famous *Pearl*, which a local historian,
Cromwell, writing in 1825, says was " one of the finest vessels of
its kind in the kingdom " ; he also laid the foundations of a
century of fame and glory for Wivenhoe, which, as a direct
result of the genius of Sainty, exemplified in that yacht, was
transformed from a home of smugglers and fishermen into a
fashionable yachting centre, which *The Field* in 1876 described as
rivalling the Medina or Haslar Creek. So numerous were the
successors of the *Pearl* that every man bar one of her original
crew is said to have become the master of a yacht.

The *Pearl* has been misdescribed (notably in the *Victoria County History*) as a lugger, and it has also been stated in print that she never raced.    There remains, however, an actual account of one race in which she took part, against the noted R.Y.S. clipper *Arrow*.    This occurred in 1826, and we are lucky to have a first-hand description of it, given by Mr Charles Ratsey, of Cowes, in 1888.    He says :

> In 1826 Mr Joseph Weld challenged the Marquis of Anglesey to sail the *Arrow* against the *Pearl* for five hundred pounds.   The Marquis at that time had the *Pearl* and a smaller vessel of forty tons called the *Liberty*, whilst Mr Weld had the *Arrow* and the *Julia* of forty tons.   It was arranged that the *Arrow* should sail against the *Pearl* and the *Liberty* against the *Julia*, and as the *Pearl* won her match and the *Julia* hers, no money passed.   Lord Anglesey in accepting the challenge said, "If *Arrow* should beat *Pearl* I will burn her as soon as we get back !"   As it was, the *Pearl* won by a fluke.

A narrow escape from an ignominious end !

Another challenger, the *Mosquito*, is recorded as having sailed through the *Pearl's* lee, upon which the Marquis politely dipped his ensign to the yacht that had weathered him for the first time in his experience—a mild and courteous reaction from an old warrior.

In 1828 a 538-ton naval sloop named *Pearl* was built by Sainty. She was to the Marquis's design, but—alas that the footnote should prove such an anticlimax to the tale !—she was a failure.   The second Marquis's brother, Lord Alfred Paget, was one of the best-known figures in Victorian yachting and a pillar of the Harvey firm with *Mystery* (1842), *Rosalind*, and *Xantha* (built at Wivenhoe in 1865 and later renamed *Gertrude*).   The family connexion was retained right up to a few years before the Second World War, when a member of the Paget family was racing the old Maldon smack *Columbine* in the Essex regattas.

It was not in the name of Sainty, however, that the shipyard was to flower to the height of its glory, for in 1832 Thomas Harvey took over from the aged smuggler, who died in 1844 and is commemorated by a stone subsequently erected in Wivenhoe churchyard, describing him as " Builder of the Marquis of Anglesey's yacht *Pearl*."

This Harvey founded in 1849 a branch at Ipswich, where several famous yachts were built, and about 1857 the firm became

Thomas Harvey and Son, John Harvey (father of Sir John Martin-Harvey, the famous actor-manager, who was born and spent his early years at Wivenhoe) having gone into partnership with his father. From now on a succession of famous racing schooners, yawls, and cutters was launched from its ways. Between 1860 and 1881 there appeared the *Audax, Joan, Ariadny, Water Lily, Elsie, Anemone, Snowdrop, Pandora, Dagmar* (a 33-ton cutter built for King Edward VII when Prince of Wales), *Edwina, Egidie, Druid, Rose of Devon, Alexandra, Island Home, Resolute, Hope, Dauntless, Sea Belle* (eulogized by *The Field* in 1877 as " unequalled for stiffness and weatherliness " by any other schooner ever built), *Shear Water, Spindrift, Rosabelle* (a yawl whose name was carried by one of the last big steam yachts to winter at Wivenhoe), *Miranda* (a very famous 130-ton schooner), *Bakalvum, Rose, Gannet,* and *Chloris.*

When the *Audax* came out she was regarded as a duffer, and in the autumn they lengthened her stern and added more lead to her keel. Wivenhoe Church was being restored at that time, and some of the leaden coffins are said to have been smuggled into the shipyard and run into the keel. After that she beat everything she met ! While lying at Erith the skipper of the *Audax*, Captain Rayner, had a tiff with the owner, who ordered the yacht to be taken to the Colne instead of competing in the Channel race, Cowes to Torquay, which was a disappointment to all on board as it meant a gold cup containing a hundred sovereigns. So instead of going to Colne the skipper telegraphed and entered for the race. The owner, opening his copy of *The Times*, saw that his yacht had won the cup, and all disagreements were soon forgotten.

The fifty-nine-ton cutter *Volante* had the distinction of racing against the schooner *America* in 1851, but, coming into collision with the *Freak*, she gave up the race. The following year she won the Royal Thames Yacht Club cup, and ten years later she was lengthened in the bow and raced with great success till 1869, when she dragged ashore on Ryde sands and was wrecked.

*Miranda* was noted as ' the cutter with two masts,' for though she was schooner-rigged her huge mainsail took the heart out of her competitors, and played its part in bringing to an end the halcyon days that schooner-racing had seen in the seventies.

One of the most famous of all yachts connected with Wivenhoe was Sir Thomas Brassey's auxiliary schooner *Sunbeam*, which signed a Colne-side crew for her famous voyage round the world.

In 1863 there was built here a little schooner which was to be immortalized by Edward Fitzgerald, the translator of Omar Khayyám, who took her to Woodbridge and named her *Scandal* because "nothing travelled so fast out of that port." The schooner's next owner, Sir Cuthbert Quilter, with supreme lack of humour platitudinously rechristened her *Sapphire*, and, converted first to cutter and then to ketch, she was knocking about Brightlingsea, the South Coast, and London River till 1928.

In the seventies Wivenhoe had reached the peak of its fame, and it is pleasant to pause and attempt to form a picture of the place in that golden age. As well as the crack yachts that were coming off the ways at Harvey's at the rate of two a year, and from James Husk's lower down the quay, cutter-rigged smacks for the local fishing were being built at both yards, together with trading vessels and some ketch smacks for Yarmouth. William Wyatt, the West Mersea shipwright, served his apprenticeship on these sixty-five years ago, and has told me their keelsons were seventy feet long, all in one piece of timber.

The place had its own ropery, Browne's, which was brought there from Nacton, in Suffolk, in 1770. The factory adopted steam-power in the very early days, but its enterprise was part of its undoing, for the primitive boiler burst and blew the whole place to pieces, killing three people, including the proprietor's son. All three are buried in one grave in Wivenhoe churchyard. You could hardly blame the old boiler, for a heavy clock-weight had been hung on the safety-valve! The rebuilding after the explosion crippled the business, for there was no insurance at the time, and the ropery finally shut down about 1900. In its time it supplied the rigging for the *Pearl* and many another good ship.

One of its last proprietors has told me of his belief that the *Royal George*, the King's yacht, was also built at Wivenhoe some time before the *Pearl*.

> There was an old man living at Wivenhoe when I was there [he said] who was a seaman in her, and proud of the fact that King William had spoken to him. When I asked him what the King had said his reply was, " Get out of my way, boy, damn yer ! "

Sailing-barges were comparatively uncommon so far from London in those days, pride of place being taken by the ' billy-boys,' tubby, cutter-rigged eighty-tonners engaged in the North Country coal trade. Nine or ten of these were owned in Wivenhoe, in addition to five or six North Countrymen which visited the Colne.

There were also about a dozen larger colliers owned in the village, one of these, the *Arabian*, being barque-rigged, and the rest brigantines, brigs, and ketches. Most famous of the fleet was the *Jessie Annandale*, a brigantine more fully described in Chapter XVI. As well as working locally in the coal trade, these vessels made voyages to Spain for nuts, Quebec for wood, Jamaica for rum, and elsewhere. Though they seldom touched Wivenhoe throughout the year, they aimed always to get a home freight for Christmas—a tradition which persists still among bargemen, with whom a chance of Christmas at home is good enough reason to throw away a fair wind to London. The largest of them was the 400-ton *Lady de Crespigny*, built at the shipyard (the de Crespigny family hailed from Wivenhoe, though later it was resident at Maldon), and one of the most curious was the barquentine *Saracen's Head*, which was converted from the lightship of that name.

When in the coal trade these vessels used to load ballast at the ballast quays, giving them the name by which they are known to this day, since, unlike barges, they could not sail light. If possible they took sand, which was a paying freight, sometimes loading a pony on top for the mines, but, failing this, they had to be content with shingle, which they unloaded in the sea outside the harbour. It was not unknown for a vessel to be caught by an off-shore wind when in this lightened trim, and being unable to make harbour to have to run all the way back to the Colne for fresh ballast.

The Yarmouth smacks at this time sailed to the port where many of them had been built, bringing cod, and half-a-dozen Norwegian timbermen might be seen unloading out of the square timber ports in their bows into lighters for Colchester, while thirty to forty yachts of between twelve and fifty tons and about eight of over a hundred tons were stationed there, in addition to the big schooners, which, cruising afield in the summer, returned annually to hibernate in the berths below the town, so that from autumn to spring the sea-wall from Wivenhoe to Alresford was one long line of them.

Many tales persist of the eccentricity of life aboard these floating palaces, though none can rival that of the crazy millionaire Mr Bayard Brown, whose 800-ton *Valfreya* lay for years in the Colne Estuary with steam up, ever ready to start on a voyage round the world, though her anchor always remained fast in Essex mud. Visitors coming alongside would be welcomed with gifts of largesse or pelted with lumps of coal according to the mood of her owner, and as this was always unpredictable a visit was spiced with a sporting element of chance. The *Varuna* was another famous steam yacht, so large that she had to lie always off Brightlingsea.

Wivenhoe smacks showed the influence of the ' English-cutter' type yacht produced in the town, and were long, lean, deep, and narrow compared to the " cod's-head-mackerel-tail " type favoured at Mersea and Tollesbury. At this time there were about twenty-five of them. They were all busy in the winter ' stow-boating' for sprats and fishing for the mussels and ' King Harrys' (a small variety of scollop which clung mussel-like to stones) which were then found in profusion on the Colne Bar and Bench Head, whence they have since disappeared utterly. They also went ' five-fingering ' on the Kent coast—dredging starfish for manure.

The bulk of the sprats caught in those days went for manure. Sprat-canning is a recent innovation, though pickling in barrels with salt, bay-leaves, and spices, mostly for Germany, Russia, Holland, and Norway, was introduced before 1914, and in 1833 there was even an abortive project to light London with gas made from sprat-oil ! The use of sprats for manure is often held up as an example of a wicked waste of good foodstuffs, and so, indeed, it was, though in its defence it should be remembered that we have been less inclined to be critical of the equal folly of failing to feed the land. In those days, when land-starvation was less prevalent, a ninety-ton trading-vessel joined in the spratting, lying to her station till she had perhaps twenty tons aboard, all for manure. When she ran home before a fair wind Wivenhoe knew of her coming before she was in sight. Seven or eight thousand bushels of sprats would be lying on Wivenhoe Quay in heaps. " You

knew you were in Wivenhoe in winter-time with your eyes shut "
is one description of the aroma prevailing.

Traditionally sprats are in for the Lord Mayor's Show ; indeed,
November 9 was known as Sprat Day, when the little fish were
called the " weaver's beef," being the nearest to a sirloin the
penurious Colchester bay- and say-makers could put upon their
tables.    The sprat is always at its best before Christmas, when it is
so fat it will fry in its own oil.    The war winters, however, have
proved the worst in memory for sprats, and after three blank
seasons fears were in 1945 being expressed that yet another Essex
fishery had come to an inexplicable end.

In good years, by contrast, phenomenal hauls are made.    In
the winter of 1885–86 the smacks went out light one ebb-tide, and
one was seen returning on the next flood with deck awash.    A
Wivenhoe veteran recalled how as a lad he ran to tell this to his
father, who surmised she had been in trouble and sent him out to
see if the crew were pumping.    But they were not.    They had
found sprats in the Colne and had brought up and put their gear
over.    Hardly were they below when they felt the strain of ropes
surging, and with that tide they practically filled the smack.    The
miraculous draught continued when they put to again on the
young flood, and soon they had holds full and a few bushels left
on deck.    And there they were back again, each man twelve
pounds the richer in a few hours, and soon behind them came the
rest, all equally successful.

The Wivenhoe *Christine* has several times landed over 400
bushels.    Once the smack left Wivenhoe in the morning, put
to in the Swire Hole (off the north eye of the Buxey), and
loaded so quickly that she was in Harwich in time to put the
cargo on the train that night.

Often the stow-boaters sold their catches to the Leigh bawleys.
On a lucky day one might sell two nets full in quick succession
for twenty-five pounds each in this way.    The smackmen reckon
three or four bushels to a ' cod,' and sometimes take 165 cod in a
net.    Seven hundred bushels in a net is the greatest catch I heard
of, and sixteen hundred bushels brought home by the *Christabel*
about a record freight.    In those old days prices fell as low as
threepence a bushel for manure, though in times of scarcity
twenty shillings a bushel has been paid.

Staunch vessels and good gear were needed to lie out in the winter anywhere in the Thames Estuary and then sail home in such trim in the gales that arise so quickly. I have often wondered what a smack felt like under sail, loaded till her decks were awash, as the spratters and five-finger dredgers sailed, but I have been told they handled well. One boat, however, came to grief in a curious fashion. She was pitching her way home when, as she dipped her head to a steep one, her slippery deadweight slid forward, broke down the cabin bulkhead, and slithered into the forepeak. Whereupon she went down by the head, and her wreck long remained a particularly awkward ' fast ' to trawlermen along the north edge of the Buxey Sand.

In summer some ten of these Wivenhoe smacks were laid up while their crews manned yachts. The rest went in for shrimping in the Wallet and Whitaker and along the Buxey and Gunfleet Sands, and in the autumn trawled for plaice there and on the Bench Head. In 1882–83, however, oyster brood was very plentiful, and most of the smackmen were earning all those summers three to four pounds a week (which, it should be remembered, was equivalent to double that to-day) dredging it on ' Pont,' as the Mersea flats are called in interesting reminiscence of the Roman name for the Blackwater, ' Panta.'

Five or six which were owned by members of the Colne Oyster Company (men who had served an apprenticeship and had been admitted as Freemen) were engaged in that work around Pyefleet Creek. These Oyster Fishery Freemen, both in Colne and Blackwater, have always jealously exercised their right of refusing to permit their fellows to trawl for the shrimps and fish in the two estuaries. There were also a number of oyster pits at Wivenhoe which were closed after one of the oyster-poisoning scares.

The smack race in the annual regatta lasted till shortly after the First World War and was at one time naturally a tremendously keenly contested affair, for these rakish Colne smacks were real clippers. It was the custom for the champion smack to wear a gilded cock at the masthead, and this was sometimes fixed there by a hand who went aloft as the winning smack roared up to the finishing-line, a practice suggestive of counting one's cock before it is hatched.

The *Who-would-have-thought-it* (thus quaintly named by her owner on his overhearing that remark made by some one who had just learned of his ordering a new boat) was one of the first champions, followed by the *Ada* and *Fancy*, the Rowhedge *Sunbeam*, *Elsie*, the Tollesbury *Bertha*, and the *Xanthe*, the last of the racers. These were all of fifteen to twenty tons.

Such, then, was Wivenhoe in its heyday. In 1872 fire devoured most of Harvey's sheds and models, which in addition to being a loss to posterity was a crippling blow to the firm. It resumed business as the John Harvey Yacht and Ship Building Company, Ltd, but Harvey seems to have been a greater artist than businessman, and with the added competition of steel-yacht-building on the Clyde the company came to grief in 1881, and Harvey went to America, where he continued to build yachts, chiefly cutters. He died in London in 1891, by which time Wivenhoe's fame as a yachting station was undergoing eclipse.

Among later products of the yard were the famous racer *Creole*, the Marquis of Dufferin's celebrated little single-handed cruiser *Lady Hermione*, and the auxiliary mission schooner *Southern Cross*. But though a fine dry dock was made (the only one between London and Lowestoft), and railway sidings and much plant were installed, the yard was closed down in 1930. After a revival of activity in the Second World War, during which more than fifty ships were built, it lies again under sentence of extinction, Ship Builders' Securities, Ltd, its owners, having laid a forty-year embargo on building there in the supposed interest of the industry in general.

For a few hectic years of war-time activity Vosper's, bombed out of Southampton, took over Husk's old yard, but though vast new sheds were built (inevitably across the riverside right-of-way) to house their M.T.B.'s and M.L.'s that firm departed early in 1946. Wivenhoe's talents and traditions, wanted in war, are being thrown on the scrapheap for the second time.

Now the sailing-barges pass by to Colchester, but do not stop, and though a few smacks and bawleys continue under motor-power shrimping in summer and spratting in winter for the cannery, only shallow impressions in the mud by the quay remain as evidence of the berths where the deep keels of the *Xanthe* and the *Who-would-have-thought-it* once lay. There are a few boats which go fish trawling at week-ends, and a fleet of fifteen-foot one-designs is maintained largely through the keenness of those to whom the tradition of Wivenhoe is dear.

The flame that was lit by three smugglers who were released from gaol to build a cutter for a marquis has guttered and gone out at last.   It burned brightly for just a century.

THE " PEARL "

From *Yachting* (Badminton Library, Longmans, 1894)

# VII

# ALRESFORD AND THE FLOUNDER FISHERS

*The Well-mannered Railway—Sand, Romans, Rats, and Cockles—Fish Weirs and Scissors Nets—Traditional Methods and the Latest in Boats*

BELOW Wivenhoe, where the river leaves the shelter of Alresford woods and opens with a sudden splendid change of character into a bold estuary, salting-bordered, the iron railway bridge spans the entrance to Alresford Creek.

In Holland they value their waterways, and all the roads and railways rise into the air or swing round out of the way when a vessel blows a toot on its horn ; in England the humble coaster or sailing-barge has to down funnel or gear and squeeze under as best she may without inconveniencing the landlubbers. Alresford is the sole exception in these waters. Here the little Brightlingsea branch line is twiddled laboriously round whenever a barge wants to come in and get a load of sand. It is not a very important gesture on the railway's part, for, truth to tell, this is not a very dignified railway. The little tank engines with a couple of carriages clank across at a walking-pace ever since one of them nearly fell in the Creek and got all muddy. Not that I disdain the old " Whelk and Winkle." If ever you go to Brightlingsea, and cannot go by water, go by train, for the line runs all the way beside the river. I like that trip. And still more I like that line for having the manners to get out of the way and let the barges in without the trouble of lowering their gear.

It is a very lovely creek which runs up to the old water-mill by the Brightlingsea road. The old-timers of Alresford can remember when barges came up to the mill, which now stands derelict, the old wheel broken in the water where it came to rest the last day it turned. More recently, up to the First World War, the regular agricultural water-borne traffic was carried on—in with chalk and manure, out with stacks of hay and straw.

A ford runs across the Creek, providing a fine hard on which the barges were unloaded into carts which came right alongside. Once it was a busy road, this one that crossed the Creek, and along it came most of the heavy traffic to Brightlingsea, for the shortest way to Colchester is through the ford and up by Wivenhoe Cross. The big brewers' drays are particularly remembered lumbering and splashing through. Nowadays the cars must not get their feet wet and don't notice the extra distance round the head of the Creek. In the First World War came a new activity. There is a fine supply of fresh water just inside the Creek mouth, and here came the water-boat which served the naval craft based in the Colne. She kept the old bridge busy, but when she went it was idle for some years till in 1932 the Alresford Sand and Ballast Company Works was opened. This trade has brought the barges back, and to-day Wakeley's, Cremer's, and Brice's craft are frequently in and out.

What other old ships lay on that road in days before the bridge impeded entrance no one is left to recall, but I cannot doubt from its convenience that many a brig unloaded her coal there for the villages around ; many a schooner or ketch, baffled by neap-tides or northerly winds from reaching Colchester, made the best of a bad job and emptied her holds into a procession of wagons which went off straining up the hill, the carters' whips cracking and the salt water dripping from the wheels.

Both this sand works and the Freshwater Sand and Ballast quarries opposite, on the Fingringhoe shore, whence Goldsmith's ' iron pots ' carry thousands of tons of ballast to London, occupy Roman sites, and their grabs and pumps are constantly bringing up fragments of 2000-year-old jars and vessels. The old maps mark " Arch Hall " on the Fingringhoe side, a mysterious name suggesting that within the span of memory the vaulting of a Roman hypocaust may have been visible from this reach. On the Alresford side a modern house stands on the site of a Roman villa, and, indeed, encloses in its forecourt a tessellated pavement of that age. How little our taste in housing sites has changed in that time—though the Romans did forbear to scrape away half the soil and leave great gashes full of scrub, swamp, and rabbits ! The occupier of this house tried the unusual experiment before the Second World War of breeding coypus for fur. A barge

Barges in a Breeze. (*Above*) The Colchester *Falconet*, with brailed mainsail, the regular 'reefed' rig. (*Right*) One of Wakeley's craft under whole mainsail and foresail. her tops'l 'rucked'—a form of sail-shortening adopted only for a passing squall. Note the stiffness of both craft in weather that would lay any yacht over on her side.

Preparing for the
Spratting Season : the
autumn fit-out on
Brightlingsea Hard

ing out on Brightlingsea Hard : the sailing-smacks for spratting, the steam drifter for scolloping

Sprats. (*Above*) A stow-boater getting her net aboard. (*Below*) Sculling loaded ski-
through Brightlingsea Creek, crowded with spratting-smacks.

e Sprat Harvest at Brightlingsea : loading in carts for manure and in barrels for the barge to carry them away pickled for export

Sky, Land, and Water : barges at anchor in the Blackwater

Full Moon and Low Water in Brightlingsea Creek

At Wivenhoe.  (*Above*) The waterfront from the Fingringhoe bank.  On the Hard is bawley *Prima Donna*; the smack behind is the *Aefa*.  The ferry is crossing.  (*Below*) ("Truthful") Eves, retired barge skipper, enjoys a chat with a smackman.

Work and Play in Colne. (*Above*) Sailing-barges, yachts, and an oyster smack. (*Right*) Mr Mole, ferryman for fifty-two years between East Mersea and Brightlingsea. A Colne police-boat is entering Brightlingsea Creek beyond.

Oyster-dredging in Colne. (*Above*) Smacks working in fair-weather conditions. (*Belo*
The steam paddle dredger *Pyefleet*, smacks sailing up over the tide, and (*right*) dredg
hove-to.

Saltings, and a Smack dredging in the Creek beyond : a sea idyll at West Mersea

Oyster Smacks.   (*Above*) The veteran *Unity*, for seventy years Queen of the West Me
fleet, with William Wyatt, who sailed aboard her at every regatta.   (*Below*) Brightlin
craft dredging.

skipper, returning late aboard, met on the sea-wall a black rat three times as large as anything he had ever seen before—and called his mate to witness his vow to sign the pledge.

Of recent years a prolific cockle-bed has developed close by the road across the creek.  Up to ten years ago cockles were quite scarce in this place, and why they have so multiplied is a mystery.  It seems that the drift of sand from the quarry must be a cause, for the cockle is partial to sand.  Anyway, tons must have been taken each year during the war, and they seem to grow no fewer.[1]

But Alresford Creek appears to have remarkable properties, just as has the wonderful oyster-fattening Pyefleet opposite.  It supports a most interesting and, I believe, unique form of fishing.  Some half-a-dozen boats work a form of net rather resembling in shape a pair of scissors.  The cross members are wooden spars some fifteen feet long, pivoted on a bolt.  A net is stretched over the longer members (the ' blades ' of the scissors), and the contraption is lowered from the anchored boat so that the points rest on the bottom of the creek.  The ' pivot of the scissors ' rests on a spar across the boat, and after a few minutes the fisherman throws his weight on the ' handles.'  Up comes the net like a scoop, full (if you are lucky) of flounders and a few whiting.  This fishing, I believe, is practised only on the flood tide.  Sometimes it draws blank ; sometimes remarkable hauls are taken.  No one can foretell the result.  It is practised by countrymen with a countryman's love of sport.  Sometimes Pilkington's lorry-drivers " up and have a goo " in the early morning before starting work.  It cannot be claimed that the flounder is anything but the least palatable of all the flatfish, but he loses his muddy taste and puts on a bit of flesh in the spring.  It would be interesting to know the antiquity of this method, and whether it was formerly practised elsewhere in Colne and Blackwater.  It has been going on at Alresford as long as memory spans, and the latest vessel to be fitted for the purpose is built on a pair of those aeroplane petrol tanks which, brought in by the American Air Force in thousands, have been bought in hundreds for a few shillings each and turned into canoes by the Essex boys, who have fitted them with rudders, sails, and even leeboards.  One I have seen sprittie-rigged—a complete barge in miniature, tops'l and all !  Wivenhoe regatta actually

[1] I learn that in 1947 the beds are at last giving out.

staged a ' doodle-bug ' race for them in 1945, but now I fear the bottom is falling out of the craze—just as it is rusting out of most of the canoes.

A more skilful method of floundering is to grub them up with the fingers. Old George (" Dulce ") Porter, who lived in the remains of the smack *Kingfisher* by the sea-wall above Alresford Creek, was an adept at this art, which many still practise for amusement and profit in the Creek, the Roman River (Fingringhoe Creek), and elsewhere. Paddling along in a few inches of water, " Dulce " would send his fingers searching in the mud, and not only detect but grab the lurking flounder. He wore neither socks nor sea-boots, and would splash about in his old shoes and then walk off up the wall to Wivenhoe with his catch. He never caught a cold, though his old *Kingfisher* was about the roughest form of human habitation imaginable. One night he played the ancient mariner with a couple of yachtsmen in a Wivenhoe pub, and, getting them under his spell, insisted they should return and spend the night with him " aboard his yacht." Their description of the arrival at the black little *Kingfisher*, of " Dulce's " majestic invitation to " step aboard," and of their precipitate flight was worth hearing.                                        .

Near Alresford Creek I have seen the only attempt in my recollection to revive the ancient Colne fish weirs, which were the subject of dispute as long ago as the thirteenth century, when the burgesses of Colchester contested the right of the Abbot of St John's, Lord of the Manor, and John de Moveron to work seven weirs, which right the holders pleaded they and their ancestors had enjoyed from time immemorial. These weirs were presumably wattle fences shaped like a ' V,' the narrow end down-stream. Coming up with the flood, the fish would pass by ; returning on the ebb, they would be trapped. During the Second World War soldiers at Alresford erected something of the sort in wire chicken netting, but I do not know of its catching any fish. An attempt of mine at a similar contraption in the Geetings collected only jellyfish, the weight of which ultimately washed it away !

Such, then, is the mild, uneventful story of Alresford Creek. That it saw livelier nights is probable. The pleasant weather-boarded farmhouse hard by the water's edge (now two cottages) is popularly connected with smuggling activities. The family which lived there now keeps the Alresford Rose and Crown, where the landlord showed me his grandfather's old muzzle-loading punt-gun, a formidable bit of ordnance which has been in his family for more than a hundred years, and told me of the painted panels showing maritime scenes, now, alas, removed from the house, and of the great cellars reached by a conveniently inconspicuous trap in the larder floor.

The cruising yachtsman wind-bound in Colne can do worse than pass a day sailing his dinghy up its pleasant reaches, past the old smacks whose hulls, beautiful even in the last stages of decay, have been laid against the sea-wall to buttress it as breakwaters, up to the empty mill with the broken wheel, symbol of days that have gone.

# VIII

# ROUGH DAYS AT ROWHEDGE

*An Old Swin Ranger, and not One of the very Timid Kind—The Trade of the Wrecker—The Man who was his own Ferry—Birthplace of the " Firecrest "—Wild Nights at the Regatta—A Ship that crossed the Andes by Llama*

To cross the ferry from Wivenhoe to Rowhedge to-day one would not think one was entering what was perhaps once the roughest of all the Colne and Blackwater villages.

Now pale, begoggled riveters obey the siren's behest and clock in at the up-to-date little Rowhedge Ironworks, where the hammers rattle all day on tankers for the Thames and stern-wheelers for tropical rivers, and shipwrights of the adze and plane go to work on R.N.L.I. lifeboats in " the lower yard," which was formerly Peter Harris's, birthplace of Alain Gerbault's *Firecrest*. Cunis's barges lie against the sand elevator, but otherwise the only indication of Rowhedge's maritime tradition is now to be found in the village clothes-lines, which run up their poles on travellers and are belayed there, so that the housewives seem to vie with one another in seamanly instinct.

Not a single smack now lies against the quay from which sixty years ago some of the toughest mariners in Essex sailed out in forty fine vessels of up to fifty tons to mix fishing with the salvaging and wrecking which were a speciality of the place. Fifty years ago the Colne river police were warned that it was not safe to approach at least one Rowhedge smack and lay a hand on the rail, for the owner would be up on deck and make a slash at the tres-passing fingers with a chopper before he inquired the policeman's business.

Rowhedge men were mostly yachting in summer, and the smacks were fitted out when they came home in autumn. Some of the yachtsmen went to steam-boats in the winter, going up to

London after a few days' holiday, 'seeking,' as they called the time spent in dockyard lodging-houses, waiting for a ship, but others would go spratting. Like the Brightlingsea men, they were accustomed to making sure that it was an ill wind that blew nobody any good in the sandbanks of the Thames Estuary, and when it came on to blow they would get their gear on deck—but not to come home out of it. No, no—that was when things began to get interesting. They would dodge about then and wait for a wreck to occur, and if a vessel looked like shaping to get ashore, well, it was just as easy to jill over into the shallow water and encourage her to follow as to hail her to keep off.

I have been told of at least one Rowhedge smack which used to lie in the Spitway or close behind the Whitaker with her riding light pulled right up to her masthead to give the impression of a big ship brought up in the Swin, and another which shifted the position of a buoy or two, but how much of this was done on the East Coast is very difficult to decide. There may have been a great deal more than was ever revealed ; indeed, one feels there must have been, from the nature of the waters and the men, but on the evidence available this unpleasant tradition seems to have belonged more particularly to the West Coast. At any rate, whether or not they took a share in its destruction, the " Swin rangers " seldom had very long to wait for a job, and as technically no wreck was a wreck if man, dog, or cat escaped from it, one is tempted to wonder what scenes may have been enacted aboard some of those stricken craft.

A lighter lay in Colne as the official place of collection for salvaged gear, but the Rowhedge men preferred to run as much as they could ashore behind the sea-wall in Pyefleet. Willing farmers collected it there, and it lay in their barns till a favourable time came for its disposal. The wreck of the *Deutschland* on the Kentish Knock in 1875, referred to in a previous chapter, is still spoken of in Rowhedge. What is now Green's Farm was crammed with booty taken off by the smacks, and half the fishermen in the place suddenly became the possessors of fine watches which had not been presented to them.

Typical of Rowhedge hardihood was Jack Spitty, who used to sail his well-known smack *Bluebell* away down to the Channel Islands, oyster-dredging. Later in life he trawled single-handed

with the *Annie*, and when over seventy fell while working down
by the Spitway and broke two ribs. He got his trawl and sailed
home to Bradwell, where he then lived. A few years later they
found the *Annie* ashore in the Rays'n, and Jack Spitty's body lying
near her. It is believed he had been knocked overboard by the
boom.

Another time Spitty went overboard was when the *Bluebell*
was racing other smacks to a wreck on the Burrows. He was
shaking out a reef (he would have been !) when over he went.
With characteristic daredevilry he hollared out to them to throw
him the quarter-board and carry on. He hung on to that while
the *Bluebell* secured the job and, leaving a man aboard, sailed
back for him. His whole career was like that, one who remembered him told me. He would fight and drink on shore, but his
boat was always a real goer.

Best remembered of all the old Rowhedge characters, however,
is Thomas Barnard, who used to boast that he never called the
ferry twice. If it did not come at his first call he would wade
across at low water, or swim at high tide. The astonished regu-
lars of the Wivenhoe public houses grew accustomed to seeing
him enter dripping-wet from head to foot, and it was advisable to
treat his condition as entirely natural. His departure would be
followed by a roar of " Ferry ! " and a splash as he saved his penny
if it did not appear.

In his old age Barnard lost the smack *New Unity* in the gale of
January 1881, and gave to the *Essex Standard* an account of that
adventure which is still thrilling to read more than half a century
later. " Ah, sir, you may well say we have had some weather,"
old Barnard is reported as saying.

Fifty-five years man and boy have I been to sea, and as you know I
was never one of the very timid sort, for you have been with me when it
has blowed a bit, but never in my life did I see such a night as that
Monday night before that Tuesday. We were lying in Colne water,
and, fearing the floating ice was likely to injure the vessel's bottom, we
resolved to put to sea, and after crossing the Wallet we brought up
under the Buxey and reefed our sails and made all snug for the rough
night we saw coming. Just as we were going below to make some
tea, we saw a schooner go ashore on the Whitaker Spit ; so tea had to
wait, and we got under way as quickly as possible to go to her assis-
tance ; but the gale kept increasing so that it was quite impossible to

board her, the daylight being gone, and as the best we could do, all things considered, we brought up as near to her as we could and let go our anchor with fifty-five or sixty fathoms of chain cable out, hoping to be able to assist her at daybreak.

All night the gale kept increasing, and at 9.30 A.M. our cable parted and our stow-boat anchor, with fifty fathoms of chain, was lost. As soon as we got the remainder of the cable in we made the Shears light and shaped a course for Sheerness. Within ten minutes every stitch of canvas we had set was blown into ribbons, and we drove before the blast in such a snowstorm that we could not see the end of the bowsprit, and we had to get under the lee of the boat or the mast or anything we could hold on to, for to stand on deck was an impossibility, and had you attempted to get on your legs it would be at the risk of being blown overboard like an old swab, for our foresail, a brand new one, was blown clean away from everything, and as long as we could see it it never did touch the water. It did blow then. After that, though we could not see twenty fathoms ahead, we made the Mouse light, and then we knew we were on the right course for Sheerness. After this we kept feeling our way with the lead as opportunity offered, and could find we were going right away up the Medway. I was for'ard, holding on for dear life, and the wind enabled me to hear my son at the helm ask me if he was steering a right course. I said, " Keep her straight, for no sand is in our way." The New Unity could sail as well as most of them, and I knew that if we did not run into an ironclad or some other obstacle we should ultimately run into the mud on the banks of the Medway, and escape with little further damage.

But so it was not to be, and bang we went on the Grain Spit, perhaps the first instance of one of the strongest forts in the world being boarded by a fishing smack.

Quicker than I can tell you, our vessel was then blown right up against the outworks of the fort, and my son at once off boots and socks and walked along the bowsprit, which he could not have done had we not struck on the weatherside of the fort, for under other circumstances he would have been blown off like a butterfly.

I have seen some strange scenes in my time, for I am an old Swin Ranger, but never in my life did I feel as I did when I saw the dear old craft, the pride of my life, in which so much good work had been done, come broadside on the fort and crack up like an old cheese-box. Not that she was not in good order, for as we watched her break up, and I don't mind telling you I could not help shedding a tear when I saw the old craft in which, by God's help, I had been instrumental in saving hundreds of persons' lives, tossed about like an old broken match-box, but in all this I had the satisfaction of observing as she went to pieces that she was as sound as ever a vessel of her class was.

On at least one occasion the police had a fancy to interview Thomas Barnard, and as he could not be found, they were keeping a pretty sharp eye on his house. The village coal in those days used to be brought by the village's own colliers, of which Charles Crosby's *New Blossom* is well remembered. It was unloaded on the quay and shouted round the village by the crier, and was then delivered in old-fashioned sacks some six feet high. This happened to be occurring at Barnard's house that day. When the cart departed one of those tall sacks contained not coal, but Thomas Barnard !

Other contemporary Rowhedge Barnards were Turner, John, and Ben, who owned the *Morgan*, *Orange*, and *Racer* respectively.

There was a heroic and romantic side to this salvaging, but there was a sordid one too. After a good salvage, the wretched women of the village had to sit in the pubs beside the men to get a share of the money, and the boys used to run from pub to pub to see the fights. The hairy old amphibians of those days were not accustomed to satisfy their thirst on half-pints and light ales. That company had a four-and-a-half-gallon or a nine-gallon cask if they were numerous, and knocked the top off, or sometimes they stood a bath of beer on the floor and you dipped your mug in that. The place was especially wild on the night of the annual regatta, which was held alternate years here and at Wivenhoe. At both places a fair was held all down the main streets. Such days and such scenes have gone now, for better and for worse.

So much for the barbarity of Rowhedge—but the place was industrious too. As has been mentioned, the *Firecrest*, perhaps the most famous of world voyagers, was a product of Peter Harris's yard, and a typical example of a lean, deep Essex cutter she was. Gerbault came to love her, though she seems a queer choice for globe-trotting. But then Gerbault, whose rigging generally seemed to fall down before he had been under way long, was quite content to cook in his forepeak, relying on a hatch in his foredeck to reach his galley (an arrangement one would hardly fancy for week-ends), so he cannot be said to have been exacting in his taste.

But the *Firecrest* was only one of hundreds of vessels built in Rowhedge in the days when P. T. Harris and his two sons, Enos, who did nearly all the designing (though *Firecrest* was by Dixon

Kemp), and John, who managed the yard, reigned there. All kinds of yachts were turned out, and the whole area of the yard was always packed with craft of every type and size pulled out for repair and overhaul. Mill Creek and the upper wall (above Rowhedge) were also crowded in winter with larger vessels, which included the steam yachts *Walrus* and *Sunflower* and the yawls and cutters *Moine, Irona, Cariad, Gudrun, Cicely, Merry Thought, Erycina, Edwina, Chiquita, Ala, Amelia, Bingo, Clara, Coralie, Cushiedoo, Day Dawn, Doris, Elfe, Florence, Island Home, Lucina, Monara, Patience, Quadroon,* and *Siwash*. Some of these yachts were of such a size that thirty men would sign on one of them, and when they had fitted out and sailed there was hardly a man left in the village bar the shipyard workers.

Harris's numbered among their distinguished patrons Sir William Burton, and it was here Frank Cowper found his famous *Lady Harvey*, but despite what seems a wonderful connexion the yard was sold in 1916 to the Rowhedge Ironworks, Mr Harris himself going as manager to the Wivenhoe shipyard. Thus ended yachting at Rowhedge.

Under its new owners the yard has been mainly concerned with the upkeep of R.N.L.I. lifeboats, a class of work which has preserved the tradition of fine workmanship. The Rowhedge Ironworks is the successor to J. A. Houston, who enjoyed the patronage of Lord Alfred Paget, mentioned in the previous chapter, whose name is perpetuated in Rowhedge by the four Memorial Cottages which he endowed for his old yacht hands. Houston was followed by Cox and King, whose attempt to enclose a public space, with the chairman of the parish council pulling down the posts with a chain as fast as they were put up, is well remembered, and they in turn were followed by the Rowhedge Ironworks. This firm has a love for individual building puzzles, the more puzzling the better. During a South American war they were commissioned to supply a vessel which was to be dismantled and sent out entirely in small parcels which could be carried across the Andes on the back of a llama. The ship was duly built, and after the parts had been carefully marked was taken to pieces and every requirement was fulfilled. The war was over by the time the llama arrived, but it can probably safely be said that no other ship has ever made such a journey.

During the Second World War motor minesweepers and motor fishing-vessels were built at the lower yard, and the hideous but useful 'austerity' cargo coasters, with their straight lines and flat plates, at the Ironworks. In all, six coastal tankers, six M.F.V.'s, three austerity coasters, six fleet auxiliaries, and three mine-recovery launches for Turkey were completed.

Some of the famous Rowhedge smacks have been mentioned in the previous chapter. Space precludes doing justice to the brilliant hands who sailed them, and the Cranfields in particular.

May your old bones rest quietly, Jack Spitty and Thomas Barnard and all your kin, for I am sure they had little rest in your lifetime.

# IX

## MERSEA AND THE DREDGERMEN

*Where they don't go far—And why—Seventy-seven-year-old Smack
still Champion Racer—Eels, Garfish, and " Penny Herrings "—
Vanished Eel-grass—A Homeric Yachting Paradise*

AIN'T they docile little chaps ? " Such was the comment of
one of the hairy amphibians of the Colne when we spoke of the
men of Mersea. It is an amusing and revealing comment, spoken
as it was with a tolerant, smiling air of infinite disdain.

In truth, West Mersea is the wrong destination to choose if you
are in search of the heroic. Storm warriors of the deep are not
typical of the place. Its seafaring is done in quieter ways, and
though it has sent men all over the world in yachts, and its smacks
have ranged from Norwich to Falmouth, on the whole the Mersea man has generally tended towards a stay-at-home life. Oyster-
dredging is the staple, with a bit of winkling, eel-fishing, and fish-
trawling.

Perhaps it is because the place is so lovely that its men have
always had more sense than to leave it easily. Brightlingsea,
Tollesbury, and Rowhedge are all thoroughly unattractive archi-
tecturally, and even Wivenhoe's charm is largely confined to its
mellow waterfront. Their little streets are lined with square and
unappealing villas, and I fancy one could sail away from any of
them without any deep nostalgia. But at Mersea the little
weatherboard cottages lie entrancingly beneath their thatch and
tiles at odd angles to the lanes that run down to the Hard. The
smoke curls up from their chimneys at evening as the men, back
from the day's dredging, put in an hour in the garden before
taking the evening stroll up to the Victory or the White Hart.
There are smacks in Mersea which have worked hard for half a
century, and never been beyond the Bench Head buoy. I don't
blame them. Mersea is all much too good to leave.

Even the shipwrecks are friendly, intimate affairs.   In 1915 the *Evergreen* was run down by a Tollesbury smack off the north shore and sank.   Her masthead just showed at low water, and her owner came ashore disconsolate.   " I've lost my bo't," he said. And, indeed, it looked like it.   A diver could easily have slipped slings around her hull, but who was to send a diver to a little oyster dredger ?   And without a diver, how to get hold of her ? It was then that William Wyatt, the island's shipwright, remembered something told him by Jack Spitty, that famous Rowhedge character already referred to in Chapter VIII, who, when at Mersea after some shipwrighting, had described a method he employed for recovering ships' anchors and cables.   " Lost her ?" commented Wyatt.   " No, that you haven't, boy.   Not yet."

They went at it this way.   Two smacks dragged a chain under the port bilge of the wreck ; two did the same on the starboard side.   Then Wyatt slipped the heaviest iron rings he could find, one over the two chains at the bow and another over the two at the stern, holding them together as they shook the rings down. The smacks hove on their windlasses, and as the tide rose they lifted.   So, setting sail, the whole conglomeration of four smacks afloat and one beneath them blew in towards the shallow waters. Next day the *Evergreen* was on the Hard, and a week later she was at work again.   Indeed, in 1945 she was converted into a yacht. The tale is worth telling both as an instance of honest ingenuity and sea-sense, and as an example of the nice, intimate way things happen at Mersea, where everything always comes all right in the end.   No one had even got a wet shirt.

Mersea and Maldon are the only places where the Colchester smack survives entirely under sail, and though the Mersea fleet has dwindled from the seventy to eighty smacks which it comprised in its heyday to a bare dozen or so, there are some lovely vessels among them.   I have attempted to discover who was really the genius who created the present type, for eighty years ago there were no such fine craft in Mersea.   The dredging-boats in those days were a miscellaneous and motley collection of old clinker-built craft, among which the *Winkie*, *Eliza*, *Lively*, and *Emma* are remembered names.

William Wyatt's father had a fine time trying to keep these boats afloat.   Most of them had to be moored over the mud, as it would have been too much to expect them to lie afloat all night, and there were strong views as to which piece of mud acted as the best natural caulking. It is related that the elder Wyatt, on being informed by a fisherman that his boat was leaking, would inquire "Any crabs in the bilges ?" "Only little ones." "Then you let her be. When she's open enough for a good big crab to run in and out of her I'll come and do a bit to her." Then Harvey's famous yard at Wivenhoe produced the *Neptune* and Aldous's, of Brightlingsea, the *Unity*, beautifully shaped, beautifully built thir-teen-ton carvel cutters, with the lines and the gear of a yacht, and old Wyatt's bewildered comment to his son was, "Just look at them bo'ts, boy. They'll finish us. They won't *never* want nothing done to them bo'ts." He was right in his estimate of the quality of the new smacks, for the *Unity* was still working and racing at regattas at the age of seventy-seven, but wrong in his conclusion, for his son has ministered to the fleet for a lifetime, till to-day he can tell you the dimensions of almost any spar in any boat without looking up his books.

Thus I am left in doubt whether Harvey or Aldous really can claim to be the designer of the type, but I believe the *Neptune* was a year or two senior to the *Unity*, and, indeed, it would be appro-priate if the yard responsible for the *Pearl* also created these love-liest of small working craft. Harvey and Husk, of Wivenhoe, built a good number more, including *Oyster*, *March*, *Amelia*, and *Fred*, but the majority came from Aldous, including *Telegraph*, *Snowdrop*, *Wave*, *Charlotte*, and a host more.

The typical Mersea smacks ranged from eight to thirteen tons —smaller than the Colne type, but rather larger than those favoured for Maldon (though many of the Maldon boats have been bought from the Mersea fleet)—and were built from half-models without plans. Often they would be supplied on credit and were expected to repay their modest cost of perhaps ten pounds a ton in a few years' work. Aldous would not only supply the smacks, but make a generous loan towards the cost of their sails and gear on payment of quite a small 'deposit'—a remark-able anticipation of hire purchase which even the most up-to-date yacht-building yards have so far hardly dared to reintroduce.

The early smacks were clippers in every line, but later shoal draught came into fashion, and these vessels, while just as good for work, and, indeed, able to stop longer dredging on the Main on an ebb tide when the older boats had to be off into deep water, are not such superlative performers under sail, specially to windward. The old *Unity* never lost her place as scratch boat on regatta days.

What was Mersea like seventy years ago ?   Baring-Gould, in his *Early Reminiscences*, views it with a thoroughly jaundiced eye, for in the ten years that he was Rector of East Mersea (1871-81) " I cannot say that I ever liked the place or became attached to the people," he declares.   Yet, considering his aversion, his descriptions are extraordinarily vivid, as one would expect from the author of that splendidly written melodrama of Mersea, *Mehalah*.

" At a former period wild-fowl shooting was largely practised by the islanders, who had their punts painted grey," he writes.

> In these shallow boats they lay for many hours at night and contracted both ague and rheumatism.   My impression was that generations afflicted with these complaints acquired in the marshes had lowered the physique and the mental development of the islanders.   When the east wind blew the wild ducks and geese came in flocks near the coast where they were surrounded and shot.   Herons frequented the marshes in considerable numbers.   Gulls were not numerous as there were no breeding-places in rocks along the coast.

The great gulls' breeding-grounds on Rat Island and St Osyth marshes have been established only some twenty years.   It is difficult to imagine these estuaries with gulls " not numerous," and the now ubiquitous cormorant unknown.   These birds came to Essex only about forty years ago, and still seem to become increasingly numerous.   At first they were known as " Isle of Wight parsons," as they were previously common down Channel. " But why parsons ? " I asked an ancient mariner.   " Ain't you ever seen 'em stand up all in black and flap their silly wings ? " he replied.   Where the Essex cormorants breed seems a mystery, as they remain in the district through the season ; yet I have never heard of their peculiarly messy colonies being found hereabouts.

Baring-Gould continues :

> An industry exercised by the women and children of West Mersea was the collecting of winkles off the flats for the London market.   In order to enable them to walk on the wet clay they wore flat boards cut into ovals under their soles and braced tightly over the instep and about

the ankles. Walking or gliding on these, they stooped to collect the molluscs into a basket held in the left hand. Woe to such as slipped and fell. The adhesive clay held him or her fast by the arms.

Though I have been shown these old-fashioned mud pattens, I have never seen them used. Perhaps the coming of rubber thigh-boots was the end of them, as it was of the leather boots which the old-timers declare were so warm and cosy as well as so useful when they became leaky for leathering oars and masts.

Baring-Gould records that there was in his time to the seaward of East Mersea church a sort of landing-stage built, and a sandy channel had been excavated in the clay flat so that a vessel of small draught could be brought up to it. This was for the purpose of bringing coal in barges to the island, and " London muck "—that is to say, the sweepings of the London streets, which was largely used as a manure for the fields—and then the stench was horrible. Another dressing employed was one of sprats.

On such occasions [he recalls] gulls arrived in great flocks, and boys were employed to scare them away with rattles, horns, and drums. The smell when a field was fertilized with sprats was not enjoyable, but the odour was superior to London muck. From the landing-stage the barges carried away hay and straw piled high on deck for London. When the mosquitoes were out in autumn they swarmed about the trees that looked as if they were on fire and smoking. We had always to drive the pests out of the bedroom in the evening by burning laurel-leaves on red-hot coals.

Here is his account of the old Colne-mouth ferry, now closed and almost forgotten :

To reach Brightlingsea we had to descend a mile and a half to the Hard, where lived a man named Baker with his wife in an old hulk drawn up on the shingle, and there anchored. Baker or his wife rowed one across, and when the tide was out carried the passenger pick-a-back through the mud. We went often to Baker's boat and had tea with him. While tea was brewing, he would set a pail of shrimps before us on the deck and bid us fall to until his tea was ready in the cabin. Baker himself was a sober man, but his wife was often tipsy. When she returned late from Brightlingsea overcome with liquor Baker had hauled up the ladder. He emptied a pail of water over her head as she stood shouting below for admittance and left her to scold, swear, and shiver till he considered her to be sufficiently sober to be admitted. Mrs Baker wore an old red military coat over her back, shoulders, and arms. I used her in my story *Mehalah*. Elijah Rebow in that same novel was sketched from a leading Dissenter at West Mersea.

Mrs Baker had a kind of proprietorial interest in one of the island's two principal ghosts, a woman's figure which she saw near the site of an old cottage between her barge and the Dog and Pheasant. The other is the better-known ghost of the Strood, acquaintance with which is generally claimed by patrons of the near-by Peldon Rose. The interesting thing about these two ghost stories is that the former is said to be the figure of a woman " killed while the soldiers of the Parliament were in the fort," and the latter is connected with a tale of a great fight near the Strood. Now, in 1648 the soldiers of the Parliament did in fact occupy the East Mersea blockhouse, and there is a Danish burial mound near the Strood. And if you think that is a long time for a story to keep in currency consider how the Mersea people are still using the Danish name Nass (and pronouncing it with the ' a ' long) for the shoal at the entrance to their creeks.

There is a fascinating picture of Mersea seventy years ago to be reconstructed from the boyhood memories of William Wyatt, still hale and hearty in his eighty-second year. The earliest of his vivid and long-focused recollections is of the last of the London River ' peter-boats ' visiting Mersea from Barking Creek and Gravesend. These were not the true medieval peter-boat—a double-ended spritsail-rigged well-boat—but small bawley-stern cutters. With a crew of a man and two boys, they came to stop the creeks for flounders. These they drove into their nets by ' jingling ' or shaking a few metal curtain-rings hung on a line. The *Frigate* was the name of one of these craft, which was later bought by William Ham, of Wivenhoe. They lay in Thornfleet by the Oyster Company's sheds, and gave the place the name of ' Sheep's Head Bay ' because of the Cockneys' fondness for consuming this inexpensive delicacy there. For years the dredgermen kept fetching up the old heads tossed over by them.

There would be French fishermen there buying herrings for bait, and brigs, brigantines such as the *Jessie Annandale*, ketches, and schooners like the *Neptune* on the Hard with coal.

A few years later, when Wyatt was as a lad of seventeen at work in the *Monitor*, the *Sarah* was making two trips a week to Billingsgate with live eels in her well. The *Prince Albert*, a bawley and therefore less fleet, had to be content with one a week, yet even so she claimed the record of Billingsgate to West Mersea in eight-and-a-half hours, roaring down Swin with a jury square-sail set as well as her great bawley mainsail and topsail.

Many of the smacks had wells then, and, though all have since had the drilled planks removed, some still reveal the internal construction of the wells. 'Bradding' the well holes was a regular job for a boy half a century ago. He had to wriggle into the bilge as the smack lay on the mud with the well empty, and get nails across the holes which the water had made too large to retain the eels.

As the smacks neared London the eels would give notice of their objection to the taste of city water by sticking out their heads and making protesting noises. Then was the time to fish them out with nets.

Eel-boxes were rather a speciality of the elder Wyatt. He was proud of his duck punts, some of which were exported to Holland and elsewhere, so he built his eel-boxes the same way, curving up the bottom at the 'bows' to give a flare to the sides. They towed in right seaworthy fashion.

Eels were caught mostly by trawling in the long 'eel-grass' on the 'Coccum Hills,' off the Mersea shore. The trawl was of fish-trawl mesh with a close-mesh cod-end. The grass lay so thick here that no sea ever got up, and even at high water in a strong southerly wind a punt could be rowed among its gently heaving fronds. Another method of eel-fishing was with the 'bumper net,' some seventy feet long by nine feet deep, which was laid out by a man in a punt. The net was pulled in by one end, and the eels slid down into the 'keed,' or cod-end pocket, at the other end. Sometimes a man would secure a hundred-weight in an evening, the eels being up to two pounds in weight.

It was in 1881 that this came to an end. The hard frost in that winter caused ice to form around the grass at low water, and when the tide came, away floated ice, grass, and all, pulled up by the

roots.[1]   It has never come back, and for sixty years Coccum,
Mersea ' middle ooze,' and other places have been what an East
Coast man calls "just white mud," instead of carpeted with a
deep, rich grass.

Shearing for eels goes on occasionally to this day, however, and
a fascinating art it is.   The eel likes to lie up in a hole in the mud
with an exit at both ends.   The shearer threads around the holes
till a tell-tale blow reveals which is the ' live ' hole—that is, which
way his head is facing.   The shear, which looks something like
Britannia's trident, is thrust into the mud and drawn out holding
a nice fat eel between the prongs.   Eel-babbing is one of the
simplest kinds of fishing.   Tie a bit of wool on a line and offer it
to the eel ; if you are lucky he thinks it is a worm, takes a big bite
at it, and gets the wool so tangled in his teeth that all you have to
do is to pull him out.

There would be smacks lying off in the outfalls in St Peter's
Flats, which were then deep enough creeks for the purpose, their
crews ashore at low water, after winkles.   The smack *Brothers*
was making regular trips to Norwich with this cargo.

That cherished East Coast delicacy, the garfish or gorbill, was
secured in a net similar to the eel ' bumper net,' but it had the
' keed ' in the middle, and so was gathered in at both ends simul-
taneously.   Garfish were up to two feet long, with a characteristic green backbone when cooked.   The meat on the back was
reckoned a great delicacy.   At this time they were sold at three or
four for a shilling.

In winter-time some seventeen smacks would be herring drifting.   Herrings come to Mersea soon after they reach Lowestoft,
and sometimes Ray, Salcot or Sampson's Creek used to be
stopped for them.   The drifters would lay nets across the tide,
with a boat, containing a light at night, made fast to the leeward
end.   The whole lot would drift for a tide, the smacks lying close
by.   Or on fine nights, letting go at the Bench Head at low water,
they would haul between Bradwell and Tollesbury Pier on the
high water.   Sometimes the Ridge channel would be worked, or
anywhere the fish happened to be.   Irrespective of how much

[1] The eel-grass suddenly disappeared in the 1930's on the New England
coast, which is in many ways, such as its accent and its domestic architecture, so like
Essex.   The scollop fishing was spoiled.   (See *Country Editor*, by Henry Hough.)

wind there might be, the nets almost always drifted the whole tide without attention. "Penny herrings" they were called because the mesh of the net was just of a size to slip a penny through. The boys helped to get them from the nets, and as they could keep any which parted company with their heads it is feared they did not do it so cleanly as they might have done. A smack would sometimes secure as many as 28,000, but no drifting has been done for some years now.

At one time there were many mussels on the Bench Head, and at least one smack, the *Blue*, went in for dredging these, using moused dredges—that is, oyster-dredges with the hoeing blade seized with spunyarn.

These were some of the activities carried on by Mersea smacks, but all were subsidiary to the oyster dredging. All the summer this went on. In the autumn some smacks, including *Hetty*, *Wave*, *Tillie*, and *Snowdrop*, sailed away down Channel to dredge at Falmouth during the winter. Others put dredges ashore and bent fish trawls to go after plaice, dabs, and roker on the flats in early autumn, and codling and whiting in the deeper water after the first frosts dispersed the flat fish from the shallows. Then most would be laid up for a while. I do not think any Mersea smacks ever went stow-boating, except the *Priscilla*, which started a few years before the Second World War. There would be some sole-trawling during the spring spawning season (a chain often being fitted ahead of the ground rope to stir the heavy soles from the holes they love to lie in), and then back to the oystering, in the heyday of which one could stand on the high ground by Mersea church and see two hundred sail of smacks at work. There must have been a gradual increase during the last century, for in 1807 there were "established to be near two hundred fishing-vessels between eight and forty tons in Essex, an increase of more than half in thirty years." It was further stated that "last week Mr Buxton counted 130 vessels at work in sight of Mersea. In the spring they go to Hampshire and Dorset, dredging."

To-day it is but a far, faint echo of that. No longer can you be carried pick-a-back through the mud and ferried across to Brightlingsea. The dredged channel and the jetty at East Mersea are long since gone, and very rarely does a barge come to the Strood or to West Mersea Hard. You would have to look a long way for a gourmet who would discuss to-day the flavour of a garfish or a King Harry. The herring come and go in their seasons practically undisturbed, and, though oystering goes on and some winkling is done, I fear many of the elegant little smacks which went into the mud berths in 1939 will not come out again. An increasing number of those in fit condition are becoming yachts. To-day the Blackwater's broad bosom is burdened with the crippled hulls of ships which have been victims of torpedo, bomb, or mine ; its depths so infested with the carcases of ' doodle-bugs ' that the trawlermen will not risk their nets, and only one smack works. But the place is the dearest paradise on all the East Coast to that increasing host of amateur sailormen who, making their Odysseys in really little ships, have brought the great sport of yachting back full circle from the swank and swagger of Victorian days to a positively Homeric simplicity !

# X

# FARMS UNDER THE WATER

*Submarine Estates and Allotments—Mysteries of Oyster Cultivation—
Ploughing, Sowing, and Reaping under the Sea—The Placid Mollusc
incites to Violence*

YES," said the man in the guernsey and the long rubber boots
as he hauled his dredge-rope hand over hand, " this is my little
farm. I always had a fancy to save up for this patch all the years
I was yachting. Then last year I was able to buy it." The iron
frame of the dredge broke surface, was rested over the gunwale
of the boat, and dexterously swung inboard. " The funny thing
is," he said, " I've never seen it, and never shall, down under the
water there."

The net deposited on the boat's bottom boards a heap of shell,
weed, crabs, and all that medley of flora and fauna which thrive
on the sea-bed. Splash ! Over went the dredge again, and his
trained fingers were soon searching among the wet jumble. He
held out a couple of sizeable natives, a few young ones, and some
stones with young ' brood ' still growing on them. " There's a
family of natives just roused out of their beds," he said, " and for
all them as will eat them knows or cares about it, they might just
as well be growing on bushes."

It is true enough that the gourmet only spares a very occasional
thought for one of the most valued and beneficial of delicacies.
The limelight is focused on the Colchester Pyefleet Natives just
twice a year—at the ancient annual ceremony of the opening of
the Fishery, when the Mayor and Corporation gather afloat to
read a medieval proclamation and partake of the traditional gin
and ginger-bread, and at the more widely known Colchester
Oyster Feast, dating back about a century in its present form,
when the notabilities of the land, often including royalty, gather
at the Mayor's invitation to tuck away their dozens. At other

times, like so many more of the best things in life, the oyster is taken for granted.

A farm under the water ! That is not a bad description of an oyster fishery. The farmer manures, ploughs, and harrows his land, sows his seeds, thins his seedlings and transplants them from the seed-beds, prunes his fruit-trees, and finally harvests. All these operations, except, perhaps, the sowing, which the oyster looks after itself, have their counterparts in oyster cultivation, and there are other operations besides which have no parallel in agriculture.

There are the big farms, employing many hands when times are good. The famous Colchester Fishery, which actually is located at Brightlingsea, has been worked since Roman times (though then no doubt the oysters were merely picked up growing wild), and when its first Charter was granted in 1189, defining the limits of the Fishery just as they now are, it referred to the rights which the burgesses have enjoyed " from time immemorial." Incidentally, it also gave these burgesses the right to hunt the fox, the hare, and the polecat, which right they still enjoy, though polecat hunting is out of fashion now. From this fishery comes the Pyefleet Native, the most highly prized oyster aristocrat in the world, which had become so popular in the seventeenth century that an inquiry in 1638 laid down that not more than one thousand barrels a week should be taken from the Essex common grounds —and that exports should be confined to the Prince of Orange and the Queen of Bohemia !

The " juicy wallfleet " of the Blackwater was in the sixteenth century preferred even to a Colchester Native, but it was not till 1876 that the present Tollesbury and Mersea Fishery Company was formed.

Such fisheries as these and their counterparts at Whitstable, in Kent, and in the Roach and Crouch are the great estates of the submarine agricultural world. Forty years ago eighty-six smacks and a steam-dredger were at work in Colne, and it was considered this was only half the number really needed to keep the ground in condition. In 1895 two and a half million oysters were sold from here for upward of £20,000, of which Colchester Corporation received £6007 towards relief of rates. The Blackwater Company only thirty years ago had five hundred shareholding fishermen at work and was selling two million oysters annually, which went all over Europe.

But bad times fell on the great estates, both on the land and under the sea. Colchester has for years recently received nothing from its fishery, which at the present time is actually supporting only half-a-dozen pensioners, and, though before the Second World War the Blackwater had attempted to fit a second string to its bow by re-laying ' foreigners,' a succession of hard winters and the wartime impossibility of renewing imported stocks have greatly reduced its activities also. At Whitstable the spatting is no better, and they rely largely on fattening young oysters mostly born on Essex ground, while in Crouch and Roach not one dredge splashes to-day where twenty worked a quarter of a century ago.

Big farms, however, are not the only kind of fishery. There are the large private layings, such as those in Salcot and Tollesbury Creeks, bordering the famous Essex wild-fowl marshes of Tollesbury Old Hall, which keep at least the owner's smack at work ; these are the small farms. And the ' patches ' which the owner cultivates single-handed, or with his wife or son's help in a skiff, are the allotments. There are many of these throughout the miles of creeks which border both shores of the Thames Estuary—the only part of the whole country entitled to call its products native oysters—and they remain prosperous, profitable, and quite delightful undertakings.

Whether it be on the grand scale or the small, however, oyster cultivation is the same in its essentials throughout the area. The oyster starts its life by appearing first ' white-sick,' as the eggs cluster on its gills, and then ' black-sick,' as they become ready for discharge. Then there occurs what resembles a puff of smoke in the water, and a family of up to two million oysters has been born. It is one of the highest birth-rates in all nature, yet such is the infantile mortality that it is difficult to keep up stocks. For not one of those tiny offspring will survive unless it finds a clean piece of ground to alight on and fix itself on to. For this purpose the muddy bottom of the creek must be covered with ' culch,' which generally takes the form of old shell laid in spring before spatting takes place. After a few days the young ' brood ' can be seen, each the size of a pin's head on the culch, and in good years as many as two hundred can be counted on one bit of shell.

There it lies for perhaps a year, at the end of which time it may be as big as a shilling. Now when the dredge fetches up the piece of culch on which it lies, the dredgerman will take his 'cultac,' as he calls his big, blunt, dagger-shaped knife, and part oyster from culch. This 'singling' prevents the oysters crowding on each other and becoming mis-shapen as they grow. At this stage and till it is three years old the young oyster is known as 'brood,' and for the next year as 'half-ware.' At four it should be reaching marketable size and only requires fattening. A year on the fattening grounds, which in most cases are in a different place from the spatting grounds, sees our native 'fished' and ready to go into the 'pits,' the shallow ponds which are such a familiar sight on the Essex marshes, ready for market. Up to the middle of the last century many of these pits had the quality of 'greening' an oyster, but a poisoning scare brought a change of fashion (even though the green tinge was quite harmless), and what was previously considered the oyster's crowning perfection came to be regarded as a blemish.

The big fisheries mostly contain their spatting and fattening grounds within their boundaries. The small men, however, make use of the common spatting grounds, of which the most prolific is that wonderful stretch of shoal off Mersea known as 'Pont,' which fifty years ago yielded such harvests, not only of oysters, but of soles and plaice, eels and the tasty guard-fish, dabs of such crisp sweetness, and the delectable King Harrys, by which name there are few left even to recognize that once prized shell-fish.

Sometimes smacks go farther afield after brood. About thirty years ago there was a big fall of spat off the Kent coast which kept a fleet of Whitstable and Essex smacks busy, and a century ago as many as fifty sail of smacks might have been seen dredging brood in Harwich harbour and taking it to Colne, to the annoyance of the Harwich men. More venturous still, in 1808 a fleet of thirty-five Colne smacks went oyster-pirating in the Crouch. Their retreat was cut off by H.M.S. *Turbulent*, and a number of men were taken off the smacks for naval service.

Indeed, the placid oyster has always shown a knack of provoking violence. As long ago as 1285 Sandwich and Yarmouth men quarrelled over buying oysters at Brightlingsea.

In Edward III's time a fisherman was killed in a fight between men of Brightlingsea, Wivenhoe, and Alresford and men of Mersea and Tollesbury. About 1870, when some Brightlingsea smacks went to the Firth of Forth to dredge oysters off Newhaven, their skill and their gear caused so much jealousy that the Scots fishermen attacked them in boats laden with stones for ammunition. The men had to sleep under police protection, armed with hatchets and pokers, and finally a gunboat was called in to restore order. The deep-sea oysters called the Essex smacks yet farther afield, as described in Chapter III, but this obsolete fishery may really be considered a separate industry.

It will by now be becoming clear that the oysterman's dredge does not scour the bottom simply to ' catch ' the oyster for market. By the time he comes up for that purpose he has probably been in a dredge a good many times already, for although the oyster is in season only when there is an ' r ' in the month, the dredges are always busy. In fact, the dredge is plough, harrow, and hoe as well as harvester. It is continually turning over the culch, keeping it clean, free from mud, and so acceptable to the spat, and like the hoe it is assiduous in searching for the ' weeds ' on the farm—the foes of the oyster.

First of the oyster's enemies which cannot be combated short of artificial cultivation is the cold winter, which leaves such oysters as it does not kill so weakened that a poor spatting season usually ensues. Of the pests the dredge does get at, one of the worst nowadays is the American slipper limpet, which was introduced with the importation of American brood. This creature eats the oyster's food, spoils his culch, accumulates mud and weed, and is so prolific that it smothers the oysters. The dredges come up full of slipper limpets instead of oysters nowadays, and these are dumped ashore in great heaps at such places as Packing Sheds Island at Mersea. It is thought that the meat decaying out of them helps to enrich the water of Thornfleet, manuring it as it were, and the sun-bleached shell is used for culch. For some years a factory worked at Mersea crushing it for chicken grit. The war-starved Dutchmen of recent years have actually learned to eat slipper limpets, and to evolve means of extracting them mechanically from their shells. Though dainty English tastes are unlikely to find such morsels acceptable, there are possibilities in pig-, poultry-, or cattle-foods for turning the pest to good account, for it is rich in protein.

Mussels and other shell-fish are also injurious in similar ways. The mussel, by the way, is curiously little thought of in this home of the shell-fish, though Mr Ivan Pullen, of the renowned old Rose Inn, Peldon, has had considerable success fattening them in near-by Ray Creek. Five-fingers (those same starfish which were once so prized in Essex for fertilizer) inject a poison and open the weakened oysters, sea-urchins scrape off and devour the young spat, and the hated whelk-tingle bores through the shell and sucks the meat out through the hole. Crabs crush the brood with their claws and have an oyster feast at their leisure, and flat fish and even shrimps consume a lot of young brood.

Small wonder, then, that 80 per cent. of the relatively few oysters that reach the brood stage perish between their first birthday and the time of their maturity, and small wonder that when dredges are not at work the beds go to ruin as quickly as neglected agricultural land. 'Slobbed-up,' the smackmen call it as the dredges empty on deck a foul tangle of mud, weed, five-fingers, and filthy culch instead of a load of clean, spat-covered shell and a dozen nice natives in all stages of growth. The marvel is how the oyster got on so well when it adorned the Roman tables in uncultivated days two thousand years ago.

Can the oyster-farming industry hope to regain the importance it once enjoyed in days when London took enough to average twenty dozen a year for every man, woman, and child, and there were enough left to send all over Europe ? Now the Colchester native is such a rarity that it is being sold in the London oyster-bars at one and sixpence, and the old men shake their heads and say, " Those days will never return." Perhaps not, but the demand for the oyster will never cease, and there is no reason why the supply should not again be greatly developed. The fishery companies, however, with their shareholders and no capital, are curious concerns to manage, and the system under which no man who has not served his apprenticeship with the company may cast a dredge in Colne further complicates labour problems. Re-laying imported oysters—American blue-points, Britannies, Dutchmen, or Portuguese from the Tagus river—can help by supplementing sales. Though they will not spat in the chilly Thames

Estuary waters, they grow all the more rapidly for this reason, but, susceptible as they are to sudden death in a hard East Coast winter —millions perished in the Blackwater in 1941–42—they can never be more than a second-string stable companion to the thorough-bred natives ; indeed, the millions laid in the Blackwater before 1939 are in future to go to the milder waters of the West Country.

There is, however, much to be learned from experiments on the lines of those made at the Ministry of Fisheries station in North Wales. An interesting experiment to get round the ' slobbing-up ' of culch and spat by the mud was tried at Mersea in 1937 when a stone was hung from a moored smack in the spring and drawn up in late summer covered with a fine fall of spat which had been collected safe from at any rate those of its enemies con-fined to the sea-bed. There are lessons to be learned, too, from the foreign methods of spat-collecting, for in Italy the culch and the fattening-ware are slung from poles in the water ; the Dutch enclose their culch-shell in wire-netting baskets which can be lifted and shaken free of mud, and the Japanese plant a little under-sea forest of bamboo twigs.

Science, however, will not solve the main riddle of oyster culti-vation till it has determined the why and wherefore of good and bad spat falls. In Essex the period 1846–1900 produced twelve really bad seasons, twenty-six moderate, and seven good, which could not be accounted for simply by the weather. More re-cently it appeared that never again would a spat fall be seen to compare with those bumper years 1849, 1859, 1876, 1881, 1884, 1893, and 1900, for the favourable summer of 1933 quite failed to put any stop to a sterile period. Then a wonderful fall in 1935 again raised hopes and restored confidence, and spatting has been much better since. In Mersea the fall in 1945 was phenomenal, thanks to the early summer.

This is probably one of nature's secrets of which she will not easily yield up the key, yet much valuable and interesting work may be done with experiments on water temperature and salinity to remove at any rate some of the present unpredictable chan-ciness from a game that by comparison makes the arable far-mer's life seem a calling as reliable, safe, and sure as the Bank of England.

# XI

## OUT WITH THE OYSTER DREDGERMEN

Far other craft our prouder river shows,
Hoys, pinks, and sloops ; brigs, brigantines, and snows :
Nor angler we on our wide stream descry,
But one poor dredger where his oysters lie ;
He, cold and wet, and driving with the tide,
Beats his weak arms against his tarry side,
Then drains the remnant of diluted gin,
To aid the warmth that languishes within,
Renewing oft his poor attempts to beat
His tingling fingers into gathering heat.

GEORGE CRABBE

OYSTER-DREDGING can hardly be enjoyed for its own sake, as can trawling, wildfowling, and most of the inshore fishermen's occupations ; it is a great deal too much like work. But I have had some happy days at it.

It was six o'clock of a bleak, raw morning when I met two Mersea dredgermen friends on the Hard for my first taste of it. They were Charlie Hewes, one of the wisest old hands that ever chucked a dredge and sailed a smack, and that grand old Mersea character, oysterman, and wildfowler, the late " Sooty " Mussett. I recall how that half-dark Hard seemed suddenly to become alive with merry little bearded figures all jesting and chattering as if it were they who were out for a holiday, and I (a sleepy and rather morose figure just out of my warm cot) embarking on my daily round of toil.

Nor shall I ever forget how that fleet of smacks got under way. Boat alongside, anchor windlass clinking, patent blocks clickety-clicking, peak up, jib set, anchor away, foresail set ; it was going on all around me almost as quickly as I can write of it. So in the grey, early dawn that humble, exquisite little armada, perhaps fifteen of those lovely eight- to fifteen-ton carvel-built cutter smacks, some of them seventy years old, streamed off out of Thornfleet and Besom Creeks. Most of them were going to work on the Main and below Tollesbury Pier, but we were to dredge in the narrow Thornfleet Creek itself, all in among the moorings and the yachts on them.

It was all new to me. The tide was on the flood, and we sailed slowly over it down the Quarters. There Charlie put the helm down, and as she wended and " Sooty " downed staysail he took the tiller out and laid it on the deck. " She steers herself," he exclaimed with a grin. " Now chuck your dredge." I flung it over, my splash sounding to me much like theirs. " Now pull it in." I hove on the bass rope, and in it came—upside down. " Now let *me* show you," said Charlie. The deft twist which sent the dredge so that the tide, catching it, opened it out was soon acquired, and before long my dredge was as often full as empty and inverted.

" Make fast." Neatly I slipped a clove-hitch on the thole-pin stuck in the rail. Safe there, anyway. But no. " Do you get your dredge fast that'll jam and break that owd pin off," came the reproving voice. So I learned that a dredgerman's hitch is only a single round turn and the end backed over. A fast dredge then jerks out the rope, which can be slipped off the pin in a moment.

Hove to in the tideway, the smack was working. The dredge ropes quivered as she hoed three paths in the creek bed. We were working only one dredge each, though in more open water with less ' soil ' on the ground we might have had two or even four each. " Ruck your peak." She was forging ahead now under the weather mud. As the drive went out of the mainsail, she backed off obediently. " Haul your dredge." Again hand over hand on the bass rope. Heavier work than I expected, and how the bits of shell in the rope do cut the wet hands ! Ah ! At last the dredge breaks surface ; its handle is across the bulwark, a couple of shakes to clear some of the weed and water, and, grasping the wooden batten that extends the wire and string-mesh bag, I shoot out on deck old shell, weed, limpets, crabs—a fine sample of the creek's bottom. Splash ! Over goes the dredge again.

Charlie and " Sooty," fingers nimbly diving into their heaps, are tossing oysters into the wooden tub before I can find one at all ; old shells and full ones look alike to me. Charlie ferrets out half a dozen. " Nothing more there," he says. I pick up the ' sheards ' (how these chaps do love to have a fancy name for everything ; these are only bits of board such as the gardener gathers up leaves with) and bundle the rubbish overboard. Charlie's boot has given the crabs their quietus ; tingle, spawn, and limpets are in a heap for dumping later. I straighten my back and see we are drifting broadside across the bows of a moored yacht. But before I have a chance to see more it is time to haul again. " Give me trawling," I reflect. " You do get a spell at that while the net is over." The pronunciation ' drudge ' acquires a new significance.

So we work up that creek, dodging yachts by working the peak of the mainsail—down to let her drop back, up to drive her to windward—and by shifting a dredge rope to another thole, aft or forward. We have to clear the anchors of moorings, and mostly miss them, but once a dredge catches one. " Sooty " sculls off in the boat and worries it free. Back aboard, he takes up his favourite wildfowling yarn just where he dropped it.

We reach the " Gut," haul for the last time, and, setting the staysail, wend and sail back. " Come and catch hold of the wheel," says Charlie, knowing I love no sensation more than the feel of a smack's tiller against my knee. " Goo on, sail her down to the Bench Head, and we'll see if we can't get a couple of widgeon," says " Sooty." Up and down that creek. Haul. Sort. Haul. Charlie recognizes an old Brittany we caught in the last haul and trims it up with his knife to make it look like a native. " Bet that own't git past our owd foreman, though," he says. My back seems never straight ; my hands are getting rawer and rawer. I am glad when we lie to a dredge to save letting go the anchor for our ' 'levenses ' ; gladder still when dinner-time comes.

" Sooty " takes advantage of the midday tide to scull ashore to the Victory. He is as tough and wiry as a terrier. I lie down on the deck. Half-past two sees our eight-hour day done. The boats go ashore to Packing Sheds Island with oysters and ' weeds.' Then we pull in over the ebb to the Hard.

On the way they drop me at my own boat. I am kicking off

my boots and creeping into the cot I left so unwillingly that morning when I hear Charlie's comment, " I think that'll keep fine, Soot. Time for a couple of hours' digging in the garden, I reckon."

Well, you don't have to go down and dig an oyster laying, anyway !

Another very different day, a lazy, sun-drenched August morning, I was paddling up " Doitch," as they call the Little Ditch by Salcot Creek, and there found Woodham Hewes hauling his skiff up and down his laying.

It is a misleading name, skiff, for these hefty, heavily built, twenty-foot boats, with fine, wide floors and big knees and timbers, that are used in the oystering and spratting trades. Woodham had spent his young days as a yacht skipper, but his ambition had always been to own and work this piece of ground, and now he has been able to gratify it. " It's only eighty yards long and thirty yards wide," he said, " but there's five hundred pounds' worth of oysters down there."

An eighty-yard bass rope runs the length of the laying. We hauled the double-ended skiff up tide, made fast while the dredge was cast, and hauled down again, towing the dredge. Up it came, and its contents spilled over the skiff floor. The cultac was soon at work, paring the edge of the shell of the larger oysters to trim off disfiguring edges, and parting the young brood. Since the season was getting advanced, Woodham counted the number of oysters per dredge. In this way he could form an estimate of the stock. The heap of limpets and ' weeds ' grew more rapidly than the marketable oysters, but the latter made a good showing. Soon with luck he would be able to sell two hundred pounds' worth of ' ware ' to the Whitstable smack when it made its autumn visit.

It is slow and arduous work, dragging a skiff up and down, gradually moving across the ' allotment,' but it is a thorough method of cultivation. On this laying Woodham puts his marketable stock on a nice, clean patch on the edge of the mud, marked by withies, where he can come and gather them at low water.

I picked up a gleaming native oyster from the contents of the last haul. What beautiful things they are to handle ! Heavy and solid as a gold hunter watch. There is a rare satisfaction in picking out these masterpieces of nature's handiwork from the litter of old dead shells, culch, weed, and mud that comes up with them in the dredge and weighing them appreciatively in the hand. That tub-full of natives looks as attractive as a pile of newly minted sovereigns or a constellation of gems in some precious bit of jewellery.

This is a good place to pass a day like to-day. We have the world to ourselves. There lies the Blackwater estuary sparkling in the sun, the smacks at work on it beyond the salts gleaming delicately mauve with sea-lavender. Behind us the tiled roofs of Mersea bask rose-red in the sun. A few dun-birds wade and feed along the edges of the mud ; an invisible curlew calls over Wig-borough way.

" Yes," says Woodham. " I always looked forward to having this little farm under the sea." He tells me how he has recently been lucky finding a wonderful haul of spat on the common ground up by Thirslet Creek and has brought a fine lot down to his laying in his little bawley. His wife came on that expedition and shared the delight of the find. " She often comes dredging here with me," he says. " She sits there and trims them up with the knife while I work the skiff. We pass some very happy days together up here."

It all seemed to me too idyllic to be true. I decided then and there that I should like to own and work an oyster laying—if it were always like this.

One final picture. I have sailed round to that happy yachts-man's haunt, Paglesham, for a week-end cruise. And there, just below the moorings, five Mersea smacks are dredging. They come round here for a week and have to put in forty-five hours' work.

As tide and weather are kindly this evening they are working late. They are dredging only a short stretch, and it is lovely to watch them manœuvring together at such close quarters. One by one they sail up tide—one long leg, one short—and then down comes the staysail, and over go the dredges, and they come slowly working down, hauling and throwing their dredges, broadcasting the culch back in the water after each haul.   One by one as they finish their last haul they break off, gather in the mainsheet, and away each dodges among her fellows as she tacks back to start again.   There are always two or three dredging and two or three sailing back.

Nowadays they pay more here for smacks with motors, and instead of this sort of maritime country-dance in which these sailing-smacks are indulging they steam up and down like a procession of schoolgirls out for a Sunday walk.   They get more work done like that, but as I watched the sailing-smacks sheering and yawing down, laid right across the tide, I realized what a much wider path a smack dredges in this way than when she follows a straight course under power, dredging only two narrow tracks with port and starboard dredges.

I rested my chin on my hatch and watched them for hours that day, till the tide was done, and they all brought up in a cluster. Is it not such memories as these, stored up in happier days, that sustain us through times of grey strain and blank living ?

# XII

## WHERE PLOUGH MEETS SAIL

*A Sailorman Farmer of Bradwell—Barge-racing and Smuggling—Old
" Righto ! " the Sea-poacher—Sailing Families—A " Cold Owd Trip "
and a Warm Reception*

BRADWELL QUAY, across on the south side of the Blackwater, is
traditionally a meeting-place of plough and sail, the front door
for the rich farmlands of the Dengie Hundred on to that great
London highroad of other days, the sea.   The farms had their own
little back doors in the places along the great wall from St Peter's
Point to Burnham, which gave its name to the " juicy wallfleet "
oysters, where they could come alongside and exchange chalk,
stone, or London muck for stacks of hay and straw, but at
Bradwell they could come right into harbour, spring-tides or
neaps, gale or calm, and lie alongside the little quay to which a
hard road brought the carts in such plenty that to load a forty-ton
stack in a day was common.

Thus the place saw the old-time barge-owner farmer develop
to a remarkable degree, and the coming of the motor-lorry killed
the waterside traffic as completely as the railway had killed
Maldon's a century before.

I heard the story of Parker's fleet of Bradwell barges from Mr
John Parker, who, though he has now no interest afloat, retains
that breezy humour, that love of a good tale, and that spicy way
of telling it which his forbears must have drunk in with the salt
air and passed on to him.   It was his grandfather who formed the
fleet and used to rouse out his son on a blowing night to ride the
wall on his pony to see if the barges were up out of their berths.
" If they are I can't push 'em back," the lad would say.   " No,
but you can go and have a look at them," came the order, and
round that long stretch of sea-wall went rider and pony to see the
little craft lying in the outfalls (then far deeper inlets across the

Dengie Flats than you will find now) or bumping against the open walls. Luckily this did not kill young Clem Parker's love of the salt water and the barges. One day he was sent to make sure the crew were taking advantage of a fair wind and a good tide to get away from Bridgewick Outfall. They had not turned up, so Clem collected a boy from the farm to help him lay her off and blew out into the fairway. He was seventeen years old at the time, and as the wind was fair for London he decided to make a day of it. The next his father heard from him was a wire from Woolwich asking where the stack was to be delivered !

Later Mr Clem Parker not only assembled a fine fleet of twenty-six craft, but took an active interest in the barge races, especially with the *Verona* and *Veronica*, built by Shrubsole, of London, to challenge perhaps the most famous of them all, Piper's *Giralda*. As a builder could not race his own barge, the *Verona* sailed under Parker's colours—the white hand and red heart on a blue ground —and he took her Thames winnings and Shrubsole any Medway prize money. *Verona* won the Medway, but to her owner's chagrin a protest against *Giralda*, which was alleged to have used a boom to clear some lighters in the Thames race, was disallowed. So Parker and Shrubsole put their heads together and built the *Veronica*, an out-and-out racer which had a slightly rockered bottom and started with a nine-inch keel. They could do nothing with her at first, and after trying the mast in five positions they scrapped the keel. She was always an awkward barge to work with heavy freights, for with her curved keelson you could see daylight under each end when she lay aground, and thus she was a terror for straining when lying laden in a hard berth, yet she remains in Everard's fleet at Grays a formidable flyer and has won many prizes. In 1906 Parker broke the record with the *Verona* and *Veronica*, taking first and second in both Thames and Medway races in the Championship Class, while the *Violet Sybil* came first in both rivers in the Coasting Class. The barge race was a serious business, and many a tale of foul play and rule-dodging is told in Bradwell. One of the *Veronica's* rivals is said to have been detected just before the race with a door cut from her cabin to her hold, so that her crew could surreptitiously slip through and move a ton of old sails to trim her while sailing.

Mr Jack Parker made his first trip at the age of seven in the *Violet Sybil*, a barge with the useful accomplishment of taking 180 tons to sea on a draught of five-and-a-half feet. He remembers to this day how they came away from Portland, stone-loaded, and how they got into a gale off the Needles, and he was firmly put to bed by the skipper, Arthur Creeks. But they had the satisfaction running back up the Thames of meeting the same barges that had set out with them a month before, still wind-bound, and then for sheer swank the crew set every stitch the *Violet Sybil* had, and she tore through the fleet like a mad thing. "Here's your son," said the skipper on arrival. "You're lucky to get him back."

Some of the Bradwell barges were in the fantastically profitable coke trade to the French ports in the 1914–18 war.

In 1932 Clem Parker died, and his son, regretfully letting his head guide his heart, sold up the fleet. Most of them went to Wakeley's, with which firm the Parker family is connected. The *Duchess* was lost at Dunkirk, whither she was towed half full of grain, of which there was no time to empty her. This barge was always fitted out for a summer family cruise, complete with the owner's white ensign defaced with his masonic insignia. Once in the Alde they tried to make him pull that fancy drapery down —but not he! "We used to pull up the Newsons' lobster pots off Shingle Street and help ourselves," John Parker recalled, "though I believe my father kept count and wrote and paid them when we got home."

So ended Parker's barges, and the proud old hand-and-heart flag. Now only the name of one of them, the *Nellie Parker*, remains to recall the fleet. It was a sad day, but the age of the farmer-sailor is past. While still a youngster John Parker found himself during a sudden illness of his father's with the management of eight hundred acres, twenty hay-presses, each calling for three tons of hay a day, and twenty-six barges to be fixed on Mark Lane. He learned his lesson from that handful of irons in the fire, and though, when the tarmac road was relaid down to the quay, his father, he declares, would have burst a blood-vessel to see little lorries bringing all the way from Leicester the tar which had always before been carried by sea from Kent, he was prepared to accept the inevitable. He had, however, enough of sailorly good sense to rise in wrath at the sight of hundreds of lorries a day bringing sand from Rowhedge to build the aerodrome which now disfigures poor Bradwell—a round trip of forty-three miles by way of Maldon at a time of extreme petrol and rubber shortage when a few barges could have slipped the stuff across from Colne. The roads are not repaired yet from the effects of that extravagant traffic.

The chief sailing families of Bradwell were the Kirbys and the Spittys—that same tribe which counted among its members the redoubtable Jack, of Rowhedge. From his seventy-seven-year-old nephew, Aaron, I heard tales of earlier days, sitting hard by the water in the little weatherboard cottage which was formerly The Case is Altered. The price paid for the licence of that inn was, I believe, used to purchase the Spittys' coasting-barge *Water Lily*, which later became part of Parker's fleet. Aaron can recall the last of the revenue cutters, the *Mermaid*, under Captain Jenkins, and his father (who with his father before him kept The Case is Altered) brought to Bradwell the old gun-brig which did preventive duty at the creek-mouth after the cutter's day, till she was in turn removed some sixty years ago when the white cottages up the road were taken for the coastguards.

Opposite the old Case is Altered stood another Spitty home with its surprising name " Envious Hall " proudly carved on a stone in the chimney. Some connect the origin of that name with an elaborate leg-pull on a neighbour who cast a jaundiced eye on it during its construction ; some with a story of how the Spittys went and collected their own thirty-six-gallon cask and rolled it down the hill to the house when the local landlord declined to serve them ; some with the fact that by dint of building first and asking afterwards the owner paid (as the owner pays to-day) but one pound a year for his site. Now, alas, the stone has gone, removed in the last year or two by some humourless hand. So too has the board inscribed " Ancient Lights," which was solemnly used as the name of Aaron's home.

Another of Aaron's uncles, " Righto " Spitty, used to go scollop-poaching on the French coast. He carried a suit of white sails and a suit of red, and when the Frenchmen went to capture an English smack with red sails reported poaching they found only an innocent, white-sailed vessel. The skipper earned his name from his habit of putting his helm up when challenged and sailing clean away with a cheery " Righto, Frogs ! "

Besides the barges, Aaron can recall many of the ketches and schooners, the brigs and brigantines, mentioned in other chapters, including the *Banshee, Eblana, Robert Adams, Standard,* and *Jessie Annandale,* unloading against the quay.   After their time most of the freights were stacks, but sometimes a barge kept up the old tradition with a load of coal.   For many years one of the Parker barges brought the groceries and beer.   The barrels worked in a sea-way, and the men had to ease the bungs—but not so much as one skipper who eased away till the barrel was three parts empty. Then he made things worse by topping up with salt water !   He was nearly detected when the kindly landlord asked him what he would have, but he had the presence of mind to reply, " That's been a cold owd trip ; I'll have a drop of whisky "—and he was gone before they tapped that cask and the landlord vowed to throw him in the creek if ever he came back !   You always knew if there was a baby due in Bradwell when that barge arrived, because if so there would be a four gallon of stout on deck for the expectant mother.

The Kirby family provided six captains of Parker's barges, a father and five sons.   Oscar Kirby, who took command of a barge when he was only seventeen, was well served with mates from his own family, but when all five boys became skippers the old man sailed his barge home single-handed and came ashore, being held in reserve in case one of the other skippers was ill.   But John Parker always thought his father looked on Joe Kirby as senior captain of the fleet.   Now, however, only William Kirby, otherwise " Admiral Truthful," so named after Parker's one-eyed sail-maker, William Phillips, remains afloat.

Smacks lay in the creeks then too, including " Fan " Hewes's little *Fiddle,* eel-trawling and oystering, and the place has been beloved by yachtsmen for thirty years.   (Did not Aaron with fine incongruity remove his venerable cap to show me the mark of the King's hatter within it, and tell me how Mr Heath, his ' owner,' had made it for him from the self-same cloth that went into King George V's last suit ?)

I'm not going to pretend that tortuous creek has the same fas-cination to-day as when one might see the *Nellie Parker* or the

*Violet Sybil* twist her way up it with such brilliant dexterity, nor that the quaint quay with its crooked piles towering over it is so picturesque now that a sprittie's lofty gear no longer crowns it, the hand and heart lording it against the green fields and woods rising behind.

For five hundred years the creek has been busy—in 1478 the *Christopher*, belonging to the place and probably built there, sailed for Calais with a cargo of wool, one of many ships then in that trade—now only one of the little Maldon smacks uses Bradwell as a port of call. Yet more and more little amateur argosies of exploration and adventure seek it out from Burnham and Harwich and farther afield. Some spend the evening perched on its all-embracing mud-spits ; the more successful navigators in the tap-room of the Green Man. In both places, a little of the atmosphere of the old days, praise be, survives.

# XIII

## TOLLESBURY—WHERE THE YACHTSMEN COME FROM

*A Famous Racing Skipper—The Starfish Dredgers—The Toll of War
—Twice mined in a Year*

IT is the proud boast of Tollesbury that there has been at least one man from that village aboard every America's Cup challenger since *Genesta*, with the solitary exception of *Galatea*. The last of them, *Endeavour*, was in charge of Captain Ted Heard—a name synonymous with Tollesbury—who took a good many of his neighbours with him for that exciting season's racing which culminated with the *Endeavour* parting from her steam-yacht consort on the voyage home and sailing back unescorted—a feat which caused more excitement in the daily Press than in the fo'c'sle of the yacht.

It is indeed on yachting that Tollesbury's prosperity and fame are founded. For some reason the smacks of that village have produced a higher proportion of skippers and mates, mastheadmen and forepeak hands, than even Wivenhoe and Brightlingsea. Prince of them all, perhaps, was the famous Captain Sycamore, who, though a native of St Lawrence, on the other side of the Blackwater, was apprenticed to a local smack and is claimed by Tollesbury. A perfect example of a breezy, hail-fellow-well-met mariner, he commanded *Valkyrie* and some of the *Shamrocks*, and cared not a damn for anybody or anything, from royalty on board to a North Sea gale. He was described as "the most cheerful and good-natured loser of a race we ever met." What finer tribute to a man who raced to win ?

Fishing has always been largely a complementary winter occupation, and up to thirty years ago the staple catch was a curious one—none other than the common five-finger, or starfish. So greatly in demand were these for agricultural fertilizer that most of the ninety smacks which before the First World War found a livelihood for three hundred men were engaged in dredging them. A wonderfully smart fleet they were too, fitted out like yachts, and to see them racing home from the Kent coast, which was the chief dredging-ground, was something not soon forgotten. The five-finger dredgers were for many years represented on Colchester market, where the local farmers placed their orders. Five-fingers cost about thirty shillings a ton and were carted straight on the fields and ploughed in. If dug over soon after they could be seen gone to a powder like sawdust in the soil.

Four oyster dredges per man were worked, using a rather wider mesh, and Captain Drake Frost, skipper of the biggest yacht ever to come up Tollesbury Creek, the 500-ton *Alice*, told me that he recalled on one occasion leaving Tollesbury at midday, sailing to Kent, dredging all night (four men working sixteen dredges in all), and returning on the next day's tide with twelve tons aboard. He described it as hard work, but less laborious than oyster-dredging.

This trade began to diminish about twenty-five years ago, although occasionally a boat brings home a load to this day. There was then a great deal of oyster brood to be found, and the grounds off Whitstable and the Reculvers were sadly over-dredged by Essex and Kent boats. This, added to the introduction of artificial fertilizers and a long period of land-starvation, caused a turnover to spratting, and now this is the main winter occupation of most of the twenty-five or so smacks and the 150 mariners whom Tollesbury supported up to the outbreak of the last war.

Most of these smacks, which average twenty to twenty-five tons, were originally built by Aldous, of Brightlingsea. Several have been rebuilt by Drake Brothers in their yard at the head of the creek. All are now mainly dependent on motor-power, for your Tollesbury man does like to get about. Wherever there are fish he will find them, and even his rivals in Colne will admit his unique flair in this respect.

Most of the fleet laid up in the summer, but forty years ago as many as twenty to twenty-five were left to go shrimping, a trade which suits a yachting port, since a shrimper carries only two hands and a spratter, in the winter, four.

Oystering, too, is a Tollesbury trade, for the creek contains a number of good layings, and as many as three-quarters of a million have been sent away in a week, all by the little branch railway-line known throughout Essex as the "Crab and Winkle."

Nowadays a barge seldom comes up to the creek unless it be to go alongside the wall and unload stone for repairs. Up to the First World War, however, several boomie-barges were owned here, including the *James Balls* which brought coal to the Hard and to Old Hall, and the *Lord Hamilton*, *Darnett*, *Empress of India*, and *Mary Kate*. Seabrook's, the big farmers of near-by Tolleshunt D'Arcy, owned three smaller sprittie-barges, *Defender*, *Pride of Essex*, and *D'Arcy*, which were mainly engaged in stack work.

One particular feature of Tollesbury gladdened my heart, saddened by having to write *finis* to so many activities in so many places. The instinct to go to sea seems stronger here than any-where else about these waters. The war could not stop it. The Tollesbury boats were working in spite of everything all about the Thames Estuary fishing-grounds, and paid their price for their enterprise. The *Alpha*, a nearly new boat, was the first to be mined. She was trawling in the Whitaker, but, luckier than most, kept afloat and managed to reach port and was soon re-paired. Some weeks later the *Thistle* was mined in the Wallet and foundered. Her crew of two were picked up by near-by smacks, and within a few days her skipper had bought another boat and was back at work. The *Rosena* was damaged in the same place about the same time, but was towed in, the crew un-harmed. The luckiest escapes befell the crew of the *Express*, blown up on the Kentish flats near Whitstable. The skipper had his son and daughter with him, and the boat was blown to pieces. It chanced, however, that they had a punt on board, which by extraordinary good fortune was untouched, and all three scrambled into this and were picked up. A few weeks later he bought another vessel, which he named *Little Express*, but less than a year after the original escape, and within a short distance of the scene of it, the *Little Express* blew another mine, and father and son lost their lives.

These were, I believe, the only instances of war damage to Colne and Blackwater smacks, save for the Maldon *Teaser*, which was sunk in the Blackwater without injury to the crew, the *Lily*, of Mersea, lost with her owner and his wife while trawling off Bradwell Point, and the Mersea *Water Lily*, sunk at her moorings by a bomb and since repaired. The experiences of the barges in the war years are described in Chapter XXI.

# XIV

## THE SALTY TOWN OF MALDON

*Where Carriers have vanished but Smacks remain—Ghosts on a Grass-grown Quay, and the Tales they tell—Don't wear Feathers !—Toll of the Gales—Merry Youngsters of Ninety—Twenty Freights in Twenty Weeks—Big Logs and Black Diamonds*

WHEREVER I go about the Essex seaboard in search of these tales I am affected by a haunting atmosphere which is as easy to sense as it is hard to define—a nostalgic melancholy which is yet tranquil and delightful—as the deserted, grass-grown quaysides remember the busy tides of other days which brought a bustling throng of sailormen to moor along them, to lift their ringbolts and slip in the big bowlines of head and stern ropes and then to lumber them with dark coal or bright timber, straw in stacks or beer in barrels. The mud in the channels sighs as the receding tide leaves it to bubble and whisper. The ghosts of the old-timers haunt these places still, and I must somehow capture their memories of the days of tar and hemp before they flee finally to some watery Elysium worsted in the unequal struggle with outboard motors and yachts with chromium-plated deck-houses.

Nowhere are these merry old ghosts thicker than at Maldon. The Blackwater is literally and figuratively the saltiest river in England, and Maldon one of the saltiest little towns. Stand on the quay and look out down the tide-way where Northey and Osea islands hang in their ever-present blue hazy drift. At full tide water gleams through masts and rigging. Water shines in flat streaks and broad vistas. Salt water that glints and burns in the sun, rippled by the wings of gulls. The saltings go under, and little flat islands show purple with sea-lavender. Smacks lie at anchor, and beyond them small yachts, with the burly hull of a great coasting barge lording it as a seagoer among the ditch-crawlers. Burgees flick in the wind, and the curlew call. Swans float by, unruffled and supercilious. Always there are swans, sometimes ten and twenty in white flotillas. And the water shines and dances away broad and glittering to a far, green sea-wall where sits a great yellow old Essex farmhouse, and beyond that to the seaway on whose flat rim lies Northey Island, its queer, towered house sticking up like a fort, its grove of elms rising sheer from the shining water. Turn and see how the rosy-tiled roofs pile away up the hill, where the road dips headlong to the tide. These old houses were built for sailors to live in. Rows of black weatherboarded cottages for the fo'c'sle hands ; self-confident, handsome little bits of Georgian brickwork for the masters of the deep-sea ships, in the days when one went deep-sea in a 200-tonner.

It is a scene intended to be a backcloth to that grand, vigorous pattern only made by the spars of a fleet of sailing-ships. Yes, Maldon should be seen through a criss-cross of masts and yards as it used to be seen and will never be seen again. I saw it yesterday with two barge bobs lording it languidly, level with St Mary's church-tower. Maldon's entire remaining fleet was in—the *Ethel Maud* and the *Mayflower*, the mill's two barges.

Vast tracts of mud-flats lie open to the sun each ebb-tide in the river, and as the flood returns it washes the salt from them, so that the Blackwater has only the Cheshire Dee as rival for the saltiest river in the country. The water is boiled over fires kindled of the cuttings from Sadd's great saw-mills, and the resulting crystal salt is of such purity that the little industry continues to hold its own, and is famous the world over, as it has been for centuries, shaken though it was by the repeal of the salt-tax in 1825. It is the last flicker of what was an almost ubiquitous marshland business for two thousand years. The enigmatic red-hills scattered about the marshes are almost certainly evidence of it in Roman or pre-Roman times, and at Colchester it survived till about 1800, and at Manningtree for about forty years longer.

Lower down the quay the smacks have by no means decided their day is done. Fourteen little beauties I counted there, and felt better. They lean on the beach with booms slung over their port bulwarks, nets, guns, trawl beams, fish-boxes, and dredges all freely in evidence—and all fully rigged despite the ubiquitous propeller marring dead-wood, blocking slim quarter, or gashing shapely rudder.

It takes more than a war to discourage a Maldon fisherman. He can still make a good living amid the devastating rationalization of the twentieth century. The men are mostly related, and so close a guild that you may chat for long without finding out really what variety of business occupies them. In the winter winkles are a mainstay, but a bit of gunning does not come amiss, nor a codling or roker (as the Essex men call skate) in the trawl. In the summer there is oyster brood to chuck a dredge for, a haul of mullet to seine, a creek to stop for flounders, eels to trawl or ' bab ' or shear. In the autumn along come the dabs and plaice ; in the spring the soles, and don't forget the gorbills. Codling and whiting are all grist to the mill, ' spruled ' with a hand-line with a party of " them owd piskitorials " aboard, or hooked on drift-lines. Everything that swims comes up Maldon river some time or other ; trout (a speckled seven-pounder was taken near Bee-leigh Mill), porpoises, seals, sturgeons, even an occasional whale— and nothing escapes a Maldon smackman. They do say no woman dare wear a feathered hat in Maldon in the wildfowling season for fear of receiving a charge of shot.

As if that were not enough, there's always a job when the timber-ships lie at Osea Island, to take down the smack, live aboard, and lend a hand humping timber into the lighters and barges for Heybridge Basin.

Mariners of Maldon, it warms my heart to think of you. I picture your little fleet now strung out down by the island, as I stood on Mill Beach yesterday watching you, waiting for you to decide it was time to be up home as the tide flows, and set up your easy, comfortable working sails smartly for the rattling sail back.

You are among the few who so believe in your glorious means of life that it never occurred to you to desert its uncertainties and ardours for the more easily earned reward of wartime factory life.

Gladdened by this glimpse of one aspect of traditional inshore activity still so much in evidence, I turned my back on the gradually filling channel to hear some tales of the old days when all Maldon river was gloriously alive. But first let us look back a generation farther and bring the story as far as the point where living memory can take it up.

Nothing will ever reconstruct for those who never saw them the old nineteenth-century collier fleets, black little brigs and billy-boys running in ballast up the East Coast (or down to the North as they themselves called it, mindful that they were on the ebb tide), before the prevailing southerlies, loading their two hundred tons of " New Castle Coals," " Walls End Coals," " Lambton's," or whatever the brand might be, from the square-rigged keels ; putting to sea again deep-laden to roll their way back through those treacherous and difficult channels, and finally, when a northerly slant favoured, to come tumbling into London River in a swarm. At the North-east Gunfleet the Colne and Blackwater craft would part company for the Wallet, and up to Maldon might come three or four on a tide, joining " our Hoys who are always to be heard of at Fletchers Wharf, St Katherine," as the Maldon Customs Controller wrote in 1732, chiding the Board for sending " a box of stationery wares " by coach, " the coach-man being so very exorbitant in his price for carryage thereof."

Filling and backing, they would work up the river, giving the pilots a busy time, and there would be another half a thousand tons of black diamonds for the merchants in the wide area which Maldon port then served, and principally for Chelmsford gas-works, whither the journey was leisurely completed in little lighters up Heybridge Canal.

The sheer number of them must have been amazing, as was the toll of them in the winter gales. Defoe, writing two and a quarter centuries ago, says, " In the old Dutch war, I have known there has been a hundred sail of men-of-war and their attendants and between three and four hundred sail of collier ships in Har-wich," and in 1692, according to the same invaluable observer, a hundred and forty of a fleet of two hundred light coasters were wrecked on the North Norfolk coast, together with fifty ships outward-bound from the Wash—in all two hundred ships and one thousand lives lost in one night on one bit of coast. In a gale in 1770 thirty vessels were lost with all hands on Lowestoft sands ; on October 31, 1789, forty were ashore between Southwold and Yarmouth, a stretch of coast which on October 28, 1882, claimed twenty more ships ; on Christmas Eve, 1739, sixteen ships with every soul aboard were lost on the same beaches ; in December 1759 twenty-two, and in 1770 twenty-five in one December day, with two hundred lives.   On February 18, 1887, a hundred and thirty bodies came ashore within thirty miles of Yarmouth.   Five vessels were stranded in the Gunfleet alone on December 7, 1849.

Truly those days recall the words attributed to Marco Polo that " persons frequenting the sea can only be persons of desperate fortune."   How such fleets came to be caught out in those fierce winter gales may seem puzzling, for though the modern barge-man's passages are short and sheltered by comparison, it is rarely that a present-day gale finds one, let alone a fleet, at its mercy at sea.   (Some exceptions are mentioned in Chapter XXI.)

But, of course, weather forecasts were non-existent ; life, no doubt, was cheap and ships ill-found.   In fact, if one considers the nature of the voyage along a coast wicked with sandbanks and with no real shelter save exposed roadsteads between Harwich and the North it perhaps becomes clear that such work in winter was impossible without appalling risks.

The Ipswich men found the best solution at the opening of the eighteenth century, when these men still seem to have been kings of the collier trade, for Defoe records that " in the winter-time these great collier ships are always laid up, as they call it : that is to say the coal trade abates at London."   He describes two hundred ships of all sizes laid up in the Orwell from Michaelmas to Lady Day ; " The masters liv'd calm and secure with their families in Ipswich and enjoying plentifully what in the summer they got so laboriously at sea so that in the winter there might be perhaps a thousand men in the town more than in the summer."   I do not know when this eminently sensible practice went out of fashion ; I can find no recollection of it on the Essex coast.

Nor were gales the only enemies of the poor East Coast sailor-man.   In April 1780 the *Dolphin*, of Maldon, with Richard Nichols master, was taken off Flamborough Head close inshore by the French privateer *Marguerite de Sigulez*, and ransomed for three hundred guineas.

To come to a rather later day, an old cargo book of Sadd's, the Maldon merchants, chronicles the comings and goings of these craft from 1836 to 1876, forty years' salt-water history in crabbed brown ink in its tattered binding.   Many of the craft, especially in the early years, are North Country, from Whitby, Blyth, Shields, and Sunderland ; some are from the West—Swansea,

Bristol, and Chester—one or two from the Channel Islands, Chichester, Rochester, Wells, Boston, and (surprisingly rarely) London. It is, however, the Essex craft which interest us in this survey. Here are some of their forgotten names and those of their masters (unless otherwise indicated, the registry is Maldon) :

1836–1840 : *Trio* (Finch) ; *Royal Sailor* (Harland) ; *Susannah* (Smith, Colchester) ; *Fontenay* (D. Eaveney) ; *Essex* (Colchester) ; *James* (Oxford) ; *Fortitude* (James Beadle) ; *John* (Cole, Colchester).

1840–1845 : *Merton* (Nairn) ; *Coral* (Butler, Ipswich) ; *Mary Ann* (Mulhy) ; *Jason* (Joslin) ; *Nathaniel* (E. Tover) ; *Shipwright* (Newman) ; *Petrel* (Corbell, Harwich) ; *Sea Flower* (Foster, Harwich) ; *Jane* (Willett, Colchester) ; *Hebe* (Colchester) ; *Arno* (Ipswich).

1846–1856 : *Polka* (Player) ; *Victoria* (Mallaburn) ; *Faithful* (Jeffers) ; *Duchess of Kent* (Brown) ; *Wave* (Mallaburn, later Finch) ; *Duke of Sussex* ; *Britannia* (Turner, Colchester).

1857–1860 : *Buchan* (Chaney) ; *Endeavour* (Staples) ; *Mary* (Snow) ; *Olivia* (Thorne) ; *Zabina* (Durrell, Ipswich) ; *Halegon* (Osborn, Ipswich) ; *Lord Howick* (Rex) ; *Fame* (Markham) ; *Echo* (Selby) ; *Alert* (Tover).

1861–1870 : *Banshee* (Bell) ; *Yandue* (Markham) ; *Surprise* (Smee) ; *Jane* (Harper, Ipswich) ; *Charles and Thomas* (Gorbell) ; *Impulse* (Pearmain) ; *Three Sisters* (Staines) ; *Wear* (Playle) ; *Spray* ; *Elizabeth* (Turner) ; *Florence* ; *Alciope* (Hawkins) ; *Eliza Fraser* (Harlow, Wivenhoe) ; *Mayland* (Turner) ; *Onda.*

1871–1875 : *Virgo* (Chaney) ; *Belle.*

These were some of the wooden walls that carried the coals before the railway killed Maldon waterside. Most of the freights were just under 200 tons (though the Whitby *Gleaner* and the Maldon *Royal Sailor* loaded 222), at about eight shillings a ton. In later years the declining rate is noticeable (six shillings a ton was being accepted in 1866), but the sorry day had not yet come when the last leaky, ill-found survivors were to beg their way on three shillings a ton. "Meterage" of 1½d. or 1¼d. a ton is one expense always shown, and a picturesque item in the earlier accounts is the "hat money," evidently the skipper's gratuity. Generally this was a guinea or half a guinea, but on one occasion it is calculated as 5 per cent. of freight.

Ballast in one instance is shown as costing £1 14s. 6d., while there is an interesting entry for the pilotage of the *Julius*, of Danzig, from Orfordness to the Colne Bar in 1868. Mr Kersey, the pilot, earned £6 11s. 0d. for this, being £4 1s. 0d. for 13½ feet draft ; £1 5s. 0d. " boarding money," and £1 5s. 0d. " dist. money," the last two being presumably for boarding at sea and for the distance he had to return.

The continual appearance of fresh craft is rather surprising. The old *Fortitude* and *Lord Howick* go on from year to year, but the majority make quite occasional appearances. It is perhaps an indication of the hundreds of vessels which must have been in this trade, for Sadd's were handling three or four a month.

The fate of some of those whose names have disappeared may be guessed, however, from the fact that in the year 1865–66 535 colliers were lost laden, and 140 in ballast. In their poverty-stricken decline the colliers must have been a sorry fleet of floating death-traps. Lest the mere number of these wrecks blind us to what each meant in human life and suffering, here is the story of one forgotten tragedy—no worse, doubtless, than many others— the loss of the Maldon schooner *Glencoe* (140 tons) on the Ship-wash sands, between Orfordness and Harwich, on Tuesday, October 24, 1882. It was related by the Captain (John Crowland), the sole survivor of the crew of six, to the *Essex Standard*.

We struck the Shipwash on Tuesday about 4 P.M. [he said]. The wind shifted to west ; the weather was awful, and the vessel broke up in an hour after touching the sand. Finding the boat stove in, all hands took to the fore-rigging till the masts got nearly level with the water. As she heeled over, we had to return to the deck, which was then beginning to break up. The hatches were off, and a sea shot Guymer head first into the hold ; it was the last I saw of him. I tried to save him, but could not. I did get as close as I could to the hold with a rope around me, but when the sea broke over, I swung in the bight of the rope till the breath was nearly out of my body and I was forced to get back or I should have been in the same plight as he was. The hold was full of things plunging about, and I think he must have been killed directly. We then got on to the cabin-top, and I told them to get mainsail tyers and to lash themselves to the cabin-top, which they did ; but I fear they must have made slippery bends or else they would have stopped there. She was breaking up then as fast as possible, and we sat there and saw her break up. A heavy sea came and took us alto-gether, cabin-top and all, and we all went into the sea together. I found myself in the water and thought I was under the ship's bottom till I saw daylight again. I did not see anything more of the other poor fellows. I got on to the cabin-top again and put my arm through the chimney-funnel and held on that way, then I fainted away. When I came to again I found my dog sitting on my knee and licking my hands. He lived about an hour. He was not drowned but died on the raft. He was very much bruised and knocked about. I don't know how he came on the raft. He was very fond of me. I would have given anything to have saved him. It was about five in the afternoon when we were washed off, and it was ten next day before I was taken off.

Quite a number of foreigners were coming in, sometimes with tiles from Holland, but generally with timber. The *Julius* brought it at fourteen shillings a load from Danzig, the *Charlotte* and others from Christiania (now Oslo) at twenty-seven shillings. Oaks came from Rotterdam at eight shillings and sixpence, and one exciting October day in 1844 the *Swan* arrived all the way from Quebec with 219 loads at thirty-five shillings and sixpence, and various loads, in all a £598 freight. For one of the Norwegians ten and sixpence is shown for the captain, five shillings for the mate, and five shillings for the sailors, in addition to " hat money."

In the declining days of the coal-trade (1872) the *Belle*, of Maldon, seems to have worked regularly in timber to Wyburg, and her accounts showed twelve shillings for " putting twelve barges in and out " and " five shillings for customs officers " ! The *Statina*, of Maldon, in 1875 brought a freight from Hudiksvall, earning Captain Simpson a two-guinea gratuity.

The coal voyages seem to have averaged rather better than one round trip a month. Thus in 1837 the *Royal Sailor* was in on April 23, May 8, and June 15, and the *May Flower*, of Scarborough, on July 15, August 8, and September 1.

The rules of demurrage are shown in this note :

*Royal Sailor* arrived on the twelfth, was ready for work on the thirteenth of November (1841), but in consequence of the Floods was not cleared till the seventh of December and sailed on the eighth—thus after allowing ten working days and two Sundays there remains thirteen working days which the *Sailor* in consequence of the above-mentioned circumstances was detained.

For this five pounds was allowed.

Chalk was coming in at two shillings a ton, presumably in sailing-barges. In 1840–43 the *Henry, Sarah and Elizabeth*, and

*Maid of the Mill* were handling sixty-ton freights (sometimes ' white,' sometimes ' grey '), twenty-five shillings being also paid for unloading, and in one case two and a penny for " five tons iron bars."    Other vessels in later years bringing up to a hundred tons included the *William and Elizabeth, Elizabeth and Mary, James, Jesse, James and Harriet, Belvedere, Raven, Burnham, Beeleigh, Ann and Elizabeth*, and *James Cann*, all of Maldon, and the tersely named *L.S.D.*, of Colchester.

What these barges were like may be gathered from two century-old bills of sale preserved by Sadd's.    The *Sally*, of Maldon, of which in 1845 Daniel Sadd sold to John Sadd a half-share for £240 with " all and singular the masts, sails, sailyards, and anchors, cables, ropes, cords, guns, gunpowder, ammunition, small arms, tackle, apparel, boats, oars, and appurtenances," was 71·2 feet long, 16·8 feet beam, and 5·6 feet deep in the hold, a square stern sloop with a topping-up bowsprit, barge carvel-built at Horsleydown in 1779.    The *Resolution*, which changed hands in the same sale, was another barge of almost the same dimensions, built at Maldon in 1803, but in this case all " sixty-four sixty-fourth shares being all that ship or vessel " were disposed of for £480, which thus seems to have been an average price for a sailing-barge at this time.

With pictures of these tubby colliers and handy little sixty-ton barges bubbling and bobbing up the fairways, I sought out three old-timers whose memories of Maldon go back to those days— Bill Raven, one of the last of the old-time sail-makers, Jim Keeble, and Dick Quilter, names synonymous with sailing-barges in Essex.

These are men in whose boyhood the port of Maldon (including, as it then did, Southend, Rochford, Burnham, Goldhanger, and Bradwell) stood higher than 34 of the 85 English ports in registered tonnage, with 137 merchant vessels of a tonnage of 8340 registered there, in addition to 282 fishing-boats, tonnage 2289, employing 642 men.    The trading figures for the year are surprising ; no fewer than 3309 vessels with a total tonnage of 156,689 entered the port in the year (against 985 at Colchester, with a tonnage of 55,221), and 3321 cleared outwards.    This number, of course, covers all the little harbours from Southend to

THE SALTY TOWN OF MALDON 115

Goldhanger which, as mentioned, comprised the port, but even so a total of over 60 in and out every week graphically illustrates the number of little coasters about at this time. Moreover, it was claimed by the Maldoners that all figures were showing increases, while all the Colchester totals were declining.[1]

These old-timers painted me a picture of the days when the *Honest Miller* and the *Rogue in Grain* were trading as far up as Bee-leigh Mill above the Abbey, and when the *Falcon, Thomas, City of London, Brothers, New Hope, George, Burnham, Morning Star,* and *Minerva,* many of them ' swimmies,' were about their business in these waters. A safe way to rouse the old-timer is to suggest that the old swim-head barges cannot have been much good. " They'd go like mad," they declare, but generally qualify it with " off the wind." To windward their short chines handicapped them. Many of the ships in the old cargo book they recalled, and many more besides, the barque *Robert Adamson,* in with poles or firewood, the brigantine *Daring,* the boomie

[1] These figures are taken from the unsuccessful petition of 1881 by the Mayor, Aldermen, and Burgesses of Maldon against the degradation of the town to the position of a " creek " in the port of Colchester, and refer to the year 1879. Previously Maldon had occupied the more honourable position of a " member " of Colchester, ever since the disposition of the ports in 1671. Defoe (end of the eighteenth century) records that " the Ports of Harwich, Colchester, Wevenhoe, Malden, Leigh, etc. are said to be members of the port of Ipswich." This is accounted for by the fact that the Customs of the whole coast from London to Yarmouth were originally ' farmed ' by Letters Patent to a ' customer ' at Ipswich, who bid for the revenues and made what he could out of his bargain. Thus long after the end of this system Colchester Customs officers remained technically subservient to this patentee, though in practice independent of him. Similarly, Maldon's subservience to Colchester, first as member and then as creek, was more in name than practice, for the Treasury reply to the Maldon protest of 1881 shows that the Customs and Board of Trade functions continued to be exercised there. These were the Exchequer Ports. The Charter rights of the old ports provide another quite separate disposition, and the Registry Ports a third. No wonder yachtsmen, seeing " MN " on Maldon smacks and " CK " on Colchester smacks, become confused. Usually the first and last letters of a name are used for registry (" IH " for Ipswich, " HH " for Harwich), but, " CR " being used by Cromer, Colchester was allotted " CK," possibly suggest-ing Colchester Creek. This, however, involves yet more confusion, for while Colchester was a ' member ' of Ipswich, it never seems to have been a ' creek,' but perhaps the distinction was not always as firm as Maldon felt it to be in 1881. Prior to 1881 the port of Colchester ran from Walton Naze to Tollesbury Point ; Maldon from Tollesbury Point to Bilmerry Creek, near Tilbury Fort. Since 1881 the port of Colchester has extended from Walton Naze to Havengore. Wivenhoe and Brightlingsea (" Bricklesea " in the 1672 record) were always part of Colchester for Exchequer and Registry purposes.

*Pioneer*, the schooners, of which the outstanding was Soulby's three-masted *Ella*, off " down to the North " with timber, back with coal, and particularly the specially admired *Sarah Lizzie*, a little square-tops'l ketch in which Captain Laythorpe made smart passages after passing from the *Record Reign*, which famous ship shall have a section to herself.   I will here only remark in passing that Raven, whose horny hands I have seen dipping and driving a great sail needle through the massive folds of a barge's mainsail as deftly as a girl's through a silk petticoat, worked on her famous square tops'ls.

We got on to building.   John Howard was to the Blackwater what Harvey was to the Colne—consummate artist, with, I fear, a soul above such sordid matters as cost and profits.   He created the glorious class of Maldon barges represented by the *Mermaid*, *D'Arcy*, *Defender*, *Ready*, *Jacon*, *Violet*, *Emily*, and *Oak*, starting in 1876 and ending before the First World War.   The *Malvoison*, for Burnham, was one of his finest boomie-ketches, apart, of course, from the *Record Reign*.   His models were a copy of the style favoured by Gill, of Rochester, but " more cut up at the ends."   I don't want to see anything sit on the water more sweetly.   Among his smacks were the *Care*, *Faith*, *Rose*, *William*, *Maud*, *Polly*, and *Sisters* (now a yacht), fleet little yacht-like carvel craft which must have caused as great a stir when they joined the motley fleet of old tore-outs as did the first of Aldous's craft when they sailed into Mersea.

Cook, the other chief builder, built barges less elegant to the eye and less fleet-laden, being longer on the bottom, but fine, fast craft when light.   They included *Dawn*, *Robert*, *Sunbeam*, and *British King*.   He also built a few smacks.   At least one smack, the *Joseph T.*, was built by Barr and Hockham.

'Lengthening' was practised at Maldon as elsewhere.   The coaster *Thomas Stratton* had twenty feet built into her and emerged a great, slim greyhound with the lines of a smack or yacht, and a reputation for speed.

Jim Keeble recalled the day when fifty or sixty years ago he made twenty freights in twenty weeks in the *Eva Annie*, all with hay and straw, all entailing loading and unloading and a return trip light, an astonishing record.   I was interested to note that he did not, like so many, attribute it to the different weather of those days, recalling how on at least one of those twenty trips they got caught off the Whitaker after being tempted out of Shore Ends by a deceptively fine morning and went galloping up London River with a stack soaked half-way up and the topsail all adrift and racketing up and down the topmast fit to whip it out of her. They were three-handed in those days, but all three of them got so dead-beat on that busy spell that, said Jim, only the old tiller tickling his ribs kept him awake turning through Gravesend reach. " You could sleep over the old tillers better than you can over a modern wheel," he mused.

On another occasion in Shore Ends the mate of the *Eva Annie*, Jimmy Allison, feeling suddenly weak, fell down on the top of the stack. They put him below, sailed him to London, and when he was got into hospital he was declared to be the first case in England of the new illness, influenza.

These little bits of human interest delightfully enliven interviews with the old hands. There was old Dick Quilter, who, having a wager to jump Heybridge Lock, did it with the aid of a vaulting-pole, and James Rivers, a hay-cutter who went down to the pub on his eighty-eighth birthday. There he kicked the ceiling and fell over backwards " nigh busting himself laughing." They died at ninety-five and ninety-six respectively, these two, and I'm afraid they haven't been replaced.

A skipper of that breed jogged off in the *William and Lucy*, of a hundred tons burthen, to the Humber for a few coals, which was reckoned nothing remarkable with barges of that size penetrating far up the Rhine.

So we came to the heyday. Like that of the Colne, the story of the bygone Blackwater divides into the ' old days,' when a motley variety of ships, ancient ships, leaky ships, absurdly small ships, was sailing into all parts, and the later days, when, though the square yards were gone, every quay was alive and the real monarch of the Essex waters, the sailing-barge, was in her prime, in numbers and quality.

Then before the First World War, which closed so many chapters and upset so many apple-carts, Maldon had a fleet of forty-five spritties, and one or two stacks for the horses in London were going away every week. The crew had to build their own stacks, which took about forty loads of hay or straw, some fifty or sixty tons in all.    Straw was easier than hay, the trusses being longer.    In either case the building was hard work, but by dint of laying the outer ends of the trusses on the rails to give the whole thing a cant inward (after filling the holds, of course), and the generous use of ' breechings,' as they called lashings bowsed down with tackles, so secure a job was made on the wide, flat barges then favoured that seldom was a stack lost overboard.

Arriving in London, the stacks had to be broken by scrapping out the centre trusses to form a cavity in which the gear would lower away to pass below bridges, and then, of course, the whole thing had to be unloaded.    Yes, the more I think of the *Eva Annie* going through all that, loading, sailing away to London with her straw half-way up her mainmast, and the mate on top to con the course, unloading and getting back light twenty times in twenty weeks, the more I call it good going.

Chalk, ' London mixture ' (salubrious name for the farmer's stand-by), stone, beer, cargoes of all kinds littered the quays at Maldon Hythe and Heybridge Basin, and the bargemen bounced the timber down the gang-plank.    There's another lost art for you !    Every plank has its own ' period ' of bounce, and every waterman knew it.    Planks on head, away he came at the double and—bounce, bounce, bounce—the springy plank whipped him ashore.

That reminds me of the old-time way of picking a bag out of a hold.    The standing end of the whip parted into three tails, each held by one man on the deck.    Once the bag was hooked on the other end, all jumped into the hold together, their combined weight bringing the bag up on deck.    If you jumped a moment too soon you swung in the air, looking a bit silly ; if you were a moment late you landed smack on the hold ' sealing,' feeling a bit sore.

Some of the craft (including the *Record Reign*) went questing ' big logs ' up the Suffolk Alde and elsewhere, and swung five-ton trees aboard with jury derricks, heaven knows how.    It must have been hard on crews and ships.

Half a dozen hufflers were kept busy then, helping the ships up and giving them a start away, for a northerly breeze brought the colliers rolling home and a southerly slant freed the barges to come running through Rays'n and Spitway.

Barges of that period, in addition to those already mentioned, were the *Rose, Diligent, James Cann, Ann Elizabeth, William and Elizabeth, Surprise, Fanny, Two Friends, Unity,* and *Pride of Essex.*

*Wave* and *Spray* were the local 'passage-boats.' *Spray,* which was used as a tender to the *Great Eastern* during the laying of the Atlantic Cable, was said to have been built out of the pieces left after her sister was finished, just as the barge *Emma* was said to have been built from the bits and pieces from the *Record Reign.* Some details of the *Wave* will be found in Chapter XVI.

Hufflers and passage-boats are gone now ; if the occasional 'sprittie' wants a helping hand the harbour bailiff's motor-boat gives her a pluck. Her *chug-chug* breaks a silence otherwise altogether devoted to memories, for the modern motor-coaster has never found her way to Maldon. Even the ubiquitous Dutch motor-coaster never pokes her nose into these historic waters. The railway's blow proved a knock-out.

In dwelling on the decline and fall of Maldon's river, however, I would not give the impression that enterprise is deficient. In Howard's old yard Dan Webb to-day builds those little Blackwater sloops which are so justly popular ; in Sadler's old loft Taylor's cut yacht sails which are prized beyond the East Coast. And did I not in the war years see at Sadd's great works amazing craft in the making, pontoons, M.F.V.'s, M.T.B.'s, even lifeboats to be dropped from out of the skies by aircraft. Sadd's, indeed, are a firm and a family giving a happy example of how to keep pace with the present without losing pride in the past. Among their twentieth-century marvels lay their two yachts, one of which, the old yawl *Ripple,* was building on the quay when John Howard set up in business in 1876. I am afraid my eye strayed often and again from the huge and hideous M.T.B. I was inspecting to her old sleeping form, and to where near by the neglected hulls of the *Rose* and the *Oak* mouldered in the mud.

# XV

## ALL QUIET AT HEYBRIDGE BASIN

*The Calm of the Canal—Where the Eighteenth-century's Last Word
has become a Quiet Backwater—The Squall that wasn't*

AWAY down Colliers' Reach, the first reach below Maldon, lies
Heybridge Basin, its placid waters now a quiet resting-place for
yachts, some of which lie snugly afloat, sheltered from the buffets
of the tidal estuary, a few equally snugly on the bottom, their
masts and mooring-ropes alone emerging. So peaceful has been
their decease that they look more like pensioners taking a well-
earned rest than shipwrecks.

A century and a half ago this picture of sylvan tranquillity must
have been a scene of immense activity, the epitome of the com-
mercial spirit of the age, for the Chelmer and Blackwater Navi-
gation Company's canal was a-building. Maldon town, with
that short-sightedness which so often characterizes waterside
politics, was up in arms against the plan for " widening, deepen-
ing, cleansing, straightening and improving the river Chelmer "
to Heybridge Mill and cutting the new channel to the Basin, and
succeeded in preventing it from entering within the Borough
boundaries. In 1797, however, the canal was completed at a cost
of £50,000, fourteen miles from Springfield Wharf to Heybridge
Basin, with eleven locks on the way. The prospectus of 1762
estimated that " under all the disadvantages of the late war " at
least six thousand tons of coal and four thousand tons of other
goods were imported into Maldon for the use of Chelmsford—
say, four two-hundred-tonners a week for that trade alone. Land
carriage by wagon was given as eight shillings a ton ; by the canal
two shillings and two and sixpence toll, " a saving of three shillings on every ton in addition to a considerable saving of time."

Things have turned out very differently from the dreams of
the canal-builders of those days, and now only a very occasional

barge-load of timber disturbs its reedy surface.  Around its mouth, however, cluster the eel-boats which come from Holland and fill the canal with their fish-boxes, staying till all the eels are sold, and the barges to add their freights of timber to the great stacks by the tow-path, the newer vessels sailing in, proud in their bold paint and lofty gear, the old craft reduced to lighters, dumb creatures which yet recall in their lines the days when they did better than a trip down to Osea behind a motor-boat.  The smaller craft still have their tillers ; they retired before the days of wheel steering.  Some of the bigger ones with the old-fashioned chain-and-barrel steering raise great black husky sides topped by deep-sea bulwarks, and the word ' coaster ' is written all over them.

Within the locks all is as tranquil as a lady's boudoir, the un-ruffled water the mirror.  Outside the winds bluster and the tides mutter ; it is as wide and free as the other is deep and confined. Heybridge Basin is a difficult place to tear oneself away from.

Just down the wall is a club worthy of the place.  The Black-water Sailing Club is one of the few clubs which has still refrained from converting itself into a yacht club ; you cannot get a pink gin there for love nor money, but you can browse among ship photos, half-models, and a lovely model of the *Amaryllis*, in which Mulhauser, himself a member, sailed round the world.  There is a poster of the local regatta of 1859, and you can gossip with Will Chaney and old Fred Austin, who after a spell deep-sea came back home to be pilot here for forty years.

All manner of ships he has brought up the river ; " filling and backing " in a barque or a brigantine seems to him as familiar and natural a method of getting to windward as the more conven-tional tacks of the fore-and-after.  Looking out over the wall, he recalled bringing up the *Fanny* brigantine, the old *Banshee* collier, that always mentioned favourite the ketch *Eliza Annie*, Smith's ' boomies ' from Burnham, the *Dauntless* and *Emily Lloyd*, the little deep-sea Brightlingsea powder-ketch *Energy*.  These and many more he spoke of, but I particularly liked his anecdote of the notorious *Evolution*, Bentall's nearly epoch-making freak, which could not carry her sail.  (See Chapter XVI.)

We were bound up in a brigantine [he recalled] with nice, fine weather, when up off the island we saw a vessel under way hove down on her beam ends.  We looked again and thought there must be a hurricane coming.  We started getting sail off the brigantine in double quick time, and then she came by, still rail under, and still next to no wind !

I picture the bewildered mariners scratching their heads and putting the clothes on the brigantine again.

Over the wall behind the sailing-club is the place where was built perhaps the most epoch-making and revolutionary British yacht of all times, the famous *Jullanar*, to whose story let us now turn.

# XVI
## SOME NOTABLE FLIERS

*Three Famous Maldoners : " Jullanar," " Evolution," " Record Reign "*
*" Essex Lass "—" Wave "—" Jessie Annandale "*

THE story of the Blackwater's *Jullanar* is as fascinating, though in a different way, as that of the Colne's *Pearl*.

One of Maldon's industries is Bentall's, the agricultural engineers. Seventy-one years ago Mr E. H. Bentall, who from boyhood had had a proper Maldonian's love for boats, was toying with the idea of improving the shape of racers, and whittling half-models. He got one that pleased him, sent the lines (drawn by a member of the firm, Mr F. King) to Harvey, of Wivenhoe, for his comments, several of which were embodied, and in 1875 in the field behind the club-house there was laid the keel of the most noteworthy yacht ever built in Essex, the pioneer of all modern racing-yacht design, the 126-ton yawl *Jullanar*.

*Jullanar*, named after the " Princess of the Sea " in *The Arabian Nights*, was, like all racers of her time, long, deep, and lean. Her length was 110 feet 6 inches ; her beam 16 feet 10 inches. Her draft aft was 13 feet 6 inches, and forward 18 inches. Her deadwoods were cut away in a fashion never before conceived, and her keel swept in a fair curve from her water-line forward to the heel of her rudder aft, cutting out the conventional fore-foot. Thus she was free from dragging under-water wetted surface, and handy to manœuvre. Add to this that every line about her was fair and sweet, and it is no wonder that she was an eye-opener. It was fifteen years before even the great G. L. Watson caught up her ideas in the famous *Thistle*, and he was generous enough to admit that he would never have dared essay so bold a design but for the *Jullanar's* example.

Mr Bentall was a big builder of ploughs, and as the yacht's shape bore some resemblance to a ploughshare she was promptly christened *The Plough*, but it is fanciful to assume that the designer simply applied to the water the lines which so sweetly cleave the earth.

By September the yacht's " peculiar construction " was causing comment in *The Field*, and in December the hull was taken round to Wivenhoe, where Harvey decked her, rigged her, and fitted her out as a cruising yawl.

In January 1876 her owner left in her for a cruise to the Mediterranean, where she proved an excellent sea-boat. Reports of her abilities began to reach England, and in April *The Field* prophesied she would prove " a torment to everything afloat."

Curiously enough, however, Mr Bentall never raced her, but sold her within a little more than a year of her launch to Mr A. D. Macleay. She was fitted out for racing by Harvey in 1877 and won more prizes than can be mentioned. She was broken up on the Colne in the early years of this century.

Heybridge still remembers with bitter scorn how the Wivenhoe men accidentally ' launched ' the great yawl down the Colne slip at low water, letting her fall over in the mud, and hints that it was done on purpose out of neighbourly jealousy. The incident probably shows that the proper legging and propping of so rockered a vessel presented an alarming problem in those days of long, straight keels.

Why did Bentall sell the *Jullanar* ? Probably because his inventive mind was already busy on another experiment, the *Evolution*, which turned out in 1880 as complete a failure as the other was a triumph. She was designed to carry the *Jullanar's* cut-away profile to a new extreme. A ten-tonner, she was 51 feet over all (long enough for a twenty-tonner) ; 10 feet draught, and only 6 feet 6 inches beam. The conventional keel disappeared altogether, and when the lead slab which replaced it was found after a trial sail to be unable to hold her upright it was replaced by a bulb—and there was the first of the bulb-fin-keel racers, which were all the rage at the close of the century. The way she sailed has already been described. She just had not the buoyancy to carry her sail, and she lay down in the water like so many cheap toy boats. Had her design been vetted by Harvey, as was *Jullanar's*, the result might have been very different.

Yet if she was a failure, *Evolution* was a glorious failure. Like her sister, she was just fifteen years ahead of her time, and of her the generous G. L. Watson wrote " to my mind the genius, daring, and originality of Mr Bentall were even more fully displayed in the design of the unsuccessful *Evolution* than in the successful *Jullanar*." At Christmas 1893 Watson sent Bentall a half-model of his earliest racer inscribed, " From the Pupil to the Master." No tribute could have been higher, and no man more richly deserved it for his " splendid audacity and no timid reverence for precedent."

Meanwhile, as Bentall dazzled the yachting world, John Howard up at Maldon was, be it confessed, getting into debt, like many another great artist before and after him. To satisfy a syndicate of his creditors he laid down in 1890 a 275-ton ketch which was to become famous as the *Record Reign*. With her two square topsails drawing her through the water, the " Owd Rec'd," as Maldon affectionately recalls her, must in her prime have been the handsomest barge ever built. (For all her yacht-like rig she was a true flat-bottom barge, though the pier-head artist responsible for the picture reproduced opposite p. 125 has, in a laudable if snobbish attempt to flatter her, omitted her leeboards.) She must also have been one of the handiest and smartest things of her size afloat, for she would turn away from Maldon Quay when the channel was barely twice her length across, and on one occasion she left for the North on a Monday morning with a cargo of timber and was back with coal on the Saturday's tide. She was built the maximum size to enter Heybridge lock (length 112·2 feet, beam 24·15 feet), but Howard, the artist, could not bear to mar the lovely sweep of her clipper bow and figurehead, and drew her out so much that she would go through only on a big tide when the water-level was high enough to permit her to overhang the lock gates. She later passed into the hands of Sadd's, for whom she did a good deal of work in the ' big log ' trade, losing her square tops'ls, which for all their power and elegance needed a crew of seven, and becoming an ordinary ' boomie.' In her declining days she suffered the final degradation of becoming a motor-ketch, with a cut-down rig and two forty-horse-power Bolinder engines.

Her life was full of adventures. Twice she blew ashore in Holland; once (in her motoring days) through the curious mishap of having her lead-line wash overboard and foul a screw. In the First World War she was a " Q " ship; later she was in the liquor-running trade off the Norwegian coast, and finally she was lost in the Channel.

An echo of her elegance is to be seen in the well-known East Coast barge-yacht *Thoma*, which Howard designed and built with the same model in his mind.

Stevenson said that the only worth-while uses for money were to own a schooner and a private string quartet, and thanks largely to his influence the schooner has always been to the layman the romantic fore-and-aft rig. Personally I have always thought the ketch a more practical and therefore more beautiful alternative (and the cutter, in her own field, is the queen of them all), but in any case the schooner was never the logical East Coast rig with so much hard turning to windward in narrow waters to be faced, but belongs more to the American seaboards, where there is more prospect of ' soldier's winds.'

Yet schooners there were among the Essex fleet, and the most famous among them were the ' fruiters,' which sailed mostly from London and the South and West Country ports, and, owing to the perishable nature of their cargo, were sharp and fine-lined. That these craft could sail is shown by the fact that the *Matchless*, an Aberdeen schooner, went from Leith to Lerwick—285 miles—in twenty-four hours and was said to have logged $13\frac{1}{2}$ knots.

According to an article by E. Findley Smith in the *Yachting Monthly* of January 1918, when the Harveys took over the Sainty yard at Wivenhoe they started building first-class ' fruiters,' which were named after fox-hunts and voyaged to the Canaries or West Indies with coal or in ballast and brought back fruit to Wivenhoe for local markets. They were brigs as well as schooners, and some were built for the Newfoundland carrying trade. They were so sharp in section near the bilges that they had to be heavily ballasted, and one actually capsized on her way to Ballast Quay.

Several of the vessels hailed from Colchester and were locally manned. Among them was the *Essex Lass,* of which a century-

Mersea Oyster Smacks. (*Above*) Coming in from the day's work, the *George and Alice* leading. (*Left*) The *Charlotte* racing.

126

Where a Man still sets up a Sail to take him about his Business. (*Above*) Bob Howe, of Brightlingsea, off to Pyefleet packing-sheds to collect some oysters. (*Right*) William Wyatt, of West Mersea, sets up the gaff mainsail, preferred to a lug by Mersea men even for their little " winkle brigs."

on Yesterday and To-day. (*Above*) A cutter unloading at the bridge. (*Below*) Smacks and barges at the Hythe.

Graceful as Swans, whether sailing or at rest : timber-laden barges at Heybridge

oners.   (*Above*) The Colchester ' fruiter ' *Essex Lass*.   (*Below*) The Maldon coaster and passage-boat  *Wave*.

(*Above*) The *Jessie Annandale*, the brigantine which was the pride of Wivenhoe. (*Right*) The *Firecrest*, Alain Gerbault's famous world voyager, at Rowhedge, where she was built.

The *Jullanar* under canvas and on Wivenhoe Shipyard Slipway, showing her then revolutionary cut-away under-water profile

The *Record Reign*.  (*Above*) A flattering impression by a 'pier-head artist,' who has om the leeboards she carried even with this splendid rig.  (*Below*) The camera's cold recor her final days as an auxiliary ketch.  The beauty of her lines is still defiantly appa

As the Yachtsman never sees it : wintry weather in Brightlingsea Creek

'Calm as a Clock.' (*Above*)
Riding lights reflected in
Brightlingsea Creek.
(*Right*) The coming and
going of boats to the cause-
way end.

rdians of the Peace.    (*Above*) The *Prince of Wales* heads the Colchester police fleet.
(*Below*) The revenue cutter *Badger*, stationed at Bradwell in 1799.

Cargoes. (*Above*) Unloading timber at Heybridge Basin. (*Below*) An old-time ' stac
leaves Mersea Strood as the Colchester carrier crosses. The barge is the *Keeble*, the last
chester craft to retain tiller-steering. Note the old-fashioned mizzen mounted o
rudder-head, and the comparison with the modern ' stackie ' (*p.* 179).

Day of the Duck-shooting Season at West Mersea.   (*Above*) The fleet of punts off for opening cannonade.   (*Below*) A party home with their bag.   " Sooty " Mussett is the figure in oil-skins above and wearing a *Migrant* yacht jersey below.

Wildfowlers. (*Above*) Walter Linnett, of Bradwell, leaves his cottage built on the sea~
side of the wall beside the Saxon chapel. (*Below*) "Gunner" Cook, of West Me~

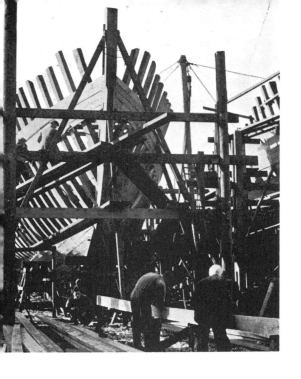

The Makers. (*Left*) Building ' wooden walls' in Wivenhoe Shipyard. The vessels are mine-sweepers, and the date 1940, but the scene has changed little in centuries. (*Below*) A barge's mainsail in Sadler's loft, Brightlingsea. " The wind costs nothing," but . . .

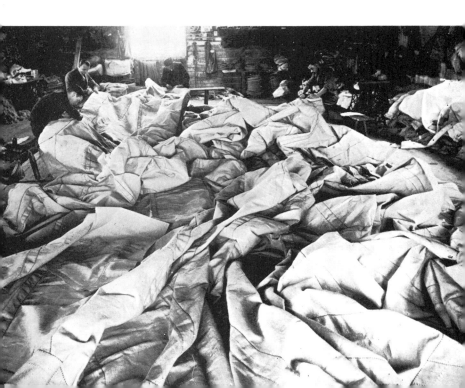

Days in a Bargeman's Life. (*Above*) The *Audrey* in tow of the Clacton lifeboat i
Whitaker. (*Below*) Modern 'stackies' leave Colchester for the Kent paper-mills
stacks of neatly baled straw. (Compare this with the old-time 'stackie,' *p. 141*

old picture, showing her entering Malta harbour, is still in existence in the possession of Captain Jones, of Rowhedge, grandson of the John Jones who was her master at the time. The master of another of these vessels was a native of Wivenhoe, Captain W. Ham, father of Captain Ham, the ex-harbour-master of Colchester. The Board of Trade certificates of these two masters, certifying them to have been " Apprentice, Mate, and Master in the foreign and coasting trade," hang together in the Nottage Institute, Wivenhoe. The ships were painted to resemble men-of-war of the period to deceive the pirates in case they were set over and becalmed on the Riff coast. In her later days the *Essex Lass* became a brig and went into the coasting trade.

Another Essex schooner of which a painting remains in existence was the Maldon *Wave*, a beauty still remembered by the ancient mariners of the upper Blackwater. Though she was smaller and more of a coaster than a deep-water clipper, such a powerful rig, with the stuns'ls shown in the smaller picture, can surely only have been designed with an eye to the carriage of perishable cargoes. The fact that the painting reproduced is by J. Petersen and the port in the background has a Scandinavian aspect suggests that at this time the *Wave* was perhaps working a timber freight from Baltic waters. Sadd's old cargo book referred to in the previous chapter shows that on October 5, 1848, the same year that this striking portrait was painted, the *Wave* made her first coal freight to her home port with 171 tons under Captain R. Mallaburn, the skipper whose name appears in the picture. It looks rather as if at first the coal trade was a winter stopgap, for after another freight in November or December of the same year the schooner does not appear again till December 1850, bringing 110 tons. Four years later, however, Captain Mallaburn made two such freights in June, but perhaps humping black diamonds at six shillings a ton was not to that master's liking, for next month Captain Finch took over. He was still in charge in 1856, when she made another summer freight, but the same month (August) she returned under Captain J. Paul, who remained in command seven years later, for in 1863 Sadd's clerk enters a note in his ledger, " The *Wave* came up to G.E.R. wharf." This was evidently an event, and no doubt a saving and convenience, for previous freights had shown charges for " use of barge " varying from 10s. 6d. to £1 15s.

Presumably the river had been improved, for in 1769 foreign ships of one hundred tons burden did not come up to the town " by the distance of nearly two miles, and there deliver their cargoes into lighters and are brought up and landed on the Merchant's own Key," the " Lawfull Key," or " Town Key," being at that time " not only ill-situated but in bad repair, and is made use of mostly for landing chalk and timber."

The experiment, however, was not often repeated, for a freight done in 1866 is the last in coal recorded, though in 1876 (now under Captain W. Carter with J. Rogers signing the receipt stamp) she did a little £26 freight of " 86 oaks, 84 elms, 57 loads 19 feet," presumably a cargo of " big logs " fetched from somewhere down the coast.

What happened to the beautiful *Wave* then ?  No doubt her stuns'ls were laid ashore and her clipper-gear cut down when she went coasting, yet it must have been a grand sight to see her slim and quite uneconomical hull going like a knife through butter past the fleet of tubby collier brigs bobbing on their leisurely way up the East Coast from the grimy coal ports of the North.  I believe, however, that unlike the *Essex Lass* she retained her original rig, for she is recalled at Maldon to-day as a schooner.

The *Wave's* birthplace was the quay wall by the old Maldon workhouse, then Sadd's property.  In 1899 *Lloyd's List* recorded her as owned by Smith, of King's Lynn.  Where she died and when I do not know, but she has the distinction of being recorded by an inn sign at Heybridge, for Skipper Paul, when he retired from the water, bought property on the main Colchester to Maldon Road which he made into a public house and named after his old ship. His nephew, Mr H. Whybrow, himself a shipwright, who now keeps the Wave, has in his tap-room two tables which came out of the old schooner's mess.

Wivenhoe's proudest memory is of the *Jessie Annandale*, a brigantine which was, I have been told, bought down Channel, leaky.  Her shrewd Essex purchaser had a good bargain, for it proved there was nothing the matter with her, bar a knot in her sternpost, and when this was made good she was tight as a bottle. She was such a handy ship that during the time she worked to Wivenhoe (1866–85) she was accustomed to sail up to the quay even in northerly winds, " filling and backing " where she could not tack, while less nimble craft lay waiting a slant off Brightling-sea or towed laboriously up behind their boats and their kedges.

The *Jessie Annandale's* first Wivenhoe cargo book, which I count among my precious possessions, opens with the resounding entry dated May 21, 1866, " First voyage of the *Jessie Annandale*. Steam from Sea £1." That was a Sunderland coal freight to Colne ; on June 18 she was up at Seaham again, and on July 5 discharging at Rochester ; by May 1867 she had successfully made ten more freights, showing profits of £2 to £20, from the North to Colne, Medway, and Orwell. Then came a voyage to Ireland. Leaving Ipswich on May the 4th, she was at Cork on the 22nd, Queenstown on the 28th, Llanelly on June the 17th, Faversham on July the 6th, and back from her adventures in the black-diamond trade the following month.

Her crew and their average month's pay consisted of master (£6 10s.), mate (£3 15s.), two seamen at £3 5s., an ordinary seaman (£2 5s.), and a lad at a shilling a day. Sometimes only one seaman was shipped, together with an apprentice receiving £1, but paid a few shillings in addition for working cargo.

Some of the entries throw light on the customs and practices of the times, as, " Paid to watchman for eleven nights, 18s." (at Cork), " Lard for mast, 2s." ; " Three men for heaving Ballast in three tides at 4s. tide, £1 4s." (the arithmetic is the skipper's) ; " Trimming ship, £1 15s." ; " Spout and plank, 3s. 6d." (these appear to have been the gear for unloading coal by hand) ; " pilot's passage money, 1s. 6d." ; " Mainsail, £22 2s. 6d." ; and " mainsail courting £1 " (was this sail dressing, or a canvas cover ?). Others delight for the richness of their phonetic spelling. " Balast and duck dues," " Pilate," and " Lawences " (allowances) follow each other to culminate in the startling charge for " Ensuring Fright " ! Yet the uneducated mariner, to whom all this writing and figuring must have been such labour, was making successful voyages to Bruges, Caen, Fécamp, Honfleur, Exmouth, Dieppe, and Dordt (Dordrecht) between the regular routine of the coal freights up and down the East Coast.

# XVII

# THE FREE TRADERS AND THE OYSTER
# PIRATES

*Colchester and Maldon Smugglers and Revenue Men—The "Repulses"
and their Dashing Contractor—The Coast Watcher that joined in the
Wars—An Enemy that was a Friend—Sailing Police Force—War on the
Oyster Poachers*

GENTLEMEN,

This is to acquaint you that we attended Mr Evens and showed him
your letter and he said you was not a Commissioner and he would go
for all of us and we offered to stop him from heven up his anker and
struck me and tore my shirt and beat me down upon the plank, and
took up a billet and swore he would knock us all down and dash out
our brains and his men were resolute likewise that our hands were
afraid to goe up with him for fear of their lives from yours to command
ROB. LONE, JOS. SCOTT, THO. MARCH, JER. HUBBERD [1]

The story of the smugglers on the Essex coast has received little
attention. It has been dismissed in the *Victoria History* of Essex as
small beer on the ground that the big ships used in the great days
of the trade on the South Coast could not be employed in Colne
and Blackwater, since the Wallet, the only approach to these
waters, was too easily guarded by a single powerful cutter. Indeed, it is probably true that for this reason the free trade in this
district never produced such bands of professional cut-throats as
the notorious Hawkhurst Gang who tortured and murdered the
Sussex Revenue men, yet the trade in Essex cannot be dismissed
as just an occasional trivial run by a smack's boat. Here, just as
elsewhere, it has gone on in varying degrees and forms since the
fourteenth century (though then the illicit traffic was outward, in
defiance of export duties), but the eighteenth saw its romantic heyday. Then it must indeed have been at least a major sideline in
the occupation of the amphibious population of the Essex marshes.

[1] *Maldon Customs Letter Book, November 17, 1741.*

As early as 1728 there is record of the offer of a reward for the capture of a gang of thirty to forty men who had badly beaten the riding officers while landing a cargo at Clacton. In 1733 some tea was seized in a farmyard near Colchester by the country folk armed with pitchforks. Disarming the Customs officer, they rescued their tea. About 1740 the Supervisor at Colchester was carried off, but was released on the promise that he would not reveal the smugglers' names. Twice at least the Colchester Customs House has actually been entered. In 1748 an armed gang of thirty men broke in and carried off fifteen thousand pounds of tea which had been seized from them shortly before. Again at 2 A.M. on the morning of April 16, 1847, the door was forced with a blacksmith's hammer and bar, and sixty oil-bags removed, containing 1514 pounds of tea seized just previously near Woodbridge Haven. The gang were traced to Hadleigh, which they reached at 6 A.M., but there, perhaps prudently, they were lost. In August 1784

in the night-time some persons did feloniously break into the room [at Maldon] where Mr Dines deposited the goods after seizure and stole from them eleven baggs of tea. . . .
P.S. the baggs now in weigh 28 lbs each.

Colchester has the interesting distinction of having been the station of the largest of all the forty-four revenue cutters stationed around the coast. This claim can be made out for the last of at least five cutters, all named *Repulse*, which between 1774 and 1800 were commanded by Daniel Harvey, of Wivenhoe. Fortunately something is known of this ship, for in 1923 Mr B. R. Leftwich, the Librarian of the Custom House, had the enterprise to visit the East Coast Custom Houses and make extracts from their letter books. To these I owe much of the information in this chapter.

The first *Repulse* was built in 1774, and had a crew of eleven men.and a boy ; the second, of 132 tons with a crew of twenty-four, followed in 1776 ; and the third, a 180-tonner with a crew of forty-two, in 1778. This vessel was wrecked on the French coast and the crew captured and fined by the Admiralty court at Calais. The Board was unsympathetic. To a petition by her mates, Martin Hopkins and John Harlow, the Board replied :

As it appears to us that the said cutter was run on shore by the willfull misconduct or negligence of the crew, unconstrained by stress of weather or the superior force of the enemy, not only out of the limits of this Duty, but on a Foreign Coast, you are to acquaint them that we reject their petition, but we agree to Martin Hopkins having a new deputation to enable him to perform his duties as mate of the new *Repulse* cutter, and herewith you will receive the same.

This new *Repulse* must have been worth seeing. She was of 210 tons, with a crew of fifty men and a boy, armed with sixteen carriage and twelve swivel guns. Keble Chatterton gives as the spar dimensions of a 150-ton cutter in 1838 : " Mast, 75 feet by 20 inches ; boom, 61 feet by $13\frac{1}{4}$ inches ; bowsprit, 55 feet by $16\frac{3}{4}$ inches ; gaff, 45 feet by $8\frac{3}{4}$ inches ; topmast, 52 feet by $9\frac{3}{4}$ inches ; spreadyard (forsquare-sail), 58 feet by $9\frac{1}{4}$ inches."

Now imagine the *Repulse* one third as big again as the vessel which carried those tremendous spars ! You may be sure she was not under-canvassed, for Harvey never intended anyone to get to windward of him. When the previous vessel was built he had given as the reason for her the fact that " he has lately found the *Repulse* cutter [*i.e.*, number two] inferior to many vessels now employed by the Smuglers." The first thing Harvey did in this giant clipper was to secure Letters of Marque, the Board stating that they had no objection to his doing so

at his own expence during the present hostilities, but we shall not consent to bear any part of the expence for any damages that may be sustained in engagements where no seizure shall be made for breach of Revenue law, and you are to enjoin him in the strictest manner not to quit his station under pretence of looking for captures.

That last warning is no doubt a reminder of the fate of the previous *Repulse*, blown ashore on the French coast when she was supposed to be keeping a sharp look-out around the Essex estuaries ; indeed, Harvey must have been a handful to the Board. In 1780 we find them inquiring into desertions from his crew, asking the collector, " whether you ever muster the Crew of this Cruizer and when, in order to see if the Commander keeps up the full Complement allowed him, which is more in number than for any of the other Cruizers in this Service, and at any other Port, from none of which the Commissioners have received any Complaints."

Whether his men deserted, however, because they did not fancy going to the wars for a livelihood, or because their Captain had artfully been employing a small crew to work his ship and drawing pay for a big one, Captain Harvey, after getting the Board to agree to spend twenty-seven pounds on alterations to his gun ports and carriages, got to sea, and was soon in action. He engaged a ship flying Dutch colours and, firing into her, killed one man and wounded another. Alas for him, the ship was a prize to H.M.S. *La Prudente*, and Harvey was up for an inquiry. Luckily for him and James Woodward, his mate, the mate of the *Argus* cutter of Harwich and the master and mate of the Sunderland brig *Blessing* corroborated his story that " the vessel in question wore all the appearance of an enemy, having Dutch colours only hoisted, and he conceived by her bearing down on him that it was an intention to board him." " But," added the Board, " you are to recommend him to use greater circumspection that the lives of his fellow-creatures may not wantonly be hazarded in future."

The circumspection was not forthcoming. Having committed the indiscretion of killing and wounding British seamen, Captain Harvey proceeded to the enormity of " providing sundry articles exceeding forty shillings for the use of the said cutter amounting to fifty-seven pounds ten shillings and fivepence halfpenny." What is more, he had been " guilty of a like offence " two years before and " admonished to pay strict attention to his printed articles," so that, added the Board, " in the present instance we consider him highly reprehensible and confirm our order for disallowing the articles in question by way of mulct upon him for his disobedience thereof, as we cannot suffer our instructions to be considered a dead letter."

But the last laugh was with Captain Harvey. Three months later he carried away the *Repulse's* mast " by the board, and for the preservation of her hull it was necessary to cutt away the whole of her rigging." So, writes the Board, "we have ordered a new mast, sails, rigging, etc., to be forthwith provided and sent you from hence." And that, I can imagine the captain commenting to himself, will cost them more than forty shillings !

Finally the fourth *Repulse* was wrecked in 1789, but another was built and served in the expedition to Holland, for which the commander, officers, and crew were paid £217. That is all we know of her or of them. In her absence the " *Mary* lugger at your port " was employed as a temporary cruiser—an unusual rig for Colne, and perhaps one of the smuggling boats of the very type which had outfooted the third *Repulse*, a poacher turned gamekeeper *pro tem*.

Several other vessels were employed during the century. Captain Roger Martin supplied by contract the *Essex* sloop (67 tons), and the *Walpole* sloop in 1729, the *Wivenhoe* smack in 1731, the *Cornelius* cutter (29 tons) in 1738, the *Princess Mary* (a 73-ton sloop with six guns and carriages, rebuilt in 1747 and increased by eight tons) in 1740, the *Good Intent* cutter (at " Bricklesea ") in 1741, and the *Mayflower* cutter in 1754. Then came our friend Harvey, who, before the *Repulses* were provided on the official establishment, supplied the *Earl of Rochford* cutter in 1774 and the *Swift* cutter in the same year.

This *Swift* cutter was laid up in February 1781 for shortage of crew, and her men put aboard the *Repulse*, of which her master, James Woodward, was mate at the time of the ill-fated engagement with the Dutch prize two years later. A month afterwards she was actually seized by smugglers, a sensation which caused the captain of the *Argus* to send an anxious request for an increase in crew lest the like befall him. She was retaken from the French and " carried into Portsmouth " a year later, when Captain Harvey had his claim " to be repaid his interest in the late *Swift* cutter " turned down on the ground that she was " the sole property of the Crown."

Under this arrangement the contractor kept the vessel in " good and sufficient repair," but the vessel remained the property of the Crown without charges for hire. The crew's pay was : master fifty pounds, mate thirty pounds, mariners fifteen pounds each, boy eight pounds, with a victualling allowance of ninepence a day each, a shilling a month each for fire and candle, and an " allowance for tallow not to exceed twenty shillings per ton in two calendar months." The cost of the 210-ton *Repulse* was from £1500 to £2200 a year, but in the three years 1781–83 her seizure values alone amounted to over £14,000.

Marryatt gives a striking picture of these cutters :

> You may know that she belongs to the Preventive Service by the number of gigs and galleys which she has hoisted up all around her. You observe that she is painted black, and all her boats are white. She is not such an elegant vessel as a yacht, and she is much more lumbered up. The guns are iron and painted black, and her bulwarks painted red ; it is not a very becoming colour, but then it lasts a long while, and the dockyard is not very generous on the score of paint. She has plenty of men, and fine men they are ; all dressed in red flannel shirts and blue trousers ; some of them have not taken off their canvas or tarpaulin petticoats, which are very useful to them as they are in the boats night and day and in all weathers.

Maldon and Burnham rivers were covered by the Colchester cutter, but had their own boats as well. The cutter *Badger* is recorded as being stationed at Bradwell in 1799, but in 1775 Thomas Shearman, the Maldon tide-surveyor, reported :

> In regard to his representation of not being able to annoy sufficiently the smugling . . . he labours under a great disadvantage by having only an open boat and situated at the distance of near eighteen miles from the mouth of the river. The Smuglers, knowing exactly what time the tides will admitt of his going down the River, and that he cannot at all times lie exposed in his open boat, which gives them fair opportunity of running or concealing their goods.

This would have been the yawl *Queen* for which Shearman was just afterwards granted two extra hands. Similarly the

> Waiter and Searcher at Burnham had acquainted us that he frequently goes on duty in the night-time, and his boat being an open boat and has nothing to keep off the inclemency of the weather, he humbly prayeth that your Honrs. will please to give an order for a tilt to be sent to him [a late use for the ancient word ' tilt,' familiar in the medieval description ' tilt-boat '].

A picture of the methods of smugglers and revenue men in this lawless corner is to be seen in the testimony of Christopher Francis, one of the boat-men of Burnham.

> He and Nicholas Billbo, the extra boatman, went out in the King's Boat to Wallis [Wallasea] Island, and there took a Farmer's small boat. Seeing a small Dover-built boat a-coming into Haven Gore Creek which they suspected to be a smugling boat who came to an anchor, they then proceeded to row up to her in order to have boarded her,

but before they could get up to her they hoisted up their sail and came
by the said Francis and Billbo, who were close alongside the said boat.
The Master, George Foxall, with three other men on board told the
said Francis and Billbo and swore if they offord to come on board they
would nock them down and held up the handspikes for that purpose,
and so they were not able to get on board. . . . Foxall is a drudgerman
and lives in the Parish of Pogglesham.

Paglesham seems to have been a great home of the trade. In
1783 (time of a " great increase " in smuggling) the Maldon
Collector stated that the practice " has been and now is to carry a
greater number of hands in their cutters than our officers dare
attack." He named as suspect " a cutter supposed to belong to
Wm. Dowsett at Paglesham, which carries ten men," a " huffler "
(the name usually reserved for a pilot or boatman rather than for
his boat), and a " cutter " of the same village ; a " smaller boat "
and " another cutter," home ports unnamed ; and " one or two
of the fishing-boats at Burnham which carry oysters to Dunkirk,"
particularly the *Sprightly*. " These above-mentioned boats frequently run goods in and about Paglesham, Burnham, and Creeks
adjacent." The reason for the smugglers' preference for Burnham over busy Colchester and Maldon is shown by the entry
made in 1777, when the master of a " foreign ship laden with deals
from Mandel in Norway came to us requesting to land his goods
at Burnham in this port. We have no president of any Fn. Goods
ever being landed at Burnham."

One of the chief reasons which made the revenue men loath to
attack smugglers was the fact that they and their families were
miserably treated should they be killed or injured. In 1742 a
seaman named Durrell was drowned out of a boat which he was
endeavouring to save while they were chasing a smuggling sloop
in the Colchester cutter ; his widow was allowed the customary
princely sum of seven pounds ten shillings for herself and thirty
shillings for each of her three children. The Board was clearly
aware of this, for when John Miles is " shot by the smuglers in
endeavouring to seize their goods " they write that " although the
allowance of fifty pounds is not strictly within the words of the
Act of Parliament," it may be paid as " that sum may likewise
prove an encouragement to officers in exerting themselves and
may intimidate the smuglers."

Tollesbury is mentioned on several occasions in these smuggling records. In 1772 the " Landing Waiter " seized a haul of silks, gloves, and ruffles in Woodrup Creek, and a reference in 1769 to the import (legally) of 500 lbs. of leaf from London reveals that there was at this time a tobacco manufactory in the village.

Mersea's connexion with the free trade is confined to one cautionary tale of William Rawlins, " boatman at Mersey Island, who is suspected to keep a correspondence with the smuglers." He was exchanged with the Burnham boatman to be " closely watched."

During the French wars the " smuglers " found a side-line in espionage, and Maldon Customs were ordered to " keep a watch on or near the Island of Mersea and the Rivers and waters of Colchester and Maldon, to hinder such persons as may attempt to embark on board the fishing-boats thereabouts, and to search fishing-boats."

The rule concerning the seizure of the " bottom " in which goods were imported led at this time to the extraordinary scheme of rebuilding the bottom of the Maldon smack *Success* into a " luggage boat."

Living memory can just stretch to recall a " Revenue cruizer," the *Mermaid* (Captain Jenkins)—a steamer built in 1853, but converted to sail in 1855—which Aaron Spitty, of Bradwell, mentions (see Chapter XII), but early in the nineteenth century the coast blockade took over the watch on the Essex coast with old gun-brigs, whose stations included Stansgate, Bradwell, Brightlingsea, and Foulness. Crews of some half a dozen coastguards occupied these insalubrious hulks, of which the old *Richmond* is still recalled lying at Stansgate up to 1870, and the *Watch Vessel 21* after her.

During the last century the free trade has, of course, been brought within bounds, but never checked. Clem Parker, of Bradwell, cheerfully instructed his barge skippers to bring him home something every time they came from " foreign," but if caught out they were to pay up on his account. One day a skipper hurried back to him in an embarrassingly public market and handed him some boxes of cigars. " But," he bellowed cheerfully, " the beggars caught me again this time, and you'll have to pay up."

One Bradwell barge sailed with a pot of tar innocently open on her fo'c'sle floor.   She brought home a load of stone from Bruges to Maldon in her hold—and a bottle or two of eau-de-Cologne well greased with tallow under the tar.   As for the *Violet Sybil*, she has a place or two so cunningly hidden in her lining that maybe the present innocent crew don't know they are there.

This was the trivial smuggling of the later nineteenth and twentieth centuries.   It was a come-down from the days when Clem Parker in his youth would come in to breakfast cursing because the free traders had had his horses out again that night.

As the trade changed and the preventive water-guard, which succeeded the coast blockade, developed into the modern coast-guards, the men took another step ashore into cottages.   They retained small sailing-craft till modern times, however ; indeed, the last pair in the district were sold out of Brightlingsea to be replaced by a motor-launch during the war.   Did I not then become the proud owner of the staunch little fifteen-foot centre-board boarding boat built for the service by James there, which has taken me many a mile about these waters collecting these tales? I have delighted in that little vessel all the more through allowing myself to indulge the fancy that she is perhaps the last of the sailing revenue ships, the lineal descendant of the piratical *Repulses*.

But I shall sail that boat no more, for as I write this chapter I have become the owner of another of the working craft of which it tells, the Colne police boat *Prince of Wales*, which I hope to restore to the original sailing condition in which, before the days of motors, she was the pride of a fleet to which let us now turn.

While the Customs men looked after the smugglers, the Colchester River Police attended to the oyster pirates.   Many yachtsmen will recall the husky little grey cutters which were always to be seen jilling about off Brightlingsea up to the Second World War, a blue-uniformed policeman at the tiller.   It looked a delightful job in summer weather, when the boats generally cruised with mainsail tack pulled well up the mast, strolling effortlessly and confidently through the water, but displaying a remarkable turn of speed when the policeman decided to go after somebody.   But in reality it was a hard life.   I say " was " because, though the suspension of the Force in 1942 was strictly a war measure, it seems unlikely it will ever be re-established, and if so never again under sail.

Night and day the patrol went on, and one boat might never come in till the next relieved her. Every two hours the men had to make contact with a point ashore on a ' beat ' as regular as that of their ' pavement-bashing ' colleagues in the town. Generally relief was effected by a flying leap from one boat to another. One of the Colne pictures I shall always carry in my mind is of two cutters swinging along side by side and a burly blue figure flying through the air from one to another, his leather sea-boots landing with a rare *clump* as he boarded. When the weather was too bad the boats were laid-to under mainsail only and left to look after themselves as the men rowed off.

Every barge that went up Pyefleet to the old wharf at the Strood, or up to the Alresford iron bridge, had to be trailed by the police boat, and despite the rough nature of the work, a Guards standard of discipline was maintained. Woe betide the man found ill-shaven, or whose journals and reports were handed in a few minutes late !

Forty years ago the River Police Force was a considerable institution. Though there may be other similar bodies, the only one I know (save the London River Police) is at Rochester. The Colne Force, which despite its Brightlingsea headquarters was always part of the Colchester Borough Police, then boasted nineteen men and a Superintendent (that dizzy rank Tom Poole characteristically secured for himself, though his successors had to be content as sergeants), and some splendid little craft, the *Victoria*, *Alexandra*, *Colne*, *Raven*, and *Prince of Wales*. All these, even the last, which at eight tons was the biggest, originally had powerful centre-boards, which made them very smart to windward, though they spoiled the cabin accommodation. They were built by Aldous, of Brightlingsea, and built to sail. Good beam, sweet lines, plenty of canvas, and low freeboard gave them a characteristically rakish look and an ability to chase anything they wanted to. Before the Second World War the *Prince of Wales* went into power, and, the others having been sold, a motor-launch of shocking ugliness was acquired. So obviously unsuitable was this *Stella*, which had Noah's own ark built on her, that the Fishery foreman refused to cross the river in her, and she too was soon sold.

Before 1890, when the River Police were established, the oysters were guarded as they are in the Blackwater to this day, by anchored watch smacks, and it used to be a dredgerman's trick to pay a friendly visit to the watch-boat, and on leaving slip loose the rowing-boat lying astern, which rendered the watchman helpless till the dredgerman cared to restore his boat as a friendly gesture with many exclamations of astonishment that he should have been so careless in securing it. To-day young oysters are to be found only on the " Binnaker," the shoal on the east shore, but in those days the whole estuary was rich with them. From East Mersea out to the Fishery Buoy runs a line, marked by small can buoys, inside which is Fishery ground. Outside, on ' Pont,' the fleets from Colne, Mersea, Tollesbury, and Maldon were wont to dredge ; inside worked the freemen for the Company.

From Elijah Ward, who joined the Force in 1912 and was Ser- geant after the retirement of Percy Small until Sidney Cranfield (grandson of the famous skipper of the *Valkyries*) took over just before the Second World War, I heard of the days when there would be a hundred smacks outside that line, and forty more within, particularly early in March, when the short ' brood sea- son ' opened. Then the fleet of freemen's smacks was so nume- rous that it could accumulate its five million oysters in Pyefleet in six weeks' work.

The two police boats constantly patrolling the line had their work cut out to prevent the " furriners " helping themselves. Though grapnels were placed beneath the buoys (and generally yielded a good harvest of dredges when lifted once a year !), the intruding smacks were constantly trying to get where the oysters lay thickest. When caught the freemen (who were not above helping themselves to their own property) were hauled before the Fishery Court held in connexion with the board meetings of the Company, but as they had a good chance of finding cousins and brothers and uncles on the jury I doubt if sentences were often savage. The River Police themselves were (for obvious reasons) seldom Colne men, but mostly came from Lowestoft. Non- freemen went to Colchester Police Court. One well-to-do de- fendant appeared there in rags and presented himself as a " poor ignorant man," but the magistrate eyed him meditatively and

commented, " I think you can afford to pay £5," which sum
the ragged one produced with alacrity from a copious wad of
notes.

On one occasion, Elijah Ward recalled, the Wivenhoe men got
into the way of paddling down in boats and punts and walking
along the mud " winkling "—only most of the " winkles " were
in oyster-shells.   They could always get away as soon as they saw
the police boat coming, and at last in desperation Sergeant
'Lijah decided to catch them another way.   He went to Wivenhoe in the train and, taking a boat, paddled down and joined in
disguised with a false beard, and needless to say wearing something different from uniform.  He got well among the pirates and
even engaged in conversation, asking if they weren't afraid of the
River Police.   " Them owd blue-bottles," came the answer ;
" they can't get within a moile of us."

" With that," recalled 'Lijah, " I straightened up and I off
whiskers.  ' Well, here's one that has,' I says, and you should
have seen 'em jump about.   ' Lor' bless us ! ' they was a-shout-
ing.   ' Come and hev a look what we got here.   That's our owd
Sergeant.' "   I can picture their consternation, for 'Lijah has, I
think, the broadest pair of shoulders I ever saw on any man,
a voice like a genial foghorn, a hand like a ham, a pair of blue
eyes to light up a dark night, and a grin you could post a
parcel in.

Any dead body, too, is the river policeman's concern if it is
found below high-water mark, but if it be drawn up above high-
water mark, even into the Wivenhoe Ferry Shelter, as once recently occurred, then it becomes the affair of the County Police.
Such are the niceties.

Though smuggling is, as I have said, the Customs men's affair,
the police often co-operated, and sometimes did well out of the
generous rewards which followed a successful capture.   Yachts
are the chief offenders, and not long before the war a visit to a
cruising yacht which had shown a strange aversion to putting into
Harwich proved very rewarding.   A Dutch motor-coaster often
proves worth a friendly visit too.

Gone are the days when the Colchester natives in their millions
kept two hundred men busy cultivating them and a score of
policemen occupied guarding them.   The rich breeding beds,

once so jealously watched, lie derelict under choking mud, and though they may yet be cleaned and restored to their old-time splendour, and again merit men to watch them, we shall not again see the jaunty little sloops and cutters cheating the tide to work up over the ebb, or running out to ' the line ' under a press of canvas to waylay some over-bold interloper.

# XVIII
## WIND AND TIDE

*The Composite Element that rules Men's Lives—Weather Superstition and Science—Sailing in Smacks and Barges—How Nature helps—Grandeur and Tedium of the Sailorman's Life*

THE finest thing ever written of the sea is Joseph Conrad's famous character study of the winds,[1] in which he declares that " the west wind reigns over the seas surrounding the coasts of these kingdoms," that the " cold, crafty easterly " seizes power and refuses to relinquish it when the blustering, benevolent monarch of the west falls into a melancholy and is caught off his guard, and that the north and south winds are " but small Princes in the dynasties that make peace and war upon the seas."

That deep-sea impression does not complete the picture in our little East Coast corner. To the square-rig skipper, outward- or homeward-bound through the chops of the Channel, the wind was fair or foul, west or east ; he could go scudding on his way, or he could thrash interminably back and forth, unable to force the passage :

> Caravans of ships to the number of three hundred or more at the very gates of the English Channel . . . while short rations became the order of the day and the pinch of hunger under the breastbone grew familiar to every sailor in that held-up fleet.

To the passage-maker among the intricate Essex sandbanks the slants are more subtle, and because both Mersea and Colne mouth lie open to the south, a gale from that direction is the most dreaded. It is the northerly too which increases the tides, and the southerly which keeps them down ; a gale hurrying the waters down round the far-away capes of Scotland sends a spring tide lapping into kitchens and parlours on Mersea Coast Road

---

[1] " Rulers of the East and West," in *The Mirror of the Sea.*

and Bradwell Street, putting out the fires at Wivenhoe gas-works, filling the cellars at the quayside inn at Maldon, and invad-ing the waterside factories at Colchester, while a southerly keeps it out of the gulls' nests on St Osyth marshes. (I have never been able to observe the so-called ' bird-tides ' which are said to occur in the nesting season, and by a charming dispensation of provi-dence to cause the springs to flow weakly during that vital season, but Mr Lewis Worsp, who, as well as being the owner of the Wivenhoe cannery and a consummate amateur seaman, is one of the wisest of the younger generation in the lore of Colne, tells me he has only once seen the gulls' nests afloat on Rat Island, which certainly floods at other times of the year.)

The bargeman, moreover, tends to think in terms more of northerly and southerly slants, the one the wind for London, the other fair to sail away down Thames, gybe through the Spitway or up Whitaker, and through the Rays'n and into the gates of the haven.

Nevertheless Conrad's contrast between the boisterous, bluster-ing but essentially friendly westerlies and the hard, relentless easterlies remains true to the coaster and small-boat sailor of the district.

In the main, the East Coast in these parts runs south-west to north-east, so that with south-westerlies prevailing the man bound down to the north counts on a fair wind. Yet nature compensates because the tides are earlier to the nor'ard by an hour in a tide's sail, so that when our sailorman at low water hardens his sheets to beat back from, say, Orfordness to Colne, he may reckon on seven hours' flood to help him with the job, whereas when he went running so gaily the other way he enjoyed only a five hours' shove from the ebb.

Rain, bad visibility, a dozen barges rolling wind-bound in Colne, and another getting the best shelter she can from the lee of Peter's Point in the Blackwater, a few more held up half-way on their passage in Shore Ends ; these are the pictures the phrase ' sou-wester ' conjures up. Yet they will soon be away. It won't last for ever, not with a sou-westerly.

But an easterly ? White caps on the short, steep waves, a hard brilliance in the air, a metallic sheen and glare on the whipped water, surf breaking over the promenade at Clacton and making

the Buxey look savage ; the " wind on the land " bringing discomfort and a lee shore everywhere and boiling up the narrows
at Osea into a little Portland Race on a spring ebb ; the home
berths empty of the barges which have managed to scrap out far
enough to bear away and go roaring up Londonward. Now
they lie baffled on their return passage in the hatefully exposed
anchorage at Southend, where the skippers wearily watch each
colourless western sunset and livid eastern sunrise for a change.
That's Conrad's " impassive tyrant " on the miniature scale of
our little sea-board, and rather than suffer his brilliant, unremit-
ing, sunlit cruelty, I would endure many a wet shirt at the
humorous pleasure of his nobler brother, who, having knocked
you down, generally eases off in time to let you pick yourself up
and dry out over the cabin stove.

But the easterly has some party manners, which he puts on in
the summer. The weather *par excellence* of this district (and I do
not know in how many other parts of the country it applies) is of
this order. You turn out to a glorious morning with a light
north-westerly wind which is never very seriously in earnest all
morning, but is just enough to help you about your business.
Round about midday, when you've earned your dinner, it clears
off to find its midday rest, and you wonder if you're in for a calm.
You're not. Soon there will be cat's-paws from the south-east,
and it will be the true wind. It will freshen into a good hefty
pusher, and it will so serve till all good mariners have made their
passage. Then it will bow, weaken, and pack up for the night—
and in the morning the programme will be repeated, perhaps
every day for weeks till the weather breaks up.

Now observe how beautifully once again nature serves.
While these conditions last the smacks in almost every one of the
little Colne and Blackwater ports have a fair wind out in the
morning and another home at night. In the old days, when the
barges went up against sea-walls and little wharves in the most
impossible places to load stacks and discharge chalk, and the
winklers slipped in and out of the Hoo outfall (that now-forgotten
hole in the Dengie flats), they were equally well served. I have
sometimes wondered at the patience of the men who went back
and forth daily from so far up-river as Wivenhoe and Rowhedge
in the days before motors, and while it is true that sometimes these

crews did spend calm days rowing laboriously on the ebb down to the Bench Head, and then rowing laboriously back on the flood, it was this combination of fair winds both ways that made the thing generally possible.

The old-timers claim that this phenomenon was far commoner in their time than now. It may have been, but I fancy it is simply less recognized and appreciated now that it is no longer so important. Having had to bicycle daily in the war years from Fingringhoe to Colchester and back, I gained plenty of acquaintance with these winds, against which I had to pedal morning and evening !

Yes—except when in the saddle of my iron horse—these two are my favourite winds. With either I can set my dinghy's lug-sail at Wivenhoe ferry and sail in an evening down to Rat Island and back for an illicit feed of gull's eggs, with only a tack or two near home. Or I can trundle back and forth like a clockwork train between the Mersea Victory and the Bradwell Green Man, and with that choice, who wants to go further and fare worse? Well, perhaps I do sometimes, and can I not enjoy then free sheets and all sail drawing from the Colne Bar to Harwich and back again ?

If I had to be so invidious as to choose between two such dear favourites I should say that while the south-easter is the gayer the northerly is the most useful of the winds. Out of Mersea or Colne it is a wind off the shore wherever you want to go, and when that is the case the man in the ten-foot dinghy feels he could sail to the South Seas.

To the bargeman wind and tides are inexplicably entangled into a sort of unnamed composite element which is second nature to him and a mystery to the mere amateur sailor. It often puzzles the yachtsmen to see barges lie in Colne in winter, while at other times with the same wind they will muster and away to London. The explanation is that with short daylight hours a morning tide makes the Spitway (where one wants to be around the low water) so awkward as not to be worth risking, and craft will often lie till the tides come round to give them a chance to get away at daylight with a reasonable prospect of being well up to Sea Reach by nightfall. Thus what is a useful wind with one tide is useless with another. As the bargemen put it, " If the wind is right the tide ain't right, and if the tide is right the wind ain't right. And if the wind and tide are both right there ain't no bloody wind."

Similarly, what is a beat up the Maplins on the flood may be turned into a fetch when the ebb pouring off the sand can be squeezed on to the lee bow, which is a fine place to have a tide—second best only to romping along with it on the lee quarter.

Much of the coaster's weather lore has become understood by the scientists and " met. men," and to-day the oldest hand gives up pacing his decks looking for " sun-dawgs "[1] in order to go below and turn on the B.B.C. forecast. But not all is known. The wise heads deny the effect of the tides on the weather, which is absurd. Time after time I have seen the weather clear or go to pieces, a squall come or a breeze die away, just on the high or low water, and nothing will shake my faith in that superstition. One day one of those who now scoff at it will find an explanation for it and claim to have discovered that of which he now denies the existence. (As to the Maldon fisherman who told me it was no use eel-fishing on the waning moon, I am less certain. It is true the herring fishermen reckon the November moon marks the season's climax, but this may be coincidence or may be cause.)

But anyway by that time these things will all be a dead language ; they will look at the clock that has stopped and tell us the time as it was—and I bet they get it wrong. Already the man with an auxiliary switches it on when the wind fails and comments smugly, " we should have been sunk without the puffer." He never notices how the wind returned half an hour later. During ten years of almost continual week-ending without an engine, I was never once so let down by my heavenly friends from the north, the south, the east, and the west as not to be home for Monday morning—though I admit sometimes I was sleepy. After all, the best auxiliary is the tide, which does the work of a million horse-power every day in the Thames Estuary, taking ships upon their way. Not that I entirely regret auxiliary engines. They make possible fresh opportunity for the enterprising cruiser, and, though they spell the end of sail to the fisherman, they take much of the heartbreaking tedium of calms out of the bargeman's life without robbing him of the glory of sailing those craft in a breeze, when they come into their own.

[1] A sun-dog is the Essex name for a rarely seen and much feared phenomenon resembling the end of a rainbow appearing near the sun.

But always there is a price to be paid.  One loses sympathy with the subtleties of the habits and manners of wind and tide. And of course when the engine becomes everything—well, one loses everything.  All the beauty and all the mystery, all the traditions of a score of centuries, vanish utterly, at once, and beyond recall.

In a comparatively few years it will be impossible to experience at first-hand the glory of a work-boat under sail, and the yachtsmen who really hear the message the sea has for them will look wistfully back at the old books and pictures and wonder what it all amounted to.

When I bought my eleven-ton Mersea smack *Charlotte* I did not know.  I had at that time a pretty little six-ton cutter built about the turn of the century at Cowes, as sweet a model as ever you saw, but too small to be manly.  I got sick of trailing my boom-end in the water in a quartering breeze and felt the *Charlotte* would be fun to amble majestically about in.  I pictured myself pushing half Burnham river in front of me and bringing up with my tarry topsides vexing the eyes of the diners in the Royal Corinthian Clubhouse.  I had not the faintest idea I was becoming master of something which, besides wide decks spacious enough to take a real stroll on, possessed the spirit of a terrier, the nimbleness of a polo pony, and the heart of a lion.

Sailing her was essentially different from handling any yacht I have known, chiefly because of her true flush deck, without cockpit of any kind, and the way it enabled her gear to be spread about. There was a deliberate certainty about all she did.  One could move about her and set up her gear unencumbered by anything obstructing action or vision.  What a different job it was walking along beside her long boom, reefing her heavy, docile, loose-footed, flax mainsail, to the struggle to roll up the fluttering folds of a laced yacht sail, one leg in the cockpit, the other seeking a hold on a rounded cabin-top.  She had hardly a shackle about her rigging, which was all rope strops and easy-fitting iron hooks. She had not a wire splice anywhere, the main shrouds being simply seized round dead-eyes.  She had hefty wooden cleats to supplement the friendly fife-rail.  It was all as ample and comfortable as an old tweed jacket.

Though I sailed her often by myself, I never led her jib sheets aft. In the narrowest creeks one could always down helm and leave the tiller in charge of the tiller-line, while one sauntered forward and tended the headsail. Hurry? Not a bit of it! Round she came, shooting ahead a smack's length, and you could stop up by the bitts as long as you liked and let her settle down on the new tack. A lee-shore anchorage amused the *Charlotte*. I well remember being caught at Queenborough and fearing I should drag ashore there, of all unattractive spots. The reefed mainsail and small jib were set, and she tacked her way up to the anchor as I got in the chain. She broke it out herself when she felt like it and went trundling away up the Medway, while I sat on the windlass and let her sort it out.

Then there were the days trawling. Running her off before the wind, we streamed the net, and then, as the helm went down, she swept round in a great arc as if to have a look at her trawl now spread out in the water to windward of her like a duchess's train. When we thought she had inspected it sufficiently we tipped the beam over, took the foresail off, and left her to tow where the soles lay thickest. She liked us to lay the tiller on deck as a gesture of handing over to her. I would this moment as soon be sitting on her weather quarter holding the trawl warp and feeling the iron heads bumping and grunting along over the Bench Head below me as anywhere in the whole wide world— though in actual fact I generally soon hopped down into the cabin to put the kettle on.

Of course, there was a price. We bumped our heads on the underside of that fine deck not once, but many times, and at night the rain drove cruelly across those wide flush decks. The lack of freeboard aft never worried me, though once when we left her for the day in Zierickzee to go into Middleburg for the fair the kindly Dutchmen were so alarmed that they put off to her, thinking her to be sinking. They were still laughing fit to bust when we got back.

The strong-willed determination of her nature made her need knowing. She never failed to perform the possible, but you couldn't ask the impossible of her. How often, till I learned to trust her, did she go ambling off for the nearest mud-spit and pile herself firmly ashore on it when the least response to my frenzied appeals to help me out of the muddle I had created would have done the trick!   To tell the truth, she was an old devil for bearing away, though she would stay round with astonishing willingness. And though the *Charlotte* took prizes in both smack and yacht races in her day, she was not as fast to windward as a really smart yacht of comparable size, but her own qualities of dependability, firmness of character, and staunch good sense gave her a character, a breeding, which may be surpassed in many respects, but cannot be exactly matched or reproduced by any yacht, even one designed in imitation.

With sailing-barges I have never been able to get on the same terms of absolutely intimate affection.   I admit that.   I love least about a barge most of the things I love most about a smack —and *vice versa*.

Almost everybody has a queer taste of anxious excitement in his mouth when he gets under way in anything over ten tons in a breeze, but in a smack the thing was always a joy.   In a barge the taste was generally too strong for me.   Partly, no doubt, this was due to my responsibility towards some one who knew more about it than ever I should ; partly to the sheer hard work involved, for the *Venta* was big and old for an amateur mate with an elderly skipper, and I always had the feeling that it was physically impossible to do the thing perfectly, with the anchor to be got, the foresail to be set, and the mainsail hooked into the traveller and sheeted out.   Perhaps one should not expect to attain perfection, but I recalled the times when, without a word exchanged between us, a friend and I had slipped the *Charlotte* out of a tight corner in a way that made us secretly hope enough people were watching.   (Yes, I forgot the times when it didn't quite come off !)   Nor would the *Venta* thread her way up a creek or a harbour with that relish the *Charlotte* displayed ; one had to coax her and sometimes threaten her, and even then in some hateful place like Bugsby's Hole she would sulk and refuse the helm for no apparent reason (generally some eddy catching one end of her long body), and we would have to use the anchor to check her in a hurry.

Indeed, close corners, where a smack so delights, can be a vexing business in a barge, though I recall instances to the contrary.

Meditating one night on the unpleasant prospect of having to turn out in the rain and unlash the stowed tops'l to sail three hundred yards up to the dock gates to windward, I was impressed when old Alfred just eased a turn off the main brails and let the mainsail drop down against the sprit. Then, with vang slacked and nothing sheeted anywhere, we cast off and, with the tide under her lee bow shoving the old box up to windward, she nosed into that dock as if drawn by a magnet.

In dock it is hell, though that isn't the barge's fault. The poor brute gets dazed by the filth and the dust and the noise, and the crew with her. Every lighter you try to warp up to proves to be a drifter, and after you have sculled off with the whole dolly-line and made fast, you find as you wind in that the beastly thing is coming to you instead of you to it. Every lighterman wants to pinch your boat-hook ; the dockers are lazy and unco-opera-tive (in London I met none whom I would except from that generalization, just as in the little country ports every man was friendly and willing to help) ; the ship you are to load from lies awkwardly or is not ready. Trimming grain is an occupation with little or nothing to be said for it, particularly when it rains and you get covered with flour plaster ; in fact, the sooner you get out again the better. It is a great moment when the old creature leaves the inert scum that fills the dock and responds to the tideway under her. Off she goes, a different ship now, with decks level with the water, moving heavily but confidently, from the light craft which entered a few days ago, decks five feet clear of the water, jaunty and free in her ways.

The ebb catches her, grasps her, holds her. She is sailing again, thank God. Down the tide-way she goes through the clutter of tugs and ships and barges, losing the wind behind factories, catch-ing it through gaps in the buildings, down to Woolwich, where the Colchester craft gather, and we exchange a hail with them lying on the buoys, a lovely vista of perhaps twenty sets of sails and spars and rigging and house flags ; down through the lighter roads of Erith, past Everard's big coasters and racers and the old training-ship at Grays, down the tedious stretch of Long Reach, by Northfleet Hope and historic Tilbury to Gravesend, where the heart is lighter still, for the tribulations of London River are astern, and the generous freedom of the broad estuary is ahead now.

And now the barge is in her element, and the smack nowhere. She settles down to it, taking it in her long stride. The *Charlotte* would be asking for a reef in Sea Reach, and it would be lively on deck. *Venta* is going like an electric train. She carries everything without noticing it, and the kettle sits on the cabin fire undisturbed. This is where size counts.

The tide fails at Southend, and over goes the hook. It is not a perfect harbour, yet she rides as quietly as a cat on a cushion. And, oh, how unspeakably blessed it is below! Unsullied by the inevitable smells and dirt of a ship with an engine, her cabin is cosy and inviting after a long and tiring day as nowhere else. The duff is in the pot. Now it is inside us. Our pipes are lit. The firelight flickers, and the lamplight gleams on the old mahogany panels of her cabin. The skipper writes up the day's log laboriously. I creep into the deep cupboard bunk—"Cert'd to Acc'date One Seaman" is carved over my head on the beam—and roll over to pass the rest of the flood tide in sleep.

Many days like that I remember. I remember too coming out of Dover and losing the wind in the Downs. An easterly breeze looked in on us about eight o'clock in the morning and got us moving again. By the time we were off the North Foreland it was fresh and getting fresher. Squaring away before it, we gave her all she had and let her go. She went. We steered in turns as the white water roared past her sides. The day glared with the bright hard sheen of the easterly weather, and the little yachts waved as we rushed past them. We hardly touched a sheet till we sheered alongside the tier at Woolwich that evening.

I recall another easterly day, wet and windy as we came out of Colne. It wasn't fit to come out, and the skippers of the anchored craft sang out as they lay rolling, "Ain't going out, are you, Alf?" Alf was uneasy. "Might have a look at it," he hailed back noncommittally. "That ain't fit," he confided to me, "but if once we bring up here we'll lay here for days, wind easterly. If we can get down the Spitways she'll do it from there." He paced uneasily about. As we came clear of Colne Point the sea started to jump all over her, but we had water over the Bar and she fetched the Spitway buoy. We had the topsail down to gybe her in Swin, but I thought when the brailed mainsail smacked that sprit across it was going to take the gear out of her. Alf was obstinate that day and insisted on steering for some six hours on end himself. As the flood made up with the wind the sea eased and lengthened, but she still yawed badly, and when we brought up, in Sea Reach, I think, he sat waiting for his supper rubbing his tired arms and cursing the barge for a " cruel owd bitch."

I recall *Venta* slipping down the Blackwater in the cool, clean autumn dawn ; *Venta* airing up in the heat of a summer evening on the last of the flood to an anchorage in Shore Ends ; giving her the anchor at Woolwich in the full bore of the spring flood-tide, and the way her 180 tons' deadweight, checking on it, tore out fathom after fathom of chain round the windlass barrel ; biting dawns, heaving on a frozen windlass handle ; days of irritation ; nights of discomfort, windbound, rolling ; fog, anxiety, gale, hard labour unending, jib-sheets that flog, brails that foul, gear that jams or, far worse, parts. . . .

Days of grandeur tearing into Harwich just in time to dodge a dusting ; sailing her in the smooth water close under the Maplins with a snorting beam wind that brought the weather chine very nearly out of the water and made her like a huge racing dinghy to handle ; nights of sheer delight ghosting through the Rays'n with the Buxey Beacon in the moon track, or pacing her spacious decks before turning in as the tide sluiced past her sides and threw up phosphorescent murmurs round her anchor chain ; the depth of sleep, such as only hard work at sea can produce, in the roomy recesses of that cavernous bunk ; the delight of a voyage done and seeing the golden cascade of precious grain run out of her. . . .

That is barging. That is what will have gone when grimy labourers bring grain to Colchester in chugging diesel coasters or towed in dumb lighters behind stolid and disdainful tugs. " You young fellows that go to sea for pleasure have earned the right to go to hell for a living," as Joshua Francis observed to me one day.

# XIX

## THE WILDFOWLERS

*By*

J. WENTWORTH DAY [1]

*Last Survivors of a Vanishing Calling—Manners and Methods, Amateur
and Professional—Great Bags of To-day and Yesterday—Shot for a Swan
by his Nephew—The Pigeons tacked to the Tree*

THE fishing-fleet which lies at the foot of Maldon's steep hill,
where the Blackwater river at full tide glints and burns in the sun,
a beaten silver shield of water, is owned and manned by men
who are among the last true fishermen-fowlers of the British
coast. These Pitts and Claydons, Handleys and Woodcrafts,
earn their livings in spring, summer, and autumn by fishing,
winkling, and oystering, and in winter by wildfowling. They
live by nets and guns, by boats and the wild creatures of marsh
and seaway. Natural men living in a natural way by the oldest
arts of mankind, the arts of the fowler and the fisher.

Each smack has one or more punts swinging on its painter or
hauled aboard, bottom up on deck, or laid like flat cigars on the
shingle strand. Those punts are built by the fishermen-fowlers
themselves—narrow, pointed fore and aft, sixteen to twenty feet
in length and from two and a half to three feet in beam. Clinker-
built, with an almost flat bottom, slightly cambered—to allow
them to be pushed easily over mud—they are, unlike the Norfolk
punts, completely open from stem to stern. The freeboard
averages from eight to ten inches. In these frail craft, so light
that a man can easily lift one, the fowlers go out on the tide, under
the moon and in the mists of dusk and dawn, to shoot duck.

Their guns, invariably muzzle-loaders, are from five to nine

[1] Author of *The Modern Fowler, King George V as a Sportsman, Sporting Adventure, Farming Adventure, Harvest Adventure*, etc.

feet in length, and they vary in weight from fifty pounds to ninety pounds. My own gun, which is kept aboard one of the smacks, is nine feet six inches long, an inch and a quarter in bore, weighs one hundred and ten pounds, and fires a pound of shot. But the average load fired is from half to three-quarters of a pound. The gun is secured in the punt by a rope passed through a hole in the butt-end of the stock and then lashed round a thwart or 'gunbeam' about a third of the way from the bows. The muzzle end of the gun rests in a shallow groove cut in the stem-post.

The gunner lies prone, often on the bare boards, sometimes on a half-sack of straw—which is reckoned 'soft practice '—and, with his eyes only a few inches above water-level, propels the punt with short hand-paddles in deep water, or with short pushing-sticks, or 'sprits,' when the water is shallow enough for their brass-shod tips to reach the mud. Thus the gunner stalks on open water up to the immense gatherings of brent geese, widgeon, mallard, and teal which 'use' the estuary in hard weather.

It is a game which needs the skin of an otter, the eyes of a hawk, the constitution of an ox, the ears of an owl, and the enthusiasm of a terrier. The man who can earn his winter livelihood at it must be a bit of a sailor, a stalker, a naturalist, a gunner, and an invincible. It is, of all sports, the most exacting and frequently the most ill-rewarded.

Big shots can be made and occasionally are made, but the average bag is from six to fifteen fowl at a shot—and a gunner may not get more than two shots in a good night and not more than one good night in a week or fortnight. I have been out on fourteen consecutive days, seen thousands of fowl, and never fired a shot—simply because wind and weather were all in favour of the fowl and against the gunner.

Yet when a professional bags, say, a score of 'heavy fowl '— widgeon or mallard—he can reckon to get about four to five pounds for them, and that sum, in the simple economics of water-side life, is worth having. But these men are more, far more, than mere market-gunners—they and their like elsewhere are among the finest sportsmen and greatest natural gentlemen alive. It has been my pleasure and privilege to know many of this small and gallant company of professional gunners—from as far south as Itchenor to as far north as Holy Island and the Cromarty Firth.

It is reliably estimated that there are not more than five purely professional punt-gunners in England and not much above 150 part-time punters. Of this number one whole-time professional —Walter Linnett, of Bradwell Chapel—and about thirty part-timers, men who fish as well as shoot, are on the Blackwater. It has always been a mighty river of punters, and Maldon Waterside its capital city.

Before, however, we consider the weighty bags of the past made by the old-timers on this noble estuary—and to me there is a nostalgic charm in looking up the feats of these great sportsmen of humble origin but magnificent skill—it is as well to consider the present state and performances of the average punt-gunner of to-day. In 1941 the International Committee for Bird Preservation, through its Wildfowl Enquiry Sub-committee, of which Dr Percy Lowe was secretary, published through the Cambridge University Press two volumes dealing with the general status of wild geese and wild duck in England and Scotland. The section on punt-gunning in England, in the first volume, gives an excellent overall picture of present-day wildfowling conditions, and the averages arrived at are well worth quoting, since they reflect most accurately the average conditions on the Essex coast to-day.

For example, the Sub-committee found that the average annual bag for a regular punt-gunner was 287 duck and geese each season. This was arrived at by comparing the bags of twenty-six punters over a series of years, choosing men from all the English coasts.

The average bag for a first-class punter, presumably a professional, who worked hard all the season in a really good locality, is given at approximately 400 duck and geese. That total, I should say, is approached by very few men on the Blackwater estuary to-day, and exceeded by still fewer.

It is interesting, *inter alia*, to notice that the largest bag recorded in any season during the twentieth century was made by four men, who, using the same double-punt, bagged no fewer than 1500 fowl. But it should be borne in mind that four men going out continually in the same punt, using it alternately, are really equal to two separate crews of two men each using two punts.

The Sub-committee records that one single-handed punter, in the winter of 1917–18, killed over a thousand fowl. It was an exceptionally hard winter, as I well remember, and there were many birds on all the Essex coast as shooting had been prohibited throughout the period of those war years. Indeed, the late Right Hon. E. G. Pretyman, of Orwell Park, Suffolk, told me at the time that his decoy pond—now one of the only five working full-time in all England—had taken no fewer than ten thousand fowl that season, which was four to five times its normal 'take.' It is interesting to note that the average annual bag of the man who made this extraordinary total was only 152 fowl in other years. Generally speaking, I should say that the average Blackwater puntsman of to-day does not bag more than from 100 to 150 fowl in a season.

What is interesting, and incidentally is borne out by the findings of the Sub-committee elsewhere, is the fact that the average old wildfowler will tell you that a good man bags 30–50 per cent. more fowl in a season to-day than the ordinary punter got, say, fifty years ago. I put this down to a number of factors, including the decrease in the number of punters, the almost total abandonment of the practice of a number of punts going out in a fleet and harassing the fowl *en masse*, the decrease in coastwise barge traffic, which formerly disturbed the birds a lot, and the complete cessation of the bad old practice of pushing what were known as "mud-sledges" over the mud-flats and firing great guns from them into the birds as they fed or rested on the flats, or along the tide-line. Thus the birds were harassed in the old days by punters afloat, by 'mud-sledgers' ashore, by bargemen who fired at them from the decks of their passing craft, and, incidentally, by a vast horde of Cockney gunners, who, following the writings of a well-known sporting journalist of the day who signed himself "Wildfowler," descended upon the Essex and Kent coasts by every train.

These people, arrayed in yachting caps and armed with 4-bores, 8-bores, and 10-bores, hired local men to take them out and discharged their artillery at random. Some of them chartered yachts on which they mounted punt-guns, ranging up to $2\frac{1}{2}$ inches in bore. I have seen one of these pieces of marine artillery, and it is truly a formidable weapon, taking a steel cartridge case, over a foot long, and firing about 2½ lb. of shot, a piece more suitable for bombarding a landward fort than for firing at ducks. One has only to read *Shooting and Fishing Trips*, by " Wildfowler," published in the seventies, to realize the manner in which the wildfowl of Kent and Essex were pursued and harried by this ignorant and voracious crew of ' sporting ' Cockneys. When they could not shoot at ducks they fired at gulls, or threw bottles overboard and banged away at them. Unfortunately there was no wildfowling Surtees to ridicule them out of existence.

To-day, apart from a few butterfly yachtsmen who sally out from Mersea and Brightlingsea, under the tutelage of local longshoremen, and discharge their borrowed weapons at frightened fowl at impossible ranges on the opening day of the season—a sort of annual holy ritual which begins in smoke, and ends, duckless, in beer—the marshes and flats are comparatively undisturbed except by the local fishermen-fowlers, 99 per cent. of whom are nature's gentlemen and behave as such, and a few amateurs, mainly Essex farmers and local business-men, who know their wildfowling code of honour and neither shoot at impossible ranges nor seek to harry the birds on any and every occasion.

Hence the gradual improvement in the numbers of birds seen and the individual bags made.

While I am on this subject of sporting behaviour, I cannot too strongly condemn those who use motor-boats, or other mechanically propelled craft, to carry punt-guns and use them therefrom. It is estimated that there are fewer than twelve power-boats mounting guns in England, but unfortunately one or two are in Essex. It is possible that they are used without their owners' really realizing that they are, in fact, offending against the true canons of the sport, which are that a puntsman should pursue his quarry under the sole power of his own or his partner's arms and paddles, that he should exercise true seamanship in approaching the birds, and seek in no way to disturb them unless, and until, he manages to manoeuvre his craft within a fair sporting range, which is generally considered to be about sixty to seventy yards, and certainly not much over eighty yards. Beyond that range he is likely, even using a powerful gun, to wound more than he kills. The true punter will endeavour to kill his birds outright and leave as few cripples as possible.

The mere noise of a motor-boat disturbs fowl, and the fact that its freeboard is so high out of the water tends to alarm them, and cause them to rise, long before the gun can be brought within fair range. The inevitable temptation, therefore, is for the punt-gunner to fire his gun the moment they jump, with the result that he wings a few and desperately frightens the rest. This practice should be prohibited by law.

Punt-gunning, although an arduous and exacting sport, is none the less unique in the quality and diversity of the surroundings into which it takes the sportsman, and the quarry which he seeks. Perhaps for that reason it has always attracted men of some artistic and literary ability, to whom the picturesque wildness of the surroundings naturally appeals. That magnificent naturalist and author the late Abel Chapman ; Colonel Peter Hawker, of immortal memory ; the late Sir Ralph Payne-Gallwey, whose books are as classic as Hawker's ; Buck, the artist, and Charles Whymper ; the late Lord Londesborough, and a host of others whose names live in literature or natural history, have all regarded punt-gunning as their favourite sport. Many of them visited the Essex coast solely for that reason.

Picture the mouth of the Blackwater as it was in that hard winter in the sixties, when that grand old Essex sportsman, fox-hunter, and wildfowler, the late Squire Thomas Kemble, of Runwell Hall, Wickford, wrote in the little book which his daughter, Miss Augusta Kemble, has kindly lent me, this passage :

> I am now going to relate what possibly sportsmen who go down at the present day for wild-fowl may not believe. I have seen the sky darkened by wild geese, covering a space of half a mile by a quarter of a mile, as thick as manure spread upon the ground, and making a noise which I could only compare with fifty packs of hounds in full cry. I have also seen seven acres at low water covered with widgeon, curlew, and ducks, making such a noise that I could not hear my brother talking to me a few yards off. Colonel Russell [the late Colonel Champion Russell, of Stubbers Hall, near Upminster] was off the coast in his yacht. He told me he had sent off to London from Maldon upwards of two tons of geese.

Such a sight can still be seen occasionally in a very hard winter. I remember in the winter of 1939–40 being in a punt off the Gold-hanger Flats at the break of dawn. We fired the great gun into a

gaggle of about fifty brent geese.   As the report boomed across
the flats another punt-gun was fired lower down the river off
Steeple Stone.   And suddenly, against the lightening apple-green
and rose-red of the eastern sky, there arose, on wing, thousands of
fowl.   They sprang from the water over three or four square
miles of estuary, and swept back and forth against the clear sky.
There were literally curtains of fowl, which seemed to be drawn
across the face of the dawn like curtains across a window.   Wild
swans, wild geese, widgeon and golden eye, mallard and teal, and
hosts of waders and plover, made one of the most magnificent
spectacles of bird life I have ever seen in these islands.   We
estimated that at least ten thousand fowl were on the wing
at once.

Our own bag of geese was only five, but had it been none that
stupendous spectacle would have made the three-mile row, and
the bitter coldness of the winter morn, more than worth such a
superb sight.   That is one of the pleasures and rewards of gunning
afloat.   The man who walks along the sea-wall with a pair of field
glasses may occasionally see trips and bunches of passing fowl.
He will see occasional skeins of geese, flapping raggedly over the
waves.   He will spring waders from the saltings, and perhaps the
lurking fox from the leeward side of the wall.   But he will see
little or nothing of the fleets and flotillas of fowl which sit out in
deep water, snooze comfortably in the deep gullies in the mud
flats, or sit sheltered out of the wind under the lee of the " cant,"
as the Essex fishermen call the miniature cliff-edge of the saltings.
The punter sees all this.   He goes low on his stomach, creeping
like a grey shadow in his little boat, nosing up the creeks and rills,
where mountains of mud make miniature Alps, and glistening
islands appear and disappear as the tide ebbs and flows.

It is a strange, wet, unearthly other-world, untouched and un-
tamed by the works of man, still the same as it was in Tudor times
or, far back, when the forgotten Trinobantian paddled his dugout
canoe, or fished from his skin-covered coracle on these ancient
seaways.

It is a thousand pities that so few chroniclers of the past recorded
the great bags and the rare fowl which were shot by " the rude
forefathers " of the Maldon and Mersea men, the " Tollesbury
chaps " and the Bradwell gunners, who, in their crazy, cranky

punts, with great lumbering guns, flintlocks, and percussion ignition, risked their lives and pitted their native skill against the wildfowl of the past.

But we have a few records to con over by the fireside on winter evenings, when the mind may dwell on the mighty days of the past. There was that great day in the winter of 1860 when thirty-two punt-gunners of the Blackwater villages, including Linnett's father, worked up to an immense gathering of brent geese off Bradwell Chapel, that ancient 'cathedral' of Bishop Cedd, the bishop of the Eastern Saxons, which still stands, earth-floored and lonely, built of the stones and narrow Roman bricks of the ancient fort of the Count of the Saxon Shore, gazing out across the waters of the North Sea which have already swallowed its eastern fortifications and ramparts.

Those thirty-two punts, commanded by Colonel Russell, lay hidden in the tall sea-asters and bentles until the tide flooded. Then they advanced in a great semicircle on the geese. Colonel Russell, whose punt was in the centre, blew a whistle at the critical moment. Every punt-gun, save one, was discharged into a body of geese estimated at between four and five thousand. No fewer than 704 dead geese were picked up, and Linnett has told me that his father remembered that there were so many that the punts could not hold them. They were loaded down to the gunwales until some of the punts swam so low in the water that they had a bare inch or two of freeboard showing. And behind them they towed strings of wild geese, knotted on their painters. Hundreds of dead and wounded got away on the tide. More than 250 were picked up in the next few days by prowling longshore gunners and village boys, who combed the tide-lines. It is safe to assume that more than a thousand geese were killed in that great onslaught which produced the record British bag of brent geese of all time.

The punts all made for Bradwell Creek, where, at the Green Man, that ancient waterside inn, standing above the quay with its great piles and anchored smacks, the bag was shared out equally. There was a great jollification of beer and tobacco, and the singing of old Essex songs of farm and tide-line, those songs which you still hear chanted in endless monotones with an occasional rousing chorus when smacksmen, bargemen, and marsh shepherds get together in the freemasonry of their immemorial crafts.

But one man had not fired his gun. He trusted to save his powder and shot, always an important economy in those days when ammunition had to be brought by carriers' carts from the gunsmith at Maldon ten miles away. He reckoned to take his share of the bag and that none would be the wiser. But a man in a neighbouring punt had noticed that there had been no flash from his gun. So the backslider was accused. His gun was examined. His guilt was proved. " So they took him by the backside, ducked his head under the pump, and hulled him out in the backyard," I was told with a chuckle.

In that same bitter winter, or it may have been the year after, another great ' community shot ' was made by eighteen gunners, who all fired together off Bradwell Chapel one moonlight night, and bagged 360 geese. Old Linnett, Johnny Basham, and Jim Chaney, of Maldon, were of the party. There was another bag of 300, another of 160, and several of over 100 to other ' community shots ' at about the same time, while " Old Stubbins," of Maldon, made the then individual record by killing fifty geese to one shot of his famous gun " Old Jubilee " off the mouth of Thurslet Creek, just west of Tollesbury Pier, where to-day the oyster-watch-boat lies at anchor.[1]

Sitting in the tiny kitchen of Linnett's little, three-roomed, wooden cottage, built of ship's timbers, which huddles, one-storied, against the ruins of that old Roman fort of Bradwell, I have heard these stories from him on winter nights while the firelight flickered on his long, brown guns, and on the stuffed ducks, glassy-eyed in their cases. Outside the North Sea night-wind whistled in the few stunted trees in his little garden, and moaned about the eaves of the old chapel, while the spume of the crinkled tide swept into his garden. For Linnett, the last of the real fowlers, lives, as befits his calling and his independence, on the *seaward* side of the sea-wall. His little home is built, with a fine gesture, on the No-man's Land of the saltings and the sea-verges.

" I lay in my punt one autumn afternoon in Gunners' Creek," he said, " and I see a great tall bird, with red legs and a crooked red

---

[1] These and other shots have been recorded in my book *The Modern Fowler* (Longmans, 1934).

beak, come stalkin' over the flats. He was a foreigner all right. I watched he for days. A rare great old bird too, four foot high. I calculated to get him. And I got him that afternoon. A flamingo, they called it—come all the way from Africa."

Nights later I was talking with Jesse Pullen, on Mersea Island. Jesse remembered the bird. " I see him fly over West Mersea church, right low, one afternoon in 1910, when we was up in the church tower, mufflin' the bells for old King Teddy VII's funeral. A rare great bird, all white and pink, and he flew over right low."

Such an occasional wanderer turns up every now and then on the Essex coast. If they are shot it is no use lamenting, for the realistic naturalist knows full well that no flamingo will breed in this country. We may, however, regret, with justice, the ravens which nested on Northey Isle as recently as the sixties, when Alf Claydon's father remembered climbing up one of those tall elms in the little grove at the head of the sea-road and taking the eggs. We may lament, too, the sea eagles which have been seen and the bitterns which come now and again to the reed beds of Old Hall Marshes, where one was shot in Dr Salter's time. The latter, indeed, might nest if they were given the chance.

Lord Lymington (now the Earl of Portsmouth) and I saw a pair of sea eagles on Langenhoe Hall Marshes in either 1930 or 1931. They were about there for a week or more. Finally one of them was shot in Kent a fortnight later. I am glad to say the shooter was fined ten pounds, and his gun was confiscated.

The kite was, almost within living memory, a bird of the Blackwater marshes. Probably the last nest was made in Essex in 1845, when Mr Round's keeper reported a " crotch-tailed puttock's " nest in Stroodland Grove, that vanished copse of tall elms which stood, so far as I can determine, near that charming old house once called Leaky Hall, and New Garden Farm. Some few old oak-trees of the Grove still stand.

I saw a marsh harrier fly off Northey Island as recently as the autumn of 1939 when we were beating home in the smack *Joseph and Mary* of Maldon, and, in the same year, from the deck of the same boat, Alf Claydon and I saw a peregrine falcon kill a pigeon with a magnificent stoop off the mouth of Steeple Creek. Both harriers and falcons turn up on the Blackwater more often than is imagined, and Linnett has seen a golden eagle sitting on a

post on the Dengie Flats as recently as 1930.    Dr Salter shot one
on Old Hall Marshes which is now in the Chelmsford Museum.
It is believed that these golden eagles, which occasionally visit the
Essex coast, are mainly immature birds *en passage* down the east
coast from Scotland to the Pyrenees and the Spanish mountain
ranges.

Mersea Island is, like Maldon, still a nest of gunners, but with
the exception of Charlie Stoker, one of the real old-timers, Harry
Banks, the oysterman, Becky D'Wit, with his quick, darting,
gipsy eyes, and Tom D'Wit, tall and gentle, there are not as many
punters as formerly.    Poor old Gunner Cook, the king of them
all, with his skull-cap and quiet, quizzical manner, died, blind,
during the Second World War.    He, indeed, was a master of the
game.    Night after night he would punt from the Fishermen's
Hard, through the " Buzzun," up past the old decoy pond on
Waldegrave's Farm, and out on to the wide, lonely East Mersea
Flats.    A rare place for black geese, but a dangerous place for all
but a skilled punter, for it is wide open to the North Sea, and if a
wind gets up the punter will find himself on a dead lee shore, in
a short sea, with no possible creek in which to hide.    Gunner
Cook made consistently good bags on those Flats, right up to
within a year of his death, which took place in 1943 or '44.    I
mourn him as a great sportsman and a natural gentleman, a man
of no pretence but of great bravery and outstanding skill.    He was
of the same mould as Walter Linnett, that quiet, blue-eyed, fair-
haired seaman-gunner with the direct Viking blood in his veins.

Mersea, however, has a number of young men who are all
making their names at punting—that irrepressible trinity of Bert
Carter, Leo Smith, and Bruce Rainbird, who shoot together with
a great $1\frac{1}{4}$-inch breech-loading gun, and, of course, Harold
Proctor, who was born in the now-vanished old Wick Farmhouse
in the middle of Langenhoe Marshes.    Harold is short, sturdy,
immensely strong, with a hand like a ham and the biceps of a
bullock.    He is a natural punt-gunner, and a born wildfowler,
one who can be trusted to carry on the traditions of this most
ancient sport in the coldest weather.

For ever immortal in the humble annals of Mersea wildfowling
are the names of " Swan " Mussett, that magnificent old patriarch
who earned his nickname because his nephew shot him one night

with a punt-gun in mistake for a wild swan. Later when his smack sank under him and " Swan " climbed to the top of the mast a few yards above the breaking waves, and refused to be taken off because, he declared, his rescuers wanted salvage, the same nephew gaily " shoved an old eel-shear up his backside " to dislodge him ! It is a great story, and I have told it at length in *Farming Adventure.*[1] Strange to say, " Swan " nurtured no grievance against " the young hound," as he affectionately called his nephew, but rather regarded these twin bloody assaults upon his person as demonstrable evidence of the uncompromising solidarity of the Mussett clan. For, indeed, these Mussetts, who are descended of the Huguenot De Mussets, are a clan in as strict and family a sense as any Highland clan. Magnificent sailors, great shots, and invincible sportsmen, they own their own houses and smacks, their oyster-beds and punt-guns, call no man master, and live in a fine, free, fearless independence. There was never yet a Mussett who was not a character. I know one, Charlie Mussett, who to this day lives in an old railway carriage with his dog and his gun, works when and where he pleases, gets drunk if he feels like it, shaves when the mood pleases him, will fight anyone who asks for it, and yet has the manners of an archduke, the essence of natural good breeding.

Prime Minister of the clan was the late and ever-to-be-mourned " Sooty." " Sooty " was master of guns, boats, oysters, and beer. His lack of knowledge of any of these laudable subjects was microscopic.

But " Sooty " was, in his latter days, no great punt-gunner. In his long boots, his old khaki field-jacket, his short oilskin top-coat and sou'wester, bearing an ancient, hammer, double-barrelled 12-bore in his hand, and a look of infinite guile upon his countenance, he stalked the creeks, peered over the sea-walls, prowled the saltings. and slew " a masterful lot of them owd ducks, and a boat-load of them web-footed owd rabbits." For when a rabbit fell to " Sooty's " gun, as many did, he always avowed that he had " copped the little beggar out on the saltings, when the tide had ketched him, and he was a-swimmin' for home ! They got paddles on 'em like Margate steamers, these here owd Mersea rabbits."

[1] Harrap, 1943.

That supreme sportsman and notable Essex character, the late Dr J. H. Salter, of Tolleshunt D'Arcy, who hunted until he was eighty, bred three Waterloo Cup winners, and was shooting ducks in his ninetieth year, had a great affection for " Sooty." " Sooty " would tell a great tale of one of their forays together.

" We'd bin and had a rare owd morning a-flightin', the owd doctor and me," " Sooty " related, " and fired away every cartridge we had.  We were a-coming back when we see ahead a tremendous lot o' dows [wood-pigeons], all settin' up in an elm-tree.  Fair covered with dows, that lil' owd elm were.  ' Good gracious, Soot,' says Dr Salter, ' I wish we had a cartridge left for them perishers ! '

" ' Do you jest wait a minute, sir,' I sez.  ' I've got some tin-tacks in my pocket, and a drop of powder left.'  So I took and loaded my old muzzle-loader with a nice charge of powder and a hand-ful of tacks, and I ups and lets fly.  ' Wot happened ? ' you ask.  Not a bird so much as moved.

" ' Good gracious, Soot,' sez the doctor, ' that weren't much of an idea.  You ain't even scared 'em.'  ' Do you jest wait a minute, sir,' I sez, and when we went up close to that owd elm, sure enough every dow was nailed on to a branch ! "

" Sooty " earned a good many pints in the Mersea Victory with that yarn, and I had heard it so often that I was listening to one retelling of it to a couple of " furrin gentlemen " with only partial attention, till the climax was reached and I was astounded to hear that the lily could be gilded.

" ' Do you jest wait a minute, sir,' I sez, and sure enough when we went close up to that owd elm, beggar me if the whole tree didn't take and fly away.  The dows was all nailed to the boughs, don't you see ! "

Poor old " Sooty " was drowned just before the Second World War.  He was out in a goose-boat, which was notoriously ' tender,' one winter afternoon on the Main when she suddenly broached-to and overturned.  " Sooty " and his ' gentleman ' gunner were both thrown into the icy water.  They clung on to the boat until " Sooty " suddenly said, " She's a-sinkin', sir.  You hang on.  You got longer to live than me.  I'll let go." And he let go.  His companion swam after him, brought him back, and a few minutes later the two of them were rescued by

Mr Augustine Courtauld, the hero of the Arctic ice-cap, who happened to be out sailing that bitter day. "Sooty" was dragged aboard his yacht, and the salt water was pumped out of him. But the cold and exposure had been too much. Another grand old Essex character had gone. He died as he had lived—game to the last.

Over the water at Tollesbury there lived, until a few years ago, a grand old native sportsman called Alf Drake, who, like the present "Admiral" Bill Wyatt, of Mersea, was a master shipwright and a great gunner. He always shot with a muzzle-loader. He kept the powder loose in the right-hand pocket of his old reefer jacket, and the shot loose in the left-hand pocket. And when he wished to load his monstrous great 8-bore he would haul a handful of powder out of the right-hand pocket, pour it down the barrel out of the small of his hand, ram down a wad of paper, and then fish a handful of shot out of the left-hand pocket.

This method, despite the ballistics experts, worked wonderfully well, until one day Alf shoved his lighted pipe into his right-hand pocket.

There was a sheet of flame, and, as the late "Shaver" Mills drily remarked to me, "That give owd Alf a taste of what the good Lord had got in store for him!" Will Leavett, Jim Frost, the Heards, and old "Shaver" Mills were, or are, all great gunners of Tollesbury. But there are no punt-gunners left in that village of yacht-skippers and deep-sea sailors unless, as I hope, young Lennox Leavett is going to follow in his father's footsteps.

Kings of the 'gentlemen gunners' in these waters when I first began to shoot there were my two very dear friends—both now, alas, dead—the late Octave, Count de la Chapelle, and Charlie Wykeham-Martin. La Chapelle was a Gascon, brought up in a family château on the shores of the Baie de la Somme. His family came to England at the fall of the Second Empire, but retained property in France. A founder and Vice-president of the Wild Fowlers' Association, he was the keenest salt-water gunner I have ever met, a man of great charm, character, and courtesy, a first-class naturalist, a brilliant shot, and one for whom no wind or tide was too foul, no night afloat too cold, and no day empty if the salt wind was on his face. He was the idol of the village, and when he died six fishermen-fowlers of Tollesbury, in blue jerseys and water-boots, carried him to the grave which they had lined with sea-lavender from the saltings he loved.

Charlie Wykeham-Martin was a son of that great Victorian shot and country gentleman, the late " Corney " Wykeham-Martin, of Leeds Castle, Kent, that dream of a feudal stronghold which rises straight out of the waters of its lake like a castle in a Tennyson poem. Charlie lived at Tollesbury, where he built his own gun-punts, made great bags of fowl, and shot snipe and partridges over a team of French poodles. He too was a man of rare courtesy, great charm, and an immense knowledge of wild-fowl and their ways. The best comment on the pair was made one day by a skipper in the Captains' Bar of the King's Head, who remarked to me : " I count there ain't another village in England can show ye two head gentlemen like them two—head gunners, head sailors, and head bird-men. They ain't amachures —they're professionals ! "

Colonel Champion Russell is long dead, and it is much to be regretted that he left no records or diary of his many years of exceptional sport on the Essex coast. I am happy to say, how-ever, that I have added his small collection of rare Essex birds to my own small museum. They include four avocets out of eight which were killed on the Blackwater ; two buzzards, one a very dark specimen ; an Egyptian goose, which one must assume had escaped from a private lake ; what appears to be a very faded specimen of a spotted crake ; and a most remarkable example of an albinistic polecat : the head and neck of the latter have gone completely white.

I also have the late Count de la Chapelle's collection, which includes a specimen of the very rare Temminck's stint ; the even rarer Harlequin duck, of which only some half a dozen specimens have been recorded from the British Isles ; a Richardson's skua : two or three eider ducks ; two spotted redshank ; and a mixed collection of less common ducks, divers, and sea-birds. These include puffins, guillemots, and little auks. In addition, I have seen in the White Swan at Maldon a stormy petrel, killed, as were all Count de la Chapelle's birds, on the Blackwater.

Not all rare birds, luckily, are shot. In the autumn of 1942 Colonel Count de Boislambert and myself definitely identified a glossy ibis on the Abberton Reservoir, and this bird used the Blackwater mud-flats regularly for a week or two. It was merely one of the many rare birds which, from time to time, turn up on the immense mud-flats of this mighty estuary. Be it said to the eternal credit of the average fisherman-fowler that he does not go out of his way to shoot a rare bird simply because it is rare. He usually takes a lively interest in anything out of the ordinary, and I have, from time to time, heard stories of all sorts of uncommon birds which I would have given my ears to have identified beyond doubt. But they were not shot, for the simple reason that the native gunner shoots for the market and for the pot, and not in order to put another rarity in a glass case. That is as it should be.

There are, praise St Hubert, still plenty of young fisherman-fowlers on the Essex flats to keep the old sport alive. There are still geese and widgeon in the dawn. There is still the lift and wheel of fowl to gladden one's eyes against the bitter, baleful glory of winter sunsets. The old fowlers die, but the young fowlers step into their mud-pattens, lie down in their fathers' punts, and push off into the fogs and snowy mists. The old fowlers have sailed on into the forgotten glories of the mighty past. But the tides still creep, the winds are bitter, and the thunder of wings in winter dawns is a fit funereal salute to those great sportsmen from humble villages, who made their unwritten history on these cold Essex waters which we love.

# XX

## THE MAN WHO SAW A SEA-MONSTER

*Disappearance of a Thirty-shilling Schooner—The Racer that sailed Backward—Record Seine-net Hauls—Seal that took Charge—Steeple-chasing Mullet*

My dear old friend Tom Poole, of Brightlingsea, Colchester's Water Bailiff and first Superintendent of River Police (how lively this collection of tales would be, had he penned it !), became part-owner of his first ship at the age of fifteen, at Southend. She was an old dinghy, the owner of which offered a half-share to anyone who would produce sails, so Tom Poole got hold of a pair of his mother's sheets. When the contract was held to include spars and rigging also, the clothes-line and props went the same way.

For half a century that boyish zest and love for the water never flagged, and Brightlingsea is not the same now he has gone. One of his last pleasures was helping to collect material for this book, and he must have a chapter in it for himself.

One night he took pencil and paper and wrote down the names of thirty-seven vessels he had owned in his life—yachts, smacks, and tugs, for his own use or for speculation. He read it through, added two more, and threw it away. "We'd never come to the end," he said.

One of the queerest of these deals was his purchase of a wrecked schooner which completely disappeared. She was the *Rennie*, of Aberdeen, which went on the Buxey Sand in 1905, bound for London with a cargo of potatoes. The smacks soon had the best of her gear and some of her cargo out of her, and she was offered for sale at Brightlingsea Custom House. Tom Poole's fondness for buying boats being known, he was asked for a bid, and £30 was suggested. " Thirty shillings would be nearer my figure," was his reply, and sure enough, after the company had dispersed, the auctioneer came up to him with, " Come on.   I've got to get this settled up and be back in London to-night.   Give us that thirty shillings, and I'll write you a receipt."

A barge skipper saw no difficulty in getting alongside and clearing fifty pounds' worth of potatoes out of the wreck, if the weather held, so it did not look a bad day's work.   But the weather did not hold.   It came up to blow a gale from the south-east, and it blew for four days.   At the end of that time there was not a trace of the *Rennie*, not a sign of a spud.   She had been well settled in the sand before the gale, and as her planking was all away from her stem on the starboard bow she could not have shifted.   Moreover, if she had done so she would only have gone into the Rays'n, and soon been detected in that much-fished channel.   No, the masts must have come out of her and been picked up by some one who kept his mouth shut, and the Buxey must have swallowed up that schooner complete in four days.

The rate at which wrecks are swallowed by the Essex sands was always remarkable, Tom Poole commented ; indeed, it used to be thought that any wreck which did not disappear pretty rapidly must be on top of another, but even so four days to swallow a schooner and leave no trace was greedy work.   Tom Poole had kept to that day a single souvenir, the *Rennie's* lignum vitæ fore-sail bowline bull's-eye, with an account of the incident pasted inside it.

Not less diverting was the tale of the *Vice Versa*.

A double-ended hack-boat belonging to the schooner *West-ward* was for sale at Brightlingsea, and examining her Tom Poole noticed what a pretty bow her stern would make.   So impressed was he that he got Aldous's to cut three feet six inches off her bow and build a transom stern instead.   Then the boat, now about twenty-two feet long, was rigged to sail backward and given the appropriate name of the *Vice Versa*.   She won the Remnant Shield in her first race, on August 19, 1930, and imme-diately became scratch boat of her class, allowing time to the cutter from Miss Carstairs' famous three-masted schooner *Sonia,* which boat was designed by Charles Nicholson !   She was ulti-mately bought by the *Sonia's* skipper.

In her time the *Vice Versa* was well-known at Brightlingsea, though not so famous as Tom Poole's *Valiant*, to which little craft through all his buyings and sellings he remained faithful for thirty-three years, racing her regularly and successfully all this time, till perhaps no boat had won so many prizes on the Colne.

Any sport on the water—racing, cruising, fishing, punt-gunning, trawling, seine-netting—appealed to Tom Poole, and he had some record hauls with the seine.

On one occasion he was fishing along the Bar so unsuccessfully that they decided that if the next haul was not luckier they would pack up, when the net began to come in alive with bass. When at last they had it in it contained 860, all of which were so identical, weighing just $2\frac{1}{2}$ lb. each, that " they might have been cast in the same mould." After they had disposed of as many as were wanted locally they sent the rest to Billingsgate, but they were delayed four days in transit. As this was July, and the fish were neither gutted nor iced, they expected nothing but a bill from the railway, but to their surprise they received a cheque for nine pounds. A Billingsgate salesman afterwards told Tom Poole, " Oh, we've got a chemical we did 'em in ; brings 'em up like new if they are not too far gone ! "

Then there was the time Tom Poole shot a seal in Brightlingsea Creek and hauled it into his punt, taking it for dead. But it wasn't, for it came to and showed signs of seeking revenge as Tom paddled home.

> That lay between me and my gun, so I couldn't reach past it [he recounted]. That bared its teeth and started to come for me. I reckoned there wasn't room for the two of us, and as I couldn't tip him over I went in myself and swam ashore. I clambered up the mud and ran down the Hard just in time to see my old punt drift by with that old seal sitting up snarling over the gunwale and looking properly savage.

On another occasion they got among eels off Bateman's Tower, at the mouth of Brightlingsea Creek. As the net came in they were pouring around the edges of it in a solid black torrent, yet they saved four and a half hundredweights. One of those present recollected the name and address of an eel-pie maker in Stratford, and a cheque for eleven pounds was the result.

These hauls were made by taking one end of the net out in a wide circle with a boat and hauling it in ashore.   When mullet are enclosed in this way they will leap the net, and a lovely sight it is on a sunny day to see them pouring over like steeple-chasers. About the only way to keep them down is to jump in oneself and splash about to scare them, or a less drastic idea is to throw bits of matting on the water.

These nets can also be laid across a creek for flounders, which are driven into them by beating the water with oars.   One end is laced up and the net pulled in by the other, for when these slothful fish slide into this rough pocket they have not the wits or energy to get out again as would a more vigorous sole or mullet.

Tom Poole told me a yarn of the only sea-monster I have heard of on the Essex coast.   He and a friend were lying in that little shingly bay just inside Walton Backwater one calm morning waiting for high water to get under way, and a holiday-maker was bathing from a boat near by, when between them appeared a creature with a neck about four feet long surmounted by a head similar to a sheep's, but larger.   It swam along, turning its head jerkily from one side to the other, and then disappeared.   It re-appeared in a very short time some five hundred yards to the east-ward, which was up-tide, since the flood was still running, and made off.

The visitor took the view that " we may just as well keep our mouths shut, for no one will believe us either in this or in any-thing we may say again."   Tom Poole, however, declared he " would face ten thousand witnesses and not be afraid of their mockery and ridicule," so confident was he of what he had seen.

His comments struck me as characteristically sensible.   " After all," he said, " a whale once gave birth to two young on the mud above Woolwich, and they turn up in these estuaries perhaps once in half a century.   A fine sturgeon was once stranded right up at Rochford and taken away in a tank on a lorry and exhibited in London, and occasionally a school of porpoises gets above London Bridge.   That shows the unaccountable way in which sea-crea-tures occasionally get off their beat.   If they had been quite iso-lated cases no one would have believed them.   There is no reason why there should not be creatures unknown to us in the sea, and what I saw was one of them making one of these unaccountable departures from its usual haunts." Both the monster described in this remarkable tale and the explanation given find a considerable degree of corroboration in the most notable book on the subject, *The Case for the Sea-serpent*, by Commander R. T. Gould, which I ascertained Tom Poole had neither seen nor heard of.

# XXI

## THE LAST FLEET

*Some Tales of the Barges of To-day—The Races—Disappearance and Revival of the ' Stackie '—Old-time Hufflers*

WHAT of the actual craft which comprise what is likely to be the last fleet of sailing-ships that Colne and Blackwater will know ?

Of the thirty-odd craft sailing under the purple-and-yellow house flag of Francis and Gilders, Ltd, or under the management of that firm before the war claimed its victims (as described in the next chapter), only two, the *Bankside* and the *Castanet*, possessed auxiliary power, a feature which is considered profitable with a skipper of sufficient enterprise to make full use of it. As the cost of initial installation is very heavy compared to the value of a barge, however, considerable extra earnings have to be made before the owners are in pocket. The custom is that the skipper pays half-cost of fuel, and the owners are responsible for the upkeep of the engine.

The *Verona* and *Varuna* are perhaps the outstanding clippers of the fleet, both having won prizes in the Thames and Medway barge races. The *Verona*, as described in Chapter XII, has the distinction of having defeated one of the most famous of all the racers, *Giralda*. These craft belong to a very attractive class, identified by the type of name, built by Shrubsole at Blackwall. Not all racers have this quality of being easy to work. There are no finer vessels afloat than the Mistley *Reminder* and *Redoubtable*, but they carry such a ' load of gear '—particularly in their huge topsails—that they have the reputation of being hard on their crews, and though they have the satisfaction of showing a clean pair of heels in light airs they often have to pick up the skirts of their sails on a wind when other barges are happy enough under full sail.

*Mildreda* (third in 1900) and *Clara* (first in 1896) are other Medway prize-winners, but it must be confessed that not all these racers will ever sail again so fast, for many of them have been ' doubled '—that is, they have had another skin of planking built on them—and this, in addition to adding weight, makes them stiff and rigid. Except perhaps for the Suffolk beach-yawls, which, in smuggling days, carried a saw to cut through their thwarts and get extra speed in a chase, no vessel is more partial to a bit of ' give ' than a barge. It was said of the Wakering brick barges that the fastest ' worked ' so much that you could hear the bricks in her hold chinking and shifting as she wriggled through a seaway. Similarly that old Wivenhoe mariner Captain Albert Turner, for many years skipper of the *Britannia*, has told me that the royal yacht was crippled when they took off the copper and drove hard wood splines into her seams, for, though it made her as tight as a bottle, it made her as solid as one too.

For half a century Maldon held a barge race at irregular intervals, apparently whenever funds were available. Usually there were three or four starters, though once at least there were five ; all trading craft registered at Maldon, starting from scratch, and sailing without restrictions. *Mermaid* won the last·race, in 1929, and once the *Saltcote Belle* took the cup outright with three successive wins. Unfortunately the records have not been preserved.

The *Emma* did a wonderful amount of sea-work for a comparatively small barge. At one time she was trading regularly to Newcastle, and on the night of the gale in which the Rye lifeboat was lost she was actually running around Dungeness with 140 tons of Portland stone. The mate was washed overboard, but saved himself by catching the lee vang, yet she steered perfectly and never lost a sail. She is—or was till she was blown to pieces— a fine example of the beautiful handy type of craft built at Maldon. I recall seeing another of these, the *Ready*,[1] cast off from the tier at Woolwich one day before the skipper had intended. She was lying head to wind and tide, with only mainsail and topsail set, yet she bore away and threaded out through the traffic with no head-sail set like a twelve-metre.

*Venta* is another Maldon barge—she was built by Howard as the *Jason*—and was once abandoned in the Channel by her crew,

[1] Since renamed *Mirosa*.

picked up by French fishermen, and towed into Boulogne. She has had her share of adventures, having been blown ashore off Newhaven beach on another occasion, after which she was ' doubled ' and given her present name.

It was in *Venta* that I served a few months as mate with Alfred Eaglestone, of Faversham, a real old coaster skipper who had been master of sea-going barges since he was eighteen. Like the *Veravia*, she is an out-and-out coaster type, quite a different proposition from the smaller barges like the *Mayland*, *Falconet*, and *General Jackson*—better at sea, with high bulwarks and good sheering ends, but less handy and unable to get up to Marriage's Mills above bridges.

The negotiating of these bridges calls for plenty of judgment. The largest barge to engage in this work measures only a few inches less between her keelson and the top of her wheel than the distance between the bed of the channel and the girders of the Hythe bridge, so the tide has to be right to a fraction if she is neither to take the ground nor knock the top spoke off the wheel.

Greatly as the present Colchester fleet of barges varies in size, however, one and all would have been considered fine, great sea-going vessels only a few decades ago, justifying quite a bit of swank on any skipper's part. There have been two tendencies at work since the First World War. On the one hand, the little wharves like Salcot, Beaumont, and Mersea Strood have come to be used less and less, and at the same time the millers have come to demand bigger and bigger ' parcels,' so that the really small barges, taking less than five hundred quarters, have become uneconomic, and most of these have been sold out of the Colchester fleet. Many of the hulls may be seen in the Heybridge canal or at Maldon being used as timber lighters, including *Rose*, *Diligent*, *Keeble*, and *Oak*, which last-named had the distinction of a beautiful elliptical stern, which was as great a delight to the eye as it was a nuisance to the skipper in dock, where it got horribly in the way. Another of these barges, the *Peace*, went lightering for a while, and was then bought for a yacht, being converted at considerable expense. She was so named because she was launched on the last day of the Crimean War.

The passing of the 450-quarter barge is to be lamented, for they were handsome and handy craft. At the other end of the scale the competition of the steamer and the motor-craft—specially the Dutch coaster—has largely driven the sailing vessel out of the long-distance trades, particularly the cross-Channel work, till now few of the Colchester skippers fancy even a trip to Dover. The result is that the big fellows and the medium fellows are now concentrating on the comparatively short trips to Colchester, Ipswich, and Norwich. On one occasion, having a midday tide and a southerly breeze, we took *Venta*, drawing seven feet six inches, over the top of the Ridge and up the Rays'n. The skipper's comment was, " I'll bet she feels uncomfortable. In her young days she wasn't afloat till she had ten fathoms under her ! "

The Dutchmen, who were the barges' chief competitors up to the Second World War, came to Colchester chiefly with Danish clay for the Moler works. The gasworks coal-trade is now carried on by Everard's nicely proportioned and hideously named motor-coasters, branded with such insults to maritime tradition as *Angularity* and *Assiduity*. Quite large vessels are now got up on spring tides, but the first time a six-hundred-tonner arrived brought scenes of great consternation to the Hythe. She arrived and unloaded successfully, but when the time came to turn her around it was found that either the ship was two feet too long or the swinging berth two feet too short. It took two tugs two tides to coax her down stern first to where she could be swung. Since then the swinging berth has been enlarged.

The decline of the small barge and the little port brings us naturally to the ' stackie.' Forty years ago barges laden with ten-foot stacks were to be seen everywhere ; then, with the decline in London horse traffic and the competition of the motor-lorry, they became rare indeed. The last few years have seen a sudden and unexpected revival, with a big demand for straw for paper-making at mills near Queenborough, in Kent. Only a few months ago I had an experience I had never expected to enjoy, of sailing thither aboard a floating straw-stack, and found all I had been told by the old-timers about the seaworthiness of barges in this extraordinary trim to be true. We went bucking and bowling across in the teeth of a strong sou'westerly, which just allowed us to fetch the East Swale. Aft at the wheel, under the lee of the stack, one hardly realized it was blowing, for with so bulky a cargo the barge was in ideal trim and as lively as a lifeboat.

Standing on top of the stack, one had to catch hold of something to avoid being rolled off, and it was remarkable from that vantage-point to watch her raising her anchor flukes clear out of the water at every lift and dipping the shackle beneath the surface at every plunge, yet she made astonishingly good weather of it and seemed quite unperturbed by the tremendous windage. The flat, beamy Maldon barges built for this work have come into their own again, and the old skippers have been busy showing their younger brethren how to take the main brails to the dolly winch above the anchor windlass forward and bury the whole deck amidship with trusses. Stack fores'ls, working on wire horses on top of the straw, have been brought out again, and all the time-honoured tricks of ' stackie ' rigging rediscovered. For all that, however, I do not know that I should care to take a stackie to windward through Gravesend and up to the Pool or above bridges, which was the usual destination in the old days. It is bad enough in those waters when you can see where you are going.

The hufflers of the old ' stackie ' days were rare characters. The pilot of Salcot Creek used to keep his fairway from filling up by ' accidentally ' putting his barge ashore at just such an angle as would send the tide scouring away over the shoal he wanted dislodged. His counterpart in the Walton backwaters, when he had to take a barge up at night, would leave his lamp in his window, and when the moment came invariably gave the stentorian order to " bear away for the harbour lights."

Tales are told too of the way these ' stackies ' used to lie about waiting for a wind to suit them. Alfred Eaglestone had made no fewer than three trips to Ipswich while a pair of them lay wind-bound at Pin Mill. On the third occasion, as he ran past with a fine northerly breeze, he sang out and asked the skipper of one of them why they did not get under way. " That ain't a mite of use, mate," came back the reply ; " we shouldn't never fetch Limehouse Reach ! "

But then old Alf, himself a Kentish man, found his great delight in stories at the expense of Essex ways—particularly while I was sailing with him.

# XXII

## PASSAGES GOOD AND BAD

High water at London Bridge,
Half-ebb in the Swin ;
Low water in Yarmouth Roads
And half-flood at Lynn.

*Coasting Bargeman's Tide-rhyme*

THE old coasting days saw some wonderful passage-making.
While sailing in *Venta* I noted from her old cargo book her
voyages in 1926. These are the trips she made : Yarmouth to
London with old rubber, and London to Newport with wheat
(January) ; Wareham to Battersea with clay (February) ; London
to Yarmouth with wheat (March) ; London to Yarmouth with
wheat (April) ; Antwerp to Poole with cement (May) ; Portland
to London with stone and Antwerp to Shoreham with tiles
(June) ; London to Shoreham with wheat (July) ; Boom to Shoreham with bricks (August) ; Neil to Isleworth with bricks (September) ; London to Poole with maize (October) ; a lightering
freight from Portland Harbour to the quay with coal, and then
Portland to Pimlico with stone (November) ; London to Newport with wheat (December).

Her skipper at this time was W. Cresswell, and she carried a
mate and a boy as third hand. She had, of course, no engine.
That was not a bad season's sailing, for in addition to the voyages
mentioned it will be seen that several long trips had to be made
light, including two out to Antwerp from London and return
trips from Yarmouth and Shoreham, which are, of course, not
included among the freights. And in addition there is all the
time spent loading and unloading, waiting for freights, and doing
the annual refits to be allowed for. Furthermore, the man who
reflects that he could have done as well in a snug, twenty-ton
cutter should realize that risks cannot be taken in a barge full
of precious grain, perhaps three thousand pounds' worth of it.

No, it cannot be said that skipper Cresswell and his mate were overpaid for their year's work, for the crew's share, based on half the total freights after certain deductions have been made, amounts to only £338. Thus, after the boy had had his two shillings a day while actually on passage, the skipper received only just over four pounds a week, and the mate just over two pounds, for the traditional allowance is "two-thirds of the crew's half for the skipper, one-third for the mate." The sailorman's lot has certainly been improved since those days, for a skipper as busy as this would now reckon to earn six or eight pounds a week.

I have often asked barge skippers how these remarkable voyages were made in former days, and invariably the answer is that the weather was far better then. Personally I am of the opinion that the weather always has appeared to be deteriorating and always will—just as there were always twice as many fish about when grand-dad was a lad. Yet I do not believe a barge without an engine could be got about in such a dashing fashion to-day, and certainly it is true that craft cheerfully ' hooked down ' at night in Swin in a way they would not do without uneasiness in the most settled weather nowadays. To-day twenty freights a year is reckoned good going, but the small barges of forty years ago did a lot better than this.

Here are a few samples of passages good and bad. When he had the *Gertrude May* Alf Eaglestone was lying in the Swale, loaded for Southampton with coal. It was just a fortnight to Christmas, and as they were likely to be away then they were spending a week-end at home in Faversham. But on going to turn in the skipper noticed a lovely little nor'-west wind, and, despite his poor wife's remonstrances, routed out his son (later skipper of the *Valdora*), who was then mate with him. Going aboard they got under way for Dover. Off the South Foreland the wind freed, and they stood on, carrying three head sails all down Channel, and made Southampton without damping their decks. While unloading there Alf was sent for by the manager of a shipyard, who was perplexed as to how to get the *Berengaria's* propellers to London. The rail would not take them in the Christmas rush, and the liner was waiting for them to be altered and refitted. A specially made wooden template showed they could just be canted to go into the *Gertrude May's* hold, and away they went again.    This time they had less easy conditions, but the well-chocked propellers were an ideal freight, and lightly loaded with the weight in the right place, low down in the barge, she was " like a little lifeboat."    Again they made the passage without a stop and spent Christmas at home after all—with a nice penny to celebrate on.    So pleased was the shipyard manager that he insisted on the *Gertrude May* taking the propellers back after the job had been done.

But it was not always so easy.    One day three barges lay in Harwich bound for Wells, in Norfolk.    The youngest skipper went out to lie out in Hollesley Bay, and the eldest commented, " That's a fine harbour.    Crazy place to go and lie."    And then, since second thoughts are not always the wisest, " If he can stand it we can."    So he went too.    As it happened the night was calm as a clock, but in the morning there were unmistakable signs of an easterly blow, and once again, as so often happens, neither skipper was going to be the one to run back first, so off they went, and when the older man passed Yarmouth he found the youngster lying at anchor in the Roads.    Soon after he parted his chain and went ashore there, where he sank.    Meanwhile the third barge was along, and the two vessels went careering on together, running through the gathering darkness under fores'ls and tops'l sheets. Wells lights went by, opening and shutting in a flash, and soon they were in the shoals of the Wash.    Here the third barge struck, and she too sank, the lifeboat taking off the crew.    The old-timer ran on through the north-west channel and into Boston Mudhole.    Even then there was no peace for him.    He had to clear out of it at four in the morning and fight the southerly gale again.    Thus he came to Wells.    " I'm glad to see you," said the broker.    " The others aren't here yet."    " Nor yet they won't be neither," was the only reply he got.

In the 108-mile-an-hour gale of November 23, 1938, the worst for eight years, nine barges (*Grecian*, *Astrild*, *Decima*, *Ailsa*, *Britisher*, *Raybell*, *Royalty*, *Cetus*, and *Una*) were all caught, having mustered together and left Yarmouth.    Ashore, dragging or running north they gave the Aldeborough and Great Yarmouth lifeboats one of the busiest days in their history.    Some were towed in by lifeboats and tugs, but, though their crews stood by them with obstinate pluck, others had in the end to be abandoned, and some which drove clear of the sands were picked up later off the coast of Germany. But as they were not Colchester or Maldon craft, that story must keep.

Nor are the adventures confined to the sea-going coaster. One Easter over forty years ago the Rochester barge *Formosa* came out of Colchester. There was a lot of wind nor'-westerly, but the men wanted to get home for the Easter Gillingham Fair. As she stood along the Maplins a snow squall hit her, and over she went. The skipper, who was below, scrambled up to find her over on her beam ends, but he and the mate got clear in the boat and were picked up. The *Alice* left Colchester on the same tide, but she went across the Rays'n and brought up off Shore Ends. Then she went over the Ridge when the tide turned, and so reached Gillingham. The men were surprised to find the *Formosa* missing, and when news of her capsize came through they went out to look for her. They found the little forty-ton double-ended barge *Hector* made fast to what they thought at first was a whale, but it turned out to be the *Formosa's* black-leaded bottom. Presently an Ipswich steam-boat came along and, getting a wire round her, towed her right in to the Shears. The gear, of course, was all torn out of her, and according to Frank Carr, who tells the tale in his *Sailing Barges*, her anchor chain was burnished bright as silver. Before the capsize the *Formosa* was a 'stumpy' (and a very smart one at that), but when she was rerigged she was given a tops'l in accordance with the trend of fashion.

A similar but more tragic event occurred about twenty years ago, when two Colchester barges, both having members of the Colchester barging family of Gosling on board, father and son, were caught in a southerly blow in the same place. The father was then mate of the *Clara*, and in that powerful barge they succeeded in beating across into the shelter of the Medway. His son, skipper of the *Excelsior*, attempted to do likewise, but by this time the sea in the tideway was too much, and the *Excelsior* capsized and sank, both hands being drowned. It is thought the boat got adrift on her hatches and ripped up the cloths, for the last vessel to see her reported her in trouble with this. The Colchester skippers now have instructions when caught by a southerly gale off Southend to blow ashore to leeward at high water and take the risk of damage rather than attempt the dash to shelter under the Kent coast.

Occasionally—marvellously seldom, it seems to me—the narrow neck of the Swin claims a victim. The wreck of the *Swan* on the Barrow was a familiar sight for some years before the war. And of course the Spitway itself has always been a trap. A weakness of the barge is that if she gets ashore and bumps, her steering is very likely to be put out of action, and several have ended their days in the Spitway after being first disabled in this way.

The 'back door,' or alternative route to the Spitway, is round the Foulness Beacon or sometimes at high water over the top of the Ridge sand into the Whitaker and the Rays'n channel. This route is favoured at certain states of wind and tide, though nothing like as much as in the days of stack-barges, when there would generally be a fleet lying at Shore Ends. During prolonged spells of bad weather these barges would take turns to sail to Burnham for provisions. But this route is also not without its pitfalls. The Whitaker is a wicked place to lie when an easterly gale contests the issue with the rushing Crouch ebb, and in the winter of 1940–41 the barge *Azariah* was swamped at anchor there and lost with her hands.

Nor is the crossing of the Ridge to be trifled with, handy route as it is if one can get to the spot at high water. One night, shortly before the war, the Colchester barge *Leslie West* attempted it and went ashore at high water. She did not float on the next day's flood, and as the tides were now taking off and there was half a gale of wind, making it unlikely that any other barge would be about to report her predicament, the skipper, J. Mumford, climbed overboard on to the sand at the next ebb and walked along the top of the Ridge to Foulness. He had to flounder his way across dykes and ditches till he got to a phone and rang up the owners. Then he started back, and I should be surprised if that skipper, getting on in years, did not feel exhausted when he got back on board after the exertion of that tramp on top of the nervous strain of the stranding (and no one who has not experienced it knows what a strain that is) and the knowledge that if he failed to find the *Leslie West* in the gathering dark there was little chance for him.

However, find her he did, and so did the barge *Alaska*, which was sent out from Colne next day with a strong crew.  Conditions were such that as they came clear of Colne Bar the fo'c'sle hatch was washed off, though the barge was, of course, light.  Even so, they got her alongside so neatly that when the two barges were aground they put hold hatches across for gangplanks, and humped across enough of the *Leslie West's* grain to lighten her, so that when next tide came she floated, and she and her consort sailed successfully home.  Even then her troubles were not over.  They moored up at Fingringhoe buoys, and Skipper Mumford went home to Colchester.  The exhausted young mate made up a good fire in the cabin and turned in.  He turned out to find the cabin on fire, so after the rest of her cargo was discharged she had to have a new cabin as well as some caulking and fastening.

One of the crew of the *Alaska* that trip was Michael Bligh, of Wivenhoe, who had a queer experience when he went to fetch the *Bankside* from Ramsgate.  He had for mate a youngster straight from one of the training-ships who had never been in a barge before, but in spite of this and the unpromising weather he got under way and was soon rolling and jumping off the North Foreland.  He had his hands too full to think of his mate for a while, and to his horror when he came to look for him he had disappeared.  He searched the barge without result, and came to the conclusion that he had been washed overboard.  An exhausting night's sail brought him to Shoebury, and there he realized that he did not even know the boy's name.  It seemed such a strange tale to take to the police that he was convinced they would decide he had done away with the lad.  Then some instinct made him open the barge's chain locker right for'd, to find the terrified lad hiding there where he had crawled in a panic.  Whether it was from this experience of mates I do not know, but the *Bankside* often used to be sailed single-handed after that.

One of the worst ordeals experienced by bargemen recently was that of the crew of Cunis's *Stour*, which left Colne sand-laden from Rowhedge one Monday morning at the end of December 1935.  The steering carried away in a breeze in the Swin, and she went ashore on the Buxey, where the crew had to take to the rigging.  There they remained for ninety-six hours, unable to get flares alight in the gale blowing.   Steamships, barges, and a fishing-boat all passed by, but they could not attract their attention. Finally, on the Saturday morning, after the two men had gone five days without food and water, they succeeded in attracting the attention of the barge *Genesta* by sounding their foghorn.   They were brought into Colchester hospital frost-bitten and exhausted.

War took a heavy toll of the Essex barges.   No fewer than five of the Colchester fleet either became total losses or suffered substantial damage from mines, wrecks, or enemy aircraft.   The first victim was the *Emma*, which in March 1941 was lying near a Norwegian steamer at Rotherhithe when the Norwegian exploded a mine.   The blast blew the stern off the *Emma*, and the mate was buried under the debris of the cabin, where he was washing up at the time.   The skipper was aft at the wheel and was thrown thirty feet against the mast.   Both had miraculous escapes from serious injury, for a 200-ton coke lighter alongside the *Emma* simply disappeared.

In December 1942 the *Gertrude May* was sailing past Clacton when she exploded a mine and sank immediately, together with the Norwegian mate.   Skipper Farrington, who was blown in the air, was picked up by the crew of another barge without a scratch.   In the same month the *Bankside* was mined off the Maplin sands, and this time the skipper was lost.   Only the after-half of the barge was left afloat with the mate, who lowered the boat from the davits and was picked up six hours later by the Tollesbury smack *Iris Mary*, plastered in flour and still in a dazed condition.   After these two disasters the firm's barges were ' wiped ' against magnetic mines.

But there were still other enemies.   The *Castanet* ran on a wreck in the Orwell in February 1943 and sank, happily without casualties.   A more tragic incident occurred the following month when the *Alaric* was machine-gunned from the air.   Six yellow-nosed fighters attacked the defenceless sailing-vessel with an inferno of machine-gun fire and cannon shells, and the skipper, Harry James Eves, died of his wounds a quarter of an hour after the attack.   His son, Adam, escaped with only a scratch.   The *Alaric* was extensively damaged, but has since been completely refitted.   Many other barges well known on Colne and Blackwater underwent similar ordeals.   One of Horlock's Mistley barges, the *Blue Mermaid*, went down within a hundred yards of where the *Gertrude May* was lost, sunk by an enemy mine and totally lost together with her crew in July 1941. The *Resolute*, of the same firm, was mined off the mouth of the Crouch in January 1943, when the skipper was rescued but the mate drowned. The steel barge *J.B.W.* (Metcalfe, London) was lost off the Maplin edge with her crew, and another vessel, the 600-ton motor-ship *Jolly Gals*, of Mistley, went down in December 1940 near the Tyne. Of Everard's coal-boats, serving the Essex gas-works, as many as nineteen were lost.

I have selected these few tales to show that neither in peace nor war is the bargeman's life all placid drifting by grassy river meads.

# XXIII

## THE FUTURE—IF ANY

*Prospects for Fishermen and Dredgermen—The Role of Marketing—*
*Barges, but No One to sail them—Will the Good Life again be valued ?*

THE preceding chapters have been concerned largely with looking
back.   As a final luxury I would ask to be allowed the indulgence
of a glance ahead to let my fancy roam over a picture of what these
unchanging estuaries may perhaps look like to generations to
come.

We have to face the fact that almost everything we have
described here appears in its present form obsolete or obsolescent.
All these smacks and barges seem destined ultimately to disappear
as surely as the brigs and peter-boats before them.   How much
does it all matter ?   In a world striving to revolutionize every
aspect of its social, economic, and political system you may say,
very little.   The world cannot stand still, and, however much
one loves the old practices, one cannot expect to see them perpetuated as museum pieces simply because they are picturesque.
Certainly this seems to be the attitude of most English people, who
view with remarkable equanimity the disappearance of sail from
around their coasts.   Old churches and mills, houses and farms,
are recorded and preserved with at least something of the attention they deserve.   Local archæological societies exist in their
interest, and a Royal Commission has surveyed them.   Yet the
fishing-boats and barges are suffered to rot in the saltings, and,
though a few enthusiasts have preserved their lines and even made
models of many types, no effort is made to preserve the actual
hulls, as has been done in Brittany, where they have preserved
some of the old Newfoundland cod schooners in the docks, their
holds fitted out with models (some life-size, using the actual ship's
boats) and panoramas showing the methods of fishing in which
they were employed.   Yet in Essex most of the old builders'

half-models have been lost or broken up. My own collection, from Wivenhoe shipyard, I rescued in the nick of time after they had been sold for firewood ! How splendid it would be if in this country we could collect actual samples of the disappearing coastal craft along the embankment at Westminster—and how unlikely ! We need a real, live maritime museum, one that will show how passing generations of sailormen have lived and worked, as well as how many silver buttons Nelson wore on his coat, just as we need real agricultural museums, but until this country acquires an appreciation of those two fundamentals, the sea and the land, we are unlikely to have either.

That is not the axe I wish to grind at the moment, however. To preserve something of the past is important ; to keep alive something of the present in the future is better.

The most constructive suggestion I have seen for the inshore fishery industry appeared in an article in *The Times* in October 1945. It suggested the establishment at the little ports (such as Tollesbury, Brightlingsea, Maldon, Wivenhoe, and Mersea) of small refrigerating plants and a sales organization consisting of a few vans which would make regular rounds of the inland villages, where the taste of fish is almost unknown, with wet fish, and perhaps in the evening fried fish as well. The refrigerators would have to take, say, five days' supply, so that bumper catches were not wasted and the housewives were not let down when a gale kept the boats in. This could be done, but I doubt if it will be while the industry is in charge of a minor department of the Ministry of Agriculture and Fisheries and of the County Sea Fisheries Committees, which are more interested in making regulations as to the mesh of nets and receiving statistics of the decline of the industry from their Fishery Officers than they are in devising bold, constructive measures for its rebuilding. The Inshore Fishing Industry Bill of 1945 offers generous loans and grants towards the cost of new boats, but I fancy the fisherman would rather have the market guaranteed and find his own boats as his father did. In default of any co-operative marketing scheme, such as the Belgian Government provided so successfully after the First World War, a few smacks will always pick up a living supplying soles, plaice, and dabs to hotels and fish-shops whose customers can distinguish fresh fish from stale. Roker will continue to be in demand for the fried-fish shops, and I trust the canners have put an end to the old wasteful slumps in sprats, but I cannot see it being a big or properly rewarded industry, for, with the exception of the roker for the 'frying to-night' merchant, the inshore man cannot compete in the Billingsgate market with the deep-sea scraper.

Oysters ought to stage a recovery, though here, again, the system of control is often obsolete and unsuitable, particularly in the case of the famous Colchester fishery. Management by town councillors and dredgermen is a decorative system in times when all goes well, but a knowledgeable board of directors with a little capital behind it would serve better when things are difficult, especially under modern conditions when the labourer expects to be rewarded for his hire. Yet I trust the oyster will re-establish himself and hold his own despite, rather than thanks to, the efforts of his cultivators, for when every healthy specimen can give birth to a family of millions, every survivor of which may in due course be worth a silver shilling, it seems clear that the world owes the oyster a living. It has refused to do without that delicacy for two thousand years, and I doubt if it ever will consent to do so. But unless nature is exceptionally well disposed, or the scientists produce some revolutionary improvements in method (and, still more difficult, persuade the dredgermen to accept them !), some modernization of organization at the sacrifice of tradition may be necessary, as has, in fact, been the tendency at Mersea.

Wildfowling has become mainly an amateur's sporting pastime, and eels, guard-fish, and herring will never again be more than a semi-sporting side-line. " King Harrys " have gone for good, and I doubt if the succulent scollops down Channel will again lure smacks from Essex to dredge them.

Sprats are a puzzle. For the first time in living memory the harvest has almost entirely failed during the war years 1942–44. Some mystery of nature may have changed the sprats' habits for ever, just as it seems the eel-grass is never going to grow again on the Essex mud. If they do return (as hauls in 1945 suggest they still may do) I doubt if the ancient and interesting system of stow-boating will be long revived. It belongs essentially to the days before power made sprat-trawling possible, and it mars the fish by crushing them in tons in the nets, leaving them inferior to those caught by the Suffolk drifters and the Poole trawlers, which can bring them ashore without even rubbing the scales off.

During the war two refugee Belgian fishermen from Ostend settled at Wivenhoe, and before long were second to none in fishing the Essex waters. They were amused at seeing stow-boating still carried on. " That is how our grandfathers caught sprats," they said. " Our fathers gave it up and worked beam-trawls ; we with our motor-smacks use otter-trawls and trawl against the tide." (Sprats, it should be remembered, usually swim head to tide.) To my regret the failure of the shoals after their arrival prevented them putting their methods to the test, but an otter-trawl seems the likeliest method for spratting in Thames Estuary channels, which are too constricted and full of traffic for drift-nets. Indeed, the beam-trawl has had its day for all kinds of fishing, and, though it has served in Essex six hundred years for certain, it is unlikely to outlast the present generation.

So much for the fishing. What about the barges ? Again it is the same tale. No form of transport has so far been developed to compete with them. They remain economically as modern as to-morrow, the one form of cargo-carrying under sail of which this can be said. Of course, the old tag that " the wind costs nothing " is quite misleading. A barge's mainsail is worth well over a hundred pounds. If she breaks her sprit there is another hundred pounds. Every time she fits out coils and coils of hemp and manilla and gallons of paint go aboard. Yet she is still a wonderful earner. She may present her owner with a bill for five hundred pounds and then work five thousand pounds' worth of freights without costing a penny. The Government-subsidized Dutchmen could beat her on some freights, but not all. She may in time have to be modified as power becomes cheaper and more efficient, but under present conditions she remains easily able to beat rail and road on her own ground. Yet no more are being built. Why ? Largely because of the problem of crews. The owners are constantly being faced with the difficulty of finding men for the barges, and will not put down capital on craft which may be laid up for this reason.

Young barge skippers are comparatively few. I know some very able ones, but they remain the exception. (One of these, by the way, found himself in the Admiralty Court following a collision.    The aged judge so angered him by asking acidly if he was not very young to be the master of a vessel that the only reply he could think of was, " Surely you are very old to be a judge." He managed to swallow the words, but became so tongue-tied that he lost his case as a result.)    The more promising young mates generally step ashore and stay there before they take charge. The reason is that since the abolition of the third hand boys are no longer brought up to barging.    Too many men ship as mates just temporarily till something better turns up.    That little bit of niggardliness in saving the third hand's two shillings a day is proving to have been one of the worst things the sailing-barge industry ever did.

In 1946 Francis and Gilders, of Colchester, with ten fewer barges than they owned at the outbreak of war, are finding the problem of crews so insoluble that the process of selling off the smallest craft has started with the disposal of the *Golden Fleece* for a yacht. Apparently the eventuality has been long foreseen, for the Colchester Harbour Master tells me he recalls his grandfather telling him there would be barges after there were men to sail them.

If the worst comes to the worst, and the last British sailing merchant vessel disappears (which to me would be a tragedy comparable with the destruction of, say, all the Tudor farm-houses in Essex), we shall probably see big lighters take the spritties' place. This has already happened in the carrying of newsprint and cement from Kent to London, and I suppose these ungainly and soulless monsters could be dragged to sea.    They would have the advantage that they could be used as floating warehouses.    A tug could bring four hundred tons of grain to Maldon or Colchester, leave it under the elevators, do another job, and call back for the empties.    It would be a more regular life than the sailorman enjoys, though I know which I should prefer.    And I know that when the brown sails no longer pass my windows on the tide I shall no longer want to live beside the Colne.

I am prepared to say good-bye without regret to the little floating slums that were the sailing-coasters of the nineteenth century, where poverty, ignorance, and filth prevailed, and to the swanky steam-yachts and holystoned clippers of the ' classic ' days of yachting, which involved such a ludicrous squandering of money, and were symbols of social and economic perversity in their contrast between conditions in the fo'c'sle and the saloon such as not even the beauty of a schooner's snowy canvas can justify, but the life of a modern barge skipper is a good life, and the wiser men know it. He lives, his own master, in a clean and healthy little home, earns good money in the wholesomest fashion, and keeps his mind alive by jogging about. He does not have to sell himself body and soul to that hard master, the sea, as does the deep-sea man, for he is unlucky if he cannot get home at least once a month. And who could be more fortunate than the owner of a flourishing little oyster farm, earning good money, working the hours God and the tides, not the clock in the factory lobby, tell him, monarch of all he surveys. " Oh, happy husbandman, did he but know his fortune ! " The worker on the bigger fisheries, too, should be able to have his lot made attractive. Oysters enjoy such a favoured position in the market that the livelihood ought always, with sound management, to be a good one—yet we have seen the straits to which some are reduced.

I therefore beg for these occupations a place in the world of to-morrow even more honoured than that which they occupied in the age that is dying. I plead that they shall cease to be regarded as the Cinderella of callings—a good corner for the boy too simple to hold his own ashore, or for old men who are quaint, entertaining, W. W. Jacobs burlesques—but rather that they shall be made attractive to the keenest and most intelligent youngsters.

At present we are naturally and properly intoxicated by the success of man's struggle to obtain decent living-rates for reasonable working-hours. It has taken generations to get as far as we have ; who shall say the present age is not right to rejoice in the fruits it has fallen to its lot to enjoy ? But there are other standards, and I for one am dreamer enough to hope that when modern education is over its teething, and when man has enjoyed his economic rights long enough to turn round and say, " A pound a day for a six-hour day is very nice—what next ? " he may find the answer in a new perspective, which, since there are no new perspectives under the sun, will prove to be as old and as young as the perspectives of the Elizabethan adventurers and their spiritual descendants ever since, and once again may perceive the virtue of valuing a job by how good it is as well as by what it brings in. A wet shirt may yet be deemed preferable to a weary mind. Indeed, there is evidence that many among the young men leaving the Forces share that view. Many a youngster, and some not so young, leaving the R.N.V.R. will never settle comfortably again on an office stool. The best of these look longingly towards the dying industries here discussed. Had we but the vision to make it possible for the fisherman or the mate of a coaster to enjoy the same standards of living and social status as the fishmonger or the shipping-office clerk, how many personal post-war problems might be solved, how much human health and happiness promoted ! And let it not be said that the intelligent and enthusiastic amateur cannot succeed in such pursuits. Have I not just returned from a capital little voyage in that pretty little barge the *Gold Belt*, the last of the small coasters, whose owner-skipper, an amateur yachtsman who had scarcely sailed aboard a barge or known the Thames Estuary before 1939, has handled and managed her with profit and pleasure throughout six years of war. I must admit he is the first amateur I have known to succeed in this undertaking, but there is no reason why he should be the last.

Of course, if all the fishing- and trading-vessels disappear off the waters there will still be the small yachts, for perversely enough probably the whole art of sailing has never been so widely understood as in the days of its decline. But best of all sports as this is, it can never replace the old callings which have bred a type of man as gentlemanly and wise in his own way as any on earth. I wish, since these chapters are intended as an inadequate ' vale ' to him, that it had been possible to devote one to recapturing for posterity the extraordinary liveliness of mind and gentility of nature which make him the salt of the earth. I cannot do it, and I am not prepared to try. Let him sleep undisturbed.

Instead I will abandon gloomy reality and pay a final wishful visit to Colne or Blackwater in A.D. 2046. There go the oyster dredgers ! Now, now—suppress that churlish instinct to comment that they don't make half such a picture as the old cutters used to under sail ! They are comely little bawleys, well kept, power-driven, and obviously prosperous. We must go aboard one presently and hear how scientific methods have improved oyster cultivation since the old days when they used to chuck culch on the muddy bottom of the creek.

Those sprits'l barges have hardly altered at all. They are steel-built though, and have a motor-windlass on the fore-deck for the anchor. They are, if anything, sweeter in build even than the old *Varuna* and *Emma*, though no doubt they have an auxiliary propeller under the quarter.

But, hello—here is something new ! What a splendid motor-coaster lying at anchor waiting for water ! No funnel. Is she electrically driven ? A Dutchman, no doubt. No, by Jove—a red ensign on her stern ! Let's go aboard. The skipper and his wife have just finished tea. The television wireless-set is tuned in to a symphony concert from some future Queen's Hall. (You smile ? Well, what did you expect to catch him doing—chewing tobacco and spitting in the stove ?) The music ends, and he picks up a book to show his wife. Why, it is this book, our book, the book we are now just finishing. "These old tales are interesting," he says. "All about some of the old craft my grand-dad used to tell me of. What things they used to get up to in the bad old days ! How ever they did it, and all under sail, beats me ! "

# INDEX

(s.b. = sailing-barge ; s.y. = steam yacht)

*Ada*, smack, 59
*Ailsa*, s.b., 182
*Ala*, yacht, 71
*Alaric*, s.b., 186
*Alaska*, s.b., 185
*Alastor*, barque, 19
*Alciope*, collier, 111
Aldous, Brightlingsea, 31, 41, 75
*Alert*, collier, 111
*Alexandra*, police boat, 139
*Alexandra*, yacht, 53
*Alice*, s.b., 183
*Alice*, s.y., 103
*Alice Watts*, s.b., 26
*Alpha*, smack, 104
Alresford, 20–21, 61 *et seq.*
*Amaryllis*, yacht, 121
*Amelia*, smack, 75
*Amelia*, yacht, 71
*America*, yacht, 53
America's Cup, 102
*Anemone*, yacht, 53
Anglesey, Henry William Paget, first Marquis of, 51
*Angularity*, m.v., 178
*Ann and Elizabeth*, s.b., 114, 119
*Anne Gallant*, 32
*Annie*, smack, 68
*Antelope*, ketch, 47
*Arabian*, barque, 55
*Ariadny*, yacht, 53
*Arno*, collier, 111
*Arnold Hirst*, s.b., 26, 27
*Argus*, revenue cutter, 133
*Arrow*, yacht, 52
*Assiduity*, m.v., 178
*Astrild*, s.b., 182
*Audax*, yacht, 53
*Azariah*, s.b., wreck of, 184

*Badger*, cutter, 135
*Bakalvum*, yacht, 53
Baker, Mr and Mrs, 47, 77–78

*Bankside*, s.b., 175, 185 ; wreck of, 186
*Banshee*, collier, 100, 111, 121
*Barbara*, 21
Barge race, 97 ; at Maldon, 176
Barges, swim-head, 24 ; boomie, 26–27 ; war toll of, 186 *et seq.*
Baring-Gould, Rev. S., 19, 76–77
Barnard, Thomas, 68
Barnard, Turner, John, and Ben, 70
Barnes, Charles, 48
Barr and Hockham, Maldon, 116
Barrow Sand, 38
Bass, in Colne, 172
*Batchelor*, smack, 39
Beckwith, Colchester, 25–26
*Beeleigh*, s.b., 114
*Belle*, collier, 111
*Belvedere*, s.b., 114
Bentall, E. H., Maldon, 123
*Berengaria*, s.s., 181
*Bertha*, smack, 59
*Bingo*, yacht, 71
' Bird-tides,' 144
Bitterns, in Essex, 163
Blackwater, 16 *et seq.*
Bligh, M., 185
*Blue*, smack, 81
*Blue Mermaid*, s.b., wreck of, 187
*Bluebell*, smack, 67, 68
Bradwell, 96 *et seq.*
Bradwell Chapel, 19
Bradwell Creek, 18
Bragg, Harry, 34
Brightlingsea, 31 *et seq.* ; memorial tablets in the church, 42 ; characters of, 47 *et seq.*
*Britannia*, collier, 111
*Britannia*, yacht, 176
*British King*, s.b., 116
*British Workman*, smack, 42
*Britisher*, s.b., 182
*Brothers*, s.b., 115
*Brothers*, smack, 80

Brown, Bayard, 56
Browne's ropery, Wivenhoe, 54
Buchan, collier, 111
Buoys, first placing of, 35
Burnham, s.b., 114, 115
Burnham, 114, 135, 136
Burton, Sir William, 71

Cap Pilar, 21
Care, smack, 116
Cariad, yacht, 71
Carter, B., West Mersea, 164
Castanet, s.b., 175 ; wreck of, 186
Cement-stone, 44–45
Cetus, s.b., 182
Channel Islands, 32, 111
Chapelle, Count de la, Tollesbury, 167
Charles and Thomas, collier, 111
Charlotte, smack, 75, 148 et seq.
Charlotte, timber ship, 113
Chiquita, yacht, 71
Chloris, yacht, 53
Christabel, smack, 34, 57
Christine, smack, 57
Christobel, yacht, 41
Christopher, wool-ship, 101
Cicely, yacht, 71
City of London, s.b., 115
Clara, s.b., 176
Clara, yacht, 71
Cockles, in Alresford Creek, 63
Colchester, 20 ; oyster fisheries, 83 et seq.
Colliers, wrecks of, 109
Colne, 20 et seq.
Colne, police boat, 139
Columbine, smack-yacht, 52
Conquest, smack, 34
Conrad, Joseph, 143
Cook, Maldon, 116
Cook, " Gunner," 164
Copperas, 45–46
Coral, collier, 111
Coralie, yacht, 71
Cormorants, breeding of, 76
Cornelius, cutter, 134
Cowper, Frank, 71
Cox and King, 71
Crampton, Walter, 34
Creole, yacht, 59
Cresswell, W., 180–181

Crowland, John, 112
Cushiedoo, yacht, 71

Dagmar, yacht, 53
Daniel, brigantine, 43
D'Arcy, s.b., 104, 116
Daring, brigantine, 115
Darling, yacht, 41
Darnett, s.b., 104
Dauntless, s.b., 121
Dauntless, smack, 38
Dauntless, yacht, 53
Davies Brothers, Brightlingsea, 49
Dawn, s.b., 116
Day Dawn, yacht, 71
Death, Charlie, Brightlingsea, 34
Decima, s.b., 182
Defender, s.b., 104, 116
Defoe, Daniel, 109
Deutschland, wreck of, 35, 67
Diligent, s.b., 119, 177
Dolphin, coaster, 110
Doris, yacht, 71
Dove, Captain, Brightlingsea, 27
Dove, yacht, 41
Drake, Alf, Tollesbury, 167
Drake Brothers, Tollesbury, 103
Druid, yacht, 53
Duchess, s.b., 98
Duchess of Kent, collier, 111
Dufferin, Frederick Blackwood, first Marquis of, 59
Duke of Sussex, collier, 111
Dutch coasters, 178
D'Wit, B. and T., West Mersea, 164

Eager, s.s., 28
Eagle, smack, 39
Earl of Rochford, cutter, 134
Eblana, coaster, 100
Echo, collier, 111
Edward, brigantine, 43
Edwina, yacht, 53, 71
Eel-boats, Dutch, 121
Eel-fishing, 79, 80
Egidie, yacht, 53
Eileen, smack, 38
Elayne, 21
Elfe, yacht, 71
Eliza, oyster boat, 74
Eliza Annie, ketch, 121
Eliza Fraser, collier, 111

*Elizabeth*, collier, 111
*Elizabeth and Mary*, s.b., 114
*Ella*, schooner, 116
*Elsie*, smack, 59
*Elsie*, yacht, 53
*Emblem*, smack, 48
*Emily*, s.b., 116
*Emily*, smack, 35, 49
*Emily Lloyd*, s.b., 121
*Emma*, oyster boat, 74
*Emma*, s.b., 119, 176, 186
*Empress*, s.b., 26
*Empress of India*, s.b., 104
*Endeavour*, collier, 111
*Endeavour*, yacht, 102
*Energy*, ketch, 121
*Erycina*, yacht, 71
*Essex*, collier, 111
*Essex*, sloop, 134
*Essex*, s.s., 28
*Essex Lass*, 126–127
*Ethel Maud*, s.b., 107
*Eva Annie*, s.b., 116
Everard's, London, 178, 187
*Evergreen*, smack, 74
*Evolution*, yacht, 121, 124
*Exact*, s.b., 26
*Excellent*, 34
*Excelsior*, s.b., wreck of, 183
*Express*, smack (Brightlingsea), 24, 48
*Express*, smack (Tollesbury), 104

*Faith*, s.b., 29
*Faith*, smack, 116
*Faithful*, collier 111
*Falcon*, s.b., 115
*Falconet*, s.b., 177
*Fame*, collier, 111
Fance, William, 48
*Fancy*, smack, 59
*Fanny*, brigantine, 121
*Fanny*, s.b., 119
*Favorite*, s.b., 26
*Fawn*, yacht, 41
*Fiddle*, smack, 100
Fingringhoe Creek, 20, 29
*Fiona*, smack, 34
Fish weirs, 64
Fitzgerald, Edward, 54
' Five-fingering,' 103
*Flamingo*, in Essex, 163
*Fleur-de-Lys*, yacht, 41

*Florence*, collier, 111
*Florence*, yacht, 71
*Fontenay*, collier, 111
*Formosa*, s.b., 183
*Fortitude*, collier, 111
*Fortitude*, s.b., 45
*Frances*, s.b., 42
Francis, David, 28
Francis, Joshua, 29
*Freak*, yacht, 53
*Fred*, smack, 75
*Friends*, sloop, 43
*Frigate*, ' peter-boat,' 78
Frost, Drake, 103
Frost, J., 167
' Fruiters,' 126

*Gannet*, yacht, 53
Garfish, 80
Geeting Creeks, 21
*Gem*, s.b., 28
*General Jackson*, s.b., 177
*Genesta*, s.b., 186
*George*, s.b., 115
Gerbault, Alain, 66
*Gertrude*, yacht, 52
*Gertrude May*, s.b., 181, 186
*Gipsy Queen*, smack, 43
*Giralda*, s.b., 97, 175
*Gleaner*, collier, 111
*Glencoe*, schooner, 112
*Gloriana*, s.b., 26
*Gold Belt*, s.b., 194
*Golden Fleece*, s.b., 192
Goldhanger Creek, 18
*Good Intent*, cutter, 134
*Gratitude*, s.b., 45
*Grecian*, s.b., 182
*Green Lettuce*, 32
*Greyhound*, ship, 39
*Greyhound*, smack, 42
*Gudrun*, yacht, 71
Gulls, breeding of, 76

*Halegon*, collier, 111
Ham, Captain W., Wivenhoe, 127
Harris, Enos, 70
Harris, John, 71
Harris, Peter, Rowhedge, 66, 70
Harvey, Wivenhoe, 52, 75, 124
Harvey, Daniel, Wivenhoe, 131–134
Hatcher, Ralph, 26

Havengore, 24, 135
Hawthorne, smack, 33
Heard, Ted, Tollesbury, 102
Heartsease, yacht, 42
Hebe, collier, 111
Hebe, smack, 32
Hector, s.b., 183
Henry, s.b., 113
Henry Grâce-à-dieu, 21
Hesper, s.b., 26
Hetty, smack, 81
Hewes, Charles, West Mersea, 90
Hewes, Woodham, West Mersea, 93
Heybridge Basin, 16, 120 et seq.
Honest Miller, s.b., 115
Honour, smack, 39
Hoo outfall, 145
Hope, yacht, 53
Houston, J. A., Rowhedge, 71
Howard, John, Maldon, 116, 125
Hufflers, 118, 179
Husk, James, Wivenhoe, 54
Hythe, Colchester, 25 et seq.

Impulse, collier, 111
Indian Chief, wreck of, 36
Ingerid, wreck of, 37
Iris Mary, smack, 186
Irona, yacht, 71
Island Home, yacht, 53, 71

J.B.W., s.b., wreck of, 187
Jabez, s.b., 26
Jacon, s.b., 116
James, collier, 111
James, s.b., 114
James and Harriet, s.b., 114
James Balls, s.b., 104
James Cann, s.b., 114, 119
James Garfield, s.b., 42
James Renford, s.s., 28
Jane, collier, 111
Jason, collier, 111
Jason, s.b., 176
Jessie, s.b., 26, 114
Jessie Annandale, brigantine, 55, 128
Joan, yacht, 53
John, collier, 111
John and Charles, ketch, 42
Jolly Gals, m.v., wreck of, 187
Jones, Captain J., 127
Joseph and Mary, smack, 163

Joseph T., smack, 116
Julia, yacht, 52
Julius, of Danzig, 111, 113
Jullanar, yacht, 123–125

Kapunda, ship, 43
Keeble, J., 116
Keeble, s.b., 177
Kemble, Squire Thomas, 159
King, s.b., 28
'King Harrys,' 56
Kingfisher, smack, 64
Kirby, family, Bradwell, 99, 100
Kite, in Essex, 163

L.S.D., s.b., 114
Lady de Crespigny, 55
Lady Harvey, yacht, 71
Lady Hermione, yacht, 59
Lady of the Isles, 49
Lawling Creek, 17
Leavett, Lennox, Tollesbury, 167
Leavett, W., Tollesbury, 167
Leslie West, s.b., 184
Liberty, yacht, 52
Lifeboats, institution of, 35
Lily, smack, 105
Linnett, W., Bradwell, 156, 161–164
Little Express, smack, 104
Lively, oyster boat, 74
Lord Hamilton, s.b., 104
Lord Howick, collier, 111
Lucina, yacht, 71

Maid of the Mill, s.b., 114
Maldon, 16, 106 et seq. ; battle of, 17
Malvoison, s.b., 116
March, smack, 75
Margaret, schooner, 26
Marquis of Huntly, salvage of, 39
Martin-Harvey, Sir John, 53
Mary, collier, 111
Mary, lugger, 134
Mary Ann, collier, 111
Mary Fortune, 32
Mary Kate, s.b., 104
Mascotte, lugger, 43
Mascotte, smack, 34
Masonic, s.b., 27, 48
Matchless, schooner, 126
Matilda Upton, 27
Maud, smack, 116

*May Flower*, collier, 113
*Mayflower*, cutter, 134
*Mayflower*, s.b., 107
*Mayland*, collier, 111
*Mayland*, s.b., 177
Mayland Creek, 17
*Mehalah* (Baring-Gould), 19, 76
*Mermaid*, s.b., 116, 176
*Mermaid*, revenue cruiser, 137
*Merry Thought*, yacht, 71
Mersea, 73 *et seq.*, 137
*Merton*, collier, 111
*Mildreda*, s.b., 176
Mills, " Shaver," Tollesbury, 167
*Minerva*, s.b., 115
*Miranda*, yacht, 53
Models, ship, 189
*Moine*, yacht, 71
*Monara*, yacht, 71
*Monitor*, smack, 79
*Morgan*, smack, 70
*Morning Star*, s.b., 115
*Mosquito*, yacht, 52
Motor-boats, 29
Mulhauser, 121
Mullet-fishing, 173
Mussels, dredging, 81 ; fattening, 88
Mussett, C., West Mersea, 165
Mussett, " Sooty," West Mersea, 90
    *et seq.*, 165, 166–167
Mussett, " Swan," West Mersea, 164 -
    165
*Mystery*, yacht, 52

NASS BEACON, 19, 78
*Nathaniel*, collier, 111
*Neddy Campbell*, smack, 43
*Nef*, wreck of, 35
*Nellie Parker*, s.b., 98
*Neptune*, smack, 75
*New Blossom*, collier, 70
*New Hope*, s.b., 115
*New Unity*, smack, wreck of, 68
*Norman*, smack, 34, 43
Northey Island, 17, 107
*Nottingham*, coaster, 32

*Oak*, s.b., 116, 177
*Odd Times*, 49
*Olivia*, collier, 111
*Onda*, collier, 111
*Orange*, smack, 70

Orman, George, 48
Osea Island, 17
Othona, 19
Oyster, deep-sea, 41 ; dredging, 81,
    83 *et seq.*, 90 *et seq.* ; enemies of, 87 ;
    imports, 89 ; spatting, 89
Oyster feasts, 83, 87, 104
*Oyster*, smack, 75
*Oyster Girl*, smack, 43

PAGET, LORD ALFRED, 52, 71
Paglesham, 94, 136
*Pandora*, hulk, 47
*Pandora*, yacht, 53
Parker, Clem, Bradwell, 97–98, 137
Parker, John, Bradwell, 96
Passage-boats, 28, 119
*Patience*, yacht, 71
Pattens (mud shoes), 76–77
*Pauncey*, 21
*Peace*, s.b., 177
*Pearl*, naval sloop, 52
*Pearl*, yacht, 41, 51–52
*Perseverance*, smack, 43
' Peter-boats,' 78
*Petrel*, collier, 111
*Pioneer*, s.b., 116
*Polka*, collier, 111
*Polly*, smack, 116
' Pont,' 21, 58
Poole, T., Brightlingsea, 49, 170 *et seq.*
Porter, George, Wivenhoe, 64
*Pride*, smack, 34
*Pride of Essex*, s.b., 104, 119
*Pride of the Colne*, s.b., 26
*Prince Albert*, bawley, 79
*Prince of Wales*, police boat, 138, 139
*Princess Mary*, sloop, 134
*Priscilla*, smack, 81
Proctor, H., 164
*Prosperous*, s.b., 29
Pullen, Ivan, 88
Pyefleet Creek, 21

*Quadroon*, yacht, 71
*Queen*, s.b., 28
*Queen*, yawl, 135
Quilter, Sir Cuthbert, 54
Quilter, Dick, Heybridge, 117

*Racer*, smack, 70
Rainbird, B., West Mersea, 164

Rat Island, 146
Ratsey, Charles, 52
Raven, police boat, 139
Raven, s.b., 114
Ravens, at Northey, 163
Raybell, s.b., 182
Ready, s.b., 116, 176
Rebecca, s.b., 26
Record Reign, s.b., 116, 125–126
Recruit, smack, 34, 43
Redoubtable, 175 ,
Reminder, s.b., 175
Rennie, schooner, 170
Repulse, revenue cutters, 131–134
Resolute, s.b., wreck of, 187
Resolute, yacht, 53
Resolution, s.b., 114
Richmond, hulk, 137
Ripple, smack, 37
Ripple, yacht, 119
River Police, Colchester, 138 et seq.
Robert, s.b., 116
Robert Adams, coaster, 100
Rogue in Grain, s.b., 115
Romulus, yacht, 41
Rosabelle, yacht, 53
Rosalind, yacht, 52
Rose, s.b., 119, 177
Rose, smack, 116
Rose, yacht, 53
Rose of Devon, yacht, 53
Rosena, smack, 104
Rowhedge, 20, 66 et seq.
Royal George, yacht, 54
Royal Sailor, collier, 111
Royalty, s.b., 182
Russell, Colonel C., 159, 161, 168

Sadd's, Maldon, 110
St Osyth, 21
Sainty, Philip, Wivenhoe, 51
Salcot, 19, 93, 177
Sales Point, 19
Sally, s.b., 114
Salmon, Fred, Brightlingsea, 49
Salmon, John, Brightlingsea, 35
Saltcote Belle, s.b., 176
Salter, Dr J. H., 163, 164, 166
Sapphire, yacht, 54
Saracen's Head, barquentine, 55
Sarah Lizzie, ketch, 116
Satanella, yacht, 41

' Salvaging,' 35, 67
Scandal, yacht, 54
Schooners, 126
Scollop-fishing, 33
Sea Belle, yacht, 53
Sea Flower, collier, 111
Sea-monsters, 173–174
Seabrook's, barge-owners, 104
Seal, at Brightlingsea, 172
Seine-netting, 172
Septaria—see Cement-stone
Shamrock, yachts, 102
Shear Water, yacht, 53
Shearing for eels, 80
Shipwright, collier, 111
Shrubsole, barge-builder, 97
Sisters, smack, 116
Siwash, yacht, 71
' Skilling,' 32–33
Smack races, 58
Smith, Leo, 164
Smugglers, 130 et seq.
Snowdrop, smack, 75, 81
Snowdrop, yacht, 53
Sonia, schooner yacht, 171
Southern Cross, mission schooner, 59
Sparling, Shedric, Brightlingsea, 34
Spindrift, yacht, 53
Spitty, Jack, 67–68, 74
Spitty family, Bradwell, 99
Sprat-fishing, 56–57
Spray, collier, 111
Spray, schooner, 119
Sprightly, smack, 136
Springfield Wharf, 120
Spy, s.b., 26
' Stackies,' 178
Standard, coaster, 100
Stansgate Point, 17
Startled Fawn, s.b., 26
Statina, timber-ship, 113
Stella, police launch, 139
Stoker, C., West Mersea, 164
Stour, s.b., wreck of, 185–186
Stow-boating, future of, 31, 180
" Stubbins, Old," 162
Success, smack, 137
Sunbeam, s.b., 116
Sunbeam, smack, 59
Sunbeam, s.y., 54
Sunflower, s.y., 71
' Sun-dawgs,' 147

*Surprise*, collier, 111
*Surprise*, s.b., 119
*Susannah*, collier, 111
*Swan*, timber-ship, 113
*Swift*, cutter, 134
Sycamore, Captain, Tollesbury, 102

*Tamesis*, yacht, 42
*Tartar*, smack, 37
Taylor's, sail-makers, 119
*Teaser*, smack, 104
*Telegraph*, smack, 75
Terschelling, 32
*Test*, smack, 34
*Thistle*, smack, 104
*Thistle*, yacht, 123
*Thoma*, yacht, 126
*Thomas*, s.b., 115
*Thomas Stratton*, coaster, 116
*Three Sisters*, collier, 111
Thurslet Creek, 18
*Tillie*, smack, 81
Tollesbury, 84, 102, 137 *et seq.*
Trawling, origin of, 31
*Trio*, collier, 111
Turner, Captain A., Wivenhoe, 176
*Two Friends*, s.b., 119

*Una*, s.b., 182
Underwood, John, Brightlingsea, 49
*Unity*, s.b., 119
*Unity*, smack, 75, 76

*Valdora*, s.b., 181
*Valfreya*, s.y., 56
*Valkyrie*, yacht, 102
*Varuna*, s.b., 175
*Varuna*, s.y., 56
*Venta*, s.b., 150 *et seq.*, 176–177, 180
*Veravia*, s.b., 177
*Verona*, s.b., 97, 175
*Veronica*, s.b., 97
*Vestal*, smack, 34
*Vice Versa*, boat, 171
*Victoria*, collier, 111
*Victoria*, police boat, 139

*Violet*, s.b., 116
*Violet Sybil*, s.b., 97
*Virgo*, collier, 111
*Volante*, yacht, 53
Vosper's, Wivenhoe, 59

*Walpole*, sloop, 134
*Walrus*, s.y., 71
Ward, Elijah, Brightlingsea, 140–141
*Watch Vessel* 21, 137
*Water Lily*, smack, 105
*Water Lily*, yacht, 53
Watson, G. L., 123, 125
*Wave*, collier, 111
*Wave*, smack, 34, 40, 75, 81
*Wave*, schooner, 119, 127
*Wear*, collier, 111
Webb, Dan, Maldon, 119
Weld, Joseph, 52
*Welfare*, smack, 34
Welham, Walter, Brightlingsea, 47
*Wesleyan*, wreck of, 40
West Rocks, 44
*Who-would-have-thought-it*, smack, 59
Wildfowling, 154 *et seq.*
*Winkie*, oyster boat, 74
*William*, smack, 116
*William*, schooner, 43
*William and Elizabeth*, s.b., 114, 119
*William and Henry*, smack, 34
*William and Lucy*, s.b., 117
Wivenhoe, 20, 51 *et seq.*
*Wivenhoe*, smack, 134
Worsp, L., Wivenhoe, 144
' Wrecking,' 67
Wyatt, William, West Mersea, 74
Wykeham-Martin, C., 167–168
Wyncoll, Spring, Fingringhoe, 49

*Xantha*, yacht, 52
*Xanthe*, smack, 59

*Yandue*, collier, 111
Yarmouth smacks, 55–56

*Zabina*, collier, 111

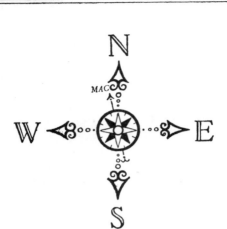

VIRLEY
SALCOT CREEK
SALCOT

TOLLESBURY ·

GOLDHANGER

MALDON

HEYBRIDGE BASIN

TO CHELMSFORD

NORTHEY I.   OSEA I.   RIVER   BLACKWAT

LAWLING CREEK   STANSGATE

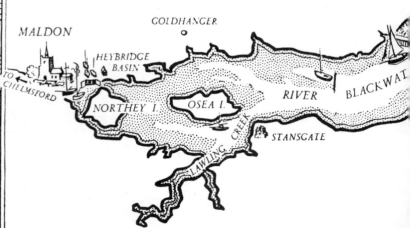

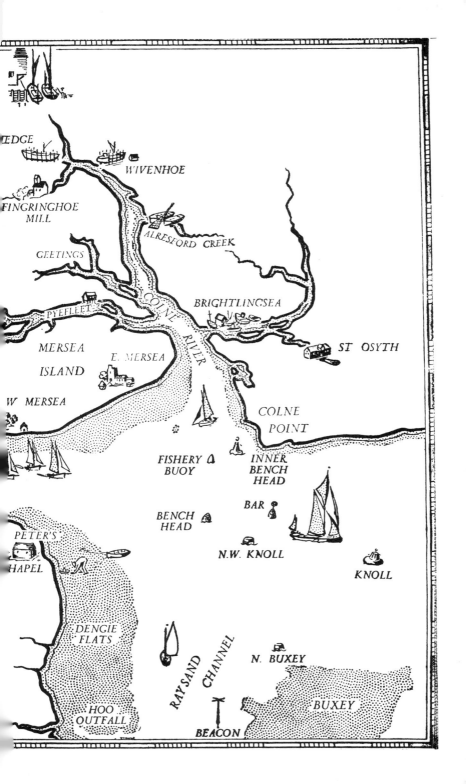